HOLY GROUND

Liturgies and worship resources for an engaged spirituality

Neil Paynter & Helen Boothroyd

WILD GOOSE PUBLICATIONS

Contents of book © the individual contributors
Compilation © 2005 Neil Paynter & Helen Boothroyd

First published 2005, reprinted 2008

Wild Goose Publications, 4th Floor, Savoy House, 140 Sauchiehall St, Glasgow G2 3DH, UK.
Wild Goose Publications is the publishing division of the Iona Community.
Scottish Charity No. SCO03794. Limited Company Reg. No. SCO96243.
www.ionabooks.com

ISBN 1 901557 88 X

Cover Illustration: 'Desert flower' © Kurt Nimmo

A catalogue record for this book is available from the British Library.

Overseas distribution:
Australia: Willow Connection Pty Ltd, Unit 4A, 3–9 Kenneth Road, Manly Vale, NSW 2093
New Zealand: Pleroma, Higginson Street, Otane 4170, Central Hawkes Bay
Canada: Novalis/Bayard, 10 Lower Spadina Avenue, Suite 400, Toronto, Ontario M5V 2Z2

Printed by Bell & Bain, Thornliebank, Glasgow

*'Spirituality is the place
where prayer and politics meet.'*

Kate McIlhagga,
a member of the Iona Community

CONTENTS

INTRODUCTION

Helen Boothroyd

The Christian scriptures resound with God's call for us to engage fully in the life of the world: being salt and light, making peace, acting justly, and showing true neighbourliness to all. *(Matthew 5:9, 13–14; Micah 6:8; Luke 10:25–37)*

Similarly, the history of liberation movements around the world is time and again a story of people of faith putting their belief into action, refusing to withdraw into a holy huddle, but sharing in the struggles of their communities for justice, for hope, for life in all its fullness *(John 10:10)*; in the here and now, in this, God's world: 'The kingdom of God is among you.' *(Luke 17:21)*

We have both been members of the resident staff group working for the Iona Community at Iona Abbey and the MacLeod Centre on the tiny Scottish island of Iona. There we had the privilege of sharing in this biblical and historical tradition of engaged spirituality through the daily work, worship and witness of the Iona Community, which is rooted in God's world, in all its beauty and pain, all its injustice and struggle, all its violence and redeeming love. This engaged spirituality is reflected in the pattern of daily worship on Iona, which focuses on the issues and concerns of the world, particularly those of the poor, the marginalised and folk caught up in conflict.

Yet it seems much harder in the worship life of many churches to introduce this element of engagement, of looking outward, of challenging in the name of God that which oppresses and degrades, and of committing ourselves to take action on these issues of the world as an essential part of our Christian discipleship. We feel that this difficulty has been partly due to a lack of suitable and readily available material to help those leading worship introduce and focus on these concerns.

Many of the liturgies and resources in this book are contributed by members and staff of the Iona Community. Some are drawn from other communities for whom an engaged spirituality is also central. Others arose from specific situations that inspired the creation of liturgy, reflection and prayer.

The liturgies can be used in their entirety as the whole or part of a worship service. Equally, it may be more appropriate on occasion simply to use part of the material within a liturgy, for example in prayers of intercession or in the ministry of the word. Some of the liturgies lend themselves particularly well to a small group gathering or to a non-church-based event, such as worship during a demonstration or campaign day. We hope that folk will be creative and adapt and use the material found here in a way that best suits their own worship situation.

HUMAN RIGHTS
HUMAN WRONGS

HUMAN RIGHTS, HUMAN WRONGS

Maxwell Craig

God created humankind in his image, in the image of God he created them;
male and female he created them. (Genesis 1:27)

You have made them a little lower than God and crowned them with glory and honour. You have
given them dominion over the works of your hands; you have put all things under their feet. (Psalm
8:5–6)

By his action in the process of creation, God has defined himself as Creator and has
accorded a special place to humankind. This is not something we have earned. So, theologically speaking, the place we have as human beings is not a right which has to be
argued for, campaigned for, maybe even fought for; rather, it's a gift, something given
without deserving and without condition. Because God has given us our valued status as
human beings, that status is never ultimately at risk.

Yet our world is full of people whose treatment is inhumane, literally less than
human. If human dignity is to be a reality in this world, then human rights have to be
asserted. How do we reconcile the lack of respect for their basic rights suffered by so
many people with the assurance that their dignity is a gift from God, which cannot be
taken from them? The Bible may help us here, both in our understanding and in our
work for justice, for human dignity and for human rights.

The Old Testament prophets

Isaiah, Amos and Micah all declared the assurance of our worth as human beings: 'Do not
fear, for I have redeemed you; I have called you by name, you are mine.' (Isaiah 43:1b)

The prophets decried the excesses of religious observance in favour of justice and
right dealing: 'I hate, I despise your festivals, and I take no delight in your solemn assem-
blies. But let justice roll down like waters and righteousness like an ever-flowing stream.'
(Amos 5:21 & 24)

Micah set out the goal of peace and of human rights, so relevant in the 21st century
when national leaders still see armed might as a means of policy: 'They shall beat their
swords into ploughshares and their spears into pruning hooks; nation shall not lift up
sword against nation; neither shall they learn war any more; but they shall all sit under
their own vines and under their own fig trees, and no-one shall make them afraid; for the
mouth of the Lord of hosts has spoken.' (Micah 4:3b-4)

The book of Deuteronomy is equally strong in its advocacy for those who are most vulnerable in any society: the widow, the child, the elderly and the stranger: 'You shall also love the stranger, for you were strangers in the land of Egypt.' (Deuteronomy 10:19)

Today our xenophobic laws use the term asylum-seekers for those who come to us as refugees and devalue and treat them shamefully in many ways. But, as Refugee Evensong reminds us, both we and our politicians need to be clear that our moral responsibility for the human rights of the strangers who seek refuge in this land is not changed, and cannot be changed, by unjust law.

The Gospel

Blessed are you who are poor, for yours is the kingdom of God. (Luke 6:21b)

Even the hairs of your head are all counted. So do not be afraid; you are of more value than many sparrows. (Matthew 10:30–31)

The life and teaching of Jesus give us much that is relevant to the global desire for human rights. Those who suffer the abuse of their rights are usually the marginalised, the poorest, those who have no battalions to back them, no wealth to buy access to a better life. And these, who might be counted losers in our society, were close to Jesus' heart. The story of the poor widow at the temple treasury may be seen not so much as a commendation of her generosity, but rather as a condemnation of the oppression of the weak in a society where, much like ours today, all too often might was equated with right.

Perhaps even more telling than his teaching was the way Jesus lived: his attitude to women, especially those whom society shunned; his concern for lepers, who were outcasts; and his delight in children, who were regarded as having no rights. These aspects of Jesus' life are so well documented that many of us today take them as normal and don't give them another thought, but in his day Jesus' advocacy of human dignity and human rights would have been highly unusual, striking, perhaps shocking.

In the last week of Jesus' earthly life, as the Cross cast its shadow ever more menacingly, two examples stand out in this regard. John 13 records Jesus washing his disciples' feet, choosing the most menial of tasks at the very time when they were arguing about what their status might be in the coming Kingdom: 'After he had washed their feet … he said to them "I have set you an example, that you also should do as I have done to you."' (John 13:12 & 15)

Thus Jesus recognised that our dignity as human beings is not dependent on an acquired status. It is a given.

In John 19 it is recorded that at the point of his deepest agony on the Cross, Jesus expressed his concern for the basic needs of another person. He saw Mary, his mother, standing at the foot of the Cross. She was about to lose her son. She faced the prospect of being homeless. Jesus required of 'the disciple whom he loved' that he provide a home for her. The response was immediate and practical: 'From that hour the disciple took her into his own home.' (John 19:27b)

Homelessness is one of the most basic deprivals of human rights. There, in the throes of execution and martyrdom, Jesus recognised that.

The Kingdom of God

The right to self-respect, dignity, self-expression and access to basic amenities is consonant with the values of the Kingdom of God. We may think this 'Kingdom' sounds too distant, more remote than the farthest outposts of space. But Jesus says no: 'The kingdom of God has come near.' (Mark 1:15) It is in our hearts and in our minds. As we live the Kingdom, human rights will become a reality: 'Do not be afraid, little flock, for it is your Father's good pleasure to give you the kingdom.' (Luke 12:32)

CARRYING THE LIGHT:

An act of prayer and thanksgiving for prisoners of conscience

John Davies

This act of worship provides an opportunity to give thanks for those who stand up for their belief in what is right, even when that results in imprisonment; to reflect on their stories; and to offer prayer for those currently held as prisoners of conscience throughout the world.

Material containing stories of prisoners of conscience, to use as indicated during the liturgy, can be obtained from Amnesty International (www.amnesty.org).

Greeting

Leader: The light shines in the darkness, and the darkness does not overcome it. *(John 1:5)*
            We come together to celebrate those whose light shines in the darkness of our world.

ALL: THE LIGHT SHINES IN THE DARKNESS, AND THE DARKNESS DOES NOT OVERCOME IT.

Leader: To reflect on their stories and offer prayers for their release.

ALL: THE LIGHT SHINES IN THE DARKNESS, AND THE DARKNESS DOES NOT OVERCOME IT.

Leader: To offer ourselves in the service of the God of light.

ALL: THE LIGHT SHINES IN THE DARKNESS, AND THE DARKNESS DOES NOT OVERCOME IT.

Prayer of thanksgiving and light

This prayer may be 'universal', as given here, or may refer to names and situations of people specifically known to the congregation. Each speaker lights a candle after saying their prayer and places it centrally. Once they have returned to their seat, the next speaker begins.

Voice A: I light a flame to give thanks for those who toast freedom in the face of oppression.

Voice B: I light a flame to give thanks for those who hold fast to their truth in the face of official denial.

Voice C: I light a flame to give thanks for those who work for the poor in the face of those who would crush them.

Voice D: I light a flame to give thanks for those who campaign for civil rights in the face of civil wrongs.

Voice E: I light a flame to give thanks for all who suffer imprisonment because of their beliefs.

Leader: Blessed are those who are persecuted because of righteousness, for theirs is the kingdom of heaven. *(Matthew 5:10)*

Silence

A Gloria is sung

Sharing stories of prisoners of conscience from scripture

Leader: God's people have been prisoners of conscience throughout human history. Let us hear the story of: *(Choose one. The scripture reading should be read by a different voice.)*:

Joseph   Genesis 39: 6–20a
Samson   Judges 16:18–21
Peter   Acts 11:27–12:5
Paul   Acts 16:16–24

Sharing stories of prisoners of conscience today

Members of the congregation share briefly no more than three stories of prisoners of conscience that are known to them, perhaps through Amnesty International reports. After each a short silence should follow.

A Psalm is sung e.g. Out of the direst depths (POPAP)

Affirmation of faith

ALL: WE BELIEVE IN GOD OUR CREATOR
Leader: Source of all light and freedom:
            who spoke to Moses through the darkness,
            who brought ancient Israel out of captivity;
ALL: WE BELIEVE IN JESUS OUR SAVIOUR
Leader: Eternally liberated from all that binds:
            who proclaimed release to the prisoners
            and recovery of sight to the blind;
ALL: WE BELIEVE IN THE SPIRIT OUR HELPER
Leader: God who is with us:
            who is our advocate, speaking for us,
            who is our comforter, offering us peace.

ALL: WE BELIEVE IN ONE GOD
            CREATOR, SAVIOUR, HELPER:
            WHO IS ALIVE AND ACTIVE
            PURSUING ALL THAT IS RIGHT
            TURNING EACH PERSON'S EYES TO THE LIGHT.

Prayers

The leader invites the congregation to offer their own prayers of intercession for prisoners of conscience or situations known to them where people are imprisoned for their beliefs. A response may be used. This time of prayer is concluded with all saying the Lord's Prayer together.

Song: Christ be our light (CG)

Carrying the light out into the world

All stand in preparation to leave. After each response, one of those who earlier lit candles and placed them centrally collects a lighted candle from the same place and walks out of the worship area, indicating the ongoing journey of faith that we share with prisoners of conscience. After the last response all the congregation follow the final candle-bearer out.

Leader: In the spirit of those we have remembered:
ALL   WE CARRY THE LIGHT OUT INTO THE WORLD.
Leader: In the confidence of faith in our Creator:
ALL: WE CARRY THE LIGHT OUT INTO THE WORLD.
Leader: In the strength of the risen Christ Jesus:
ALL: WE CARRY THE LIGHT OUT INTO THE WORLD.
Leader: In the presence of the life-giving Spirit:
ALL: WE CARRY THE LIGHT OUT INTO THE WORLD.
Leader: Sharing the faith that the darkness will end:
ALL: WE CARRY THE LIGHT OUT INTO THE WORLD.

REFUGEE EVENSONG

Woolman House Community (Alan Paxton, Kate Marks, Craig Barrett)

This liturgy is the fruit of worship and discussion led by members of the ecumenical Woolman House Community[1] with several congregations in Liverpool and elsewhere. The idea came from the autobiography of the German Lutheran theologian Dorothee Soelle *(Against the Wind: Memoir of a Radical Christian)*, in which she tells of her participation in the 'Political Evensongs' led in Cologne in the late 1960s by a group of Christians, Catholic and Protestant, who had come to believe that it was verging on blasphemy to reflect theologically without responding to that reflection in the political realm. Worship at 'Political Evensongs' took the form of political information integrated with the more familiar elements of liturgy, such as scripture readings and preaching, and included both calls for action and discussion in the congregation.

The Woolman House Community offered hospitality to refugees in Liverpool from 1999 to 2004. They began by befriending a Kosovan family whom they met at mass at a local church, and by visiting refugees housed in high-rise flats elsewhere in Liverpool, where they encountered the Rwandan man whose story is told at the beginning of the evensong. Later they helped to set up and run a drop-in for refugees, and began a visitors' group to befriend immigration detainees in Liverpool Prison and to act as bail sureties to obtain their release where possible. The Woolman House Community offered overnight hospitality to refugees coming to Liverpool from cities elsewhere in Britain for the all-important interview with the Home Office on which their claim for asylum would be judged. The 'house of hospitality' was also able to provide a longer-term home for one refugee made homeless and destitute by the Home Office system.

The Woolman House Community drew its inspiration from the Catholic Worker movement[2], which has become known not only for houses of hospitality serving poor and excluded people, but also for insisting on asking why there should be so many poor and excluded people in such rich countries. One of the ways it does this is through 'round table discussions'; a kind of public meeting that also influenced the form of this evensong.

Refugee evensong is simple in form. Worshippers are encouraged to enter into the experience of persecution, flight and exile. At its centre is a time of reflection and discussion, which is intended to lead to suggestions for putting our faith into practice. The Woolman House Community have found during these discussions that their work with refugees has enabled them to speak with an authority and conviction that they might lack if this were a subject they knew of only through reading and research. They therefore offer refugee evensong not as a ready-made service, but rather as a form of worship that can be adapted to explore whatever concern preoccupies a group and can be addressed through the experience of its members.

Opening responses

Leader: God of all, where are your children?
ALL: LET US WELCOME GOD'S CHILDREN
            WHO ARE FAR FROM HOME.
Leader: God of all, why is there crying?
ALL: LET US HEAR THE CRIES OF REFUGEES
            AND RESPOND WITH LOVE.
Leader: God of all, who is praying?
ALL: LET US PRAY WITH THE FAMILIES WHO ARE BROKEN APART,
            ASKING FOR COMFORT AND FOR JUSTICE.

Leaving home

Reader 1:   I was born in the town of Nyange in Rwanda. My mother died naturally in 1987, but my father was murdered in the killings. They also killed my first son Alain. They attacked me and thought they had killed me too. That is how I got these scars on my head and hand. It was very bad in my country so we decided to run away. We walked for seven months to get out of the country. When we got out I, my wife and child arrived in Zaire [now Democratic Republic of Congo], at a refugee camp in Goana. It was very bad in the camp. Many people were sick from cholera. Then there was a war started between the Democratic Republic of Congo and Rwanda, and they wanted to kill Rwandan people. So we tried to get out of the country into Congo-Brazzaville.

Scripture reading: Matthew 2:13–18

Leader: Close your eyes for a minute and imagine that you are being forced to leave your home ...
            You don't know if you will ever be able to come back ...
            Perhaps you are worried about other members of your family.
            What is happening to them?
            Will you see them again?
            You are leaving on foot so you can't take much with you.
            What would you take?

Song: When I needed a neighbour were you there?

Journey

Reader 1:   We tried to get to the border but there was a big lake there, and troops from the government chasing us. We had to cross over the lake with rafts that we made from trees. Many refugees fell into the water and died there. When we crossed over we arrived in Bandaka, where we waited for a ship that was taking refugees away. But the ship had just left and never came back for us. We started to walk through the bush. We had nothing to eat and had to live on what we could find on the way. The people in the villages took our money and clothes to let us pass through. We lived like that until we arrived in the country of Congo Brazzaville. I stayed with my wife and second son in a refugee camp, and my daughter was born there. I started a job, but then a big war began in Brazzaville. The President started to take the young Rwandan men out of the camp to fight in the war. Many boys died in that war, many of my friends, and when they came for me I had to run away again. My wife was left behind in the refugee camp so I didn't know what happened to her. Since that time I've had no news of her or my children.

Scripture reading: Exodus 14:5–6; 10–11; 21–23; 26–27

Leader: Think for a moment about your journey as a refugee …
            Having to escape from those who want to kill you …
            How would you get out of the country without being caught?
            Are you still in shock from what has happened to you?
            Maybe you're starting to be frightened about what will face you when you arrive somewhere new …

Song: Do not be afraid (SOGP)

In exile

Leader: There are some 23 million refugees in the world, uprooted from their homes by war, persecution or economic and political collapse. Most of these people live in countries bordering their own. Poor countries such as Pakistan and Iran are host to millions of refugees, while only a small proportion ever reach rich countries such as Britain. Other European countries have been accepting growing numbers of asylum-seekers for many years, but Britain's strong cultural links to former colonies and its reputation for fairness and tolerance also lead some to believe they will find a fair hearing in the UK.

Reader 2:   I fled from Kenya the 26th of June and applied for asylum immediately. However before I could say anything I was already condemned: as a single, young man, without any fixed address in the UK, I had all the reasons to be put in prison. For the first time in my life and whereas I hadn't committed any crime I was locked in prison like a convicted person. Can you imagine the shock and the questions raised during these first days? How long am I going to stay here? Is there somebody to help me get out? Nobody could, as nobody knew I was in prison … And the more I talked to other refugees the more depressed I felt, as some were there for six or nine months already. After one week, you realise that you are completely trapped and it becomes very hard as the fear, the anxiety and the depression begin to grow inside. I lost my sleep and began to suffer all sorts of pain like headache and backache. I didn't know what my rights were or what to expect. After two months, still no change. I missed doing simple things like going to the library or to university, having coffee with a friend or doing shopping. The depressing routine of the prison was still going on: only one shower per week, one hour of TV per week and one hour of walking per day. I thought I would die here failing to achieve anything. I heard about my father's death. I didn't eat for four days, I was crying in my room and wanted to die. People kept on visiting me and one person agreed to be my bail surety. On the 18th of September I got bail: I was free in ten minutes! I couldn't believe that in only ten minutes I was free, able to come back to real life and to build my own future. I am still haunted by that experience.

Scripture reading: Matthew 25:31–40

Leader: Now the governments of Europe are in competition to deter asylum-seekers by making their lives increasingly difficult and dangerous. In this country that can mean destitution, homelessness, and indefinite imprisonment without charge or trial, as happened to the young Kenyan man we have just heard about, who was later accepted by our government as entitled to political asylum.

Discussion

The worship leader introduces a discussion in twos and threes on the question:
How should we be responding as Christians to people seeking asylum in the UK?
After about 15 minutes, the worship leader invites people to share their comments and reflections with the whole congregation.

Closing prayer

Leader: God beyond borders,
            we bless you for strange places and different dreams
            for the demands and diversity of a wider world
            for the distance that lets us look back and re-evaluate
            for new ground where broken stems can take root, grow and blossom.
            We bless you for the friendship of strangers
            the richness of other cultures
            and the painful gift of freedom.
ALL: BLESSED ARE YOU, GOD BEYOND BORDERS.
Leader: But if we have overlooked the exiles in our midst,
            heightened their exclusion by our indifference
            given our permission for a climate of fear
            and tolerated a culture of violence
ALL: HAVE MERCY ON US,
            GOD WHO TAKES SIDE WITH JUSTICE.
            CONFRONT OUR PREJUDICE
            STRETCH OUR NARROWNESS
            SIFT OUT OUR LAWS AND OUR LIVES
            WITH THE PENETRATING INSIGHT OF YOUR SPIRIT,
            UNTIL GENEROSITY IS OUR ONLY MEASURE.
            AMEN

Song: When I needed a neighbour were you there?

Notes

[1] The Woolman House Community takes its name from the eighteenth century Quaker, John Woolman, a slavery abolitionist and advocate of a simple and non-violent style of life. Woolman was uncompromising in his opposition to war, exploitation, and the craving for wealth and power that he discerned as the seeds of war. Yet he was a gentle and humble man who succeeded in 'speaking the truth in love' without falling into the aggressive self-righteousness that can sometimes disfigure Christian witness to justice and peace.

[2] Founded in the USA in the 1930s by Dorothy Day and Peter Maurin. Catholic Worker communities sometimes engage in acts of non-violent resistance to injustice and war, and witness to the radical Gospel in courtrooms and prisons.

A VIGIL LITURGY FOR THE WORLDWIDE ABOLITION OF THE DEATH PENALTY

Iona Abbey, 1999

Helen Boothroyd and Neil Paynter

We believe that use of the death penalty is the ultimate violation of human rights, and is directly contrary to the will and purposes of God. We want to see all people of faith join together to speak out against this planned and ritualised killing by the state, wherever it still takes place.

The intention of this act of worship is to resonate with vigils held by campaigners for the abolition of the death penalty outside prisons in the United States when an execution is taking place.

Small unlit hand-held candles are placed on each seat before the service begins.

Reading: The last hours of James Terry Roach

James Terry Roach was executed in South Carolina on 10th January 1986. In 1977, when he was 17 years old, he had pleaded guilty to the murders of two teenagers and to additional charges, including sexual assault and kidnapping. He was sentenced to death despite a finding by the trial judge that he had acted under the domination of an older man, was mentally retarded and had a personality disorder.

One of his lawyers stayed with him on the night of his execution and gave the following account of those last hours:

'Although Terry was twenty-five years old by the time of his death, he seemed very childlike. In general, his demeanour and his reactions to the people around him appeared to me to comport with the finding, made at his last psychological evaluation, that his IQ was 70 – a score which placed his intellectual functioning at about the level of a twelve year old child. When his family minister showed him some prayers from the Bible that they would read together, Terry asked him which ones he thought would be especially likely to help him into heaven: his questions about this seemed based on the childish assumption that one prayer was likely to work better than another, and that he just needed some advice about which ones would work best.

'Terry was a very passive young man, and that showed all through the night. Although he was obviously very frightened, he was as cooperative as possible with the guards, and he tried to pretend that all of the ritual preparation – the shaving of his head and right leg, the prolonged rubbing in of electrical conducting gel – was all a normal sort of thing to have happen. He wanted the approval of those around him, and he seemed well aware that this night he could gain everyone's approval by being brave and keeping his fear at bay. Still, when the warden appeared in the cell door at 5.00 a.m. and read the death warrant, while Terry stood, each wrist immobilized in a manacle, known as a claw, his left leg began to shake in large, involuntary movements.

'After that, everything happened quickly. I walked to the chair with him, and talked to him as much as I could. After he had read his final statement we had a couple of last words. I left him and walked to the witness area, where I gave him a thumbs-up sign. He signaled back with his fingers, as much as the straps permitted.

'A few seconds later the current hit. Terry's body snapped back and held frozen for the whole time that the current ran through his body. After a few seconds, steam began to rise from his body, and the skin on his thigh just above the electrode began to distend and blister. His fists were clenched and very white. His body slumped when the current was turned off, and jerked erect again when it was resumed. When he was declared dead, several guards wrestled his body out of the chair and onto a stretcher, while taking care to conceal his face (no longer covered by the mask) from the view of the witnesses and me by covering it with a sheet.

'I left the death house at about this time in the company of the warden. As we stepped out of the building, I heard the whoops of a crowd of about 150 or 200 demonstrators who had apparently come to celebrate the execution, yelling and cheering outside the prison gates.'

Chant: Goodness is stronger than evil *(sung three times by all)*

Goodness is stronger than evil;
love is stronger than hate;
light is stronger than darkness;
life is stronger than death.
Victory is ours, victory is ours
through him who loved us. (LAA, TIOAU)

Archbishop Desmond Tutu

Scriptural litany *(based on Matthew 26 and 27 and John 18 and 19)*

Voice 1:   The soldiers, their officer, and the Jewish police arrested Jesus and bound him. First they took him to Annas, who was the father-in-law of Caiaphas, the high priest that year. Caiaphas was the one who had advised the Jews that it was better to have one person die for the people. Then the high priest questioned Jesus about his disciples and about his teaching. Jesus answered, 'I have spoken openly to the world; I have always taught in synagogues and in the temple, where all the Jews come together. I have said nothing in secret. Why do you ask me? Ask those who heard what I said to them; they know what I said.' When he had said this, one of the police standing nearby struck Jesus on the face, saying, 'Is that how you answer the high priest?' Jesus answered, 'If I have spoken wrongly, testify to the wrong. But if I have spoken rightly, why do you strike me?' Then Annas sent him bound to Caiaphas the high priest.

Voice 2:   Mahmoud Mohamed Taha, the 76-year-old leader of the Republican Brothers Movement in the Sudan, was arrested in January 1985. The movement advocated a new approach to Islam and had engaged in non-violent political activities. Mahmoud was charged with undermining or subverting the constitution, a capital offence. He admitted distributing leaflets calling for the repeal of Islamic laws, appealing for a peaceful solution to the conflict in southern Sudan and advocating an Islamic revival. In one day he was found guilty of subversion and sentenced to death. The Court of Appeal confirmed the sentence, ruling that he was also guilty of heresy by advocating an unacceptable form of Islam. The court gave Mahmoud one month in which to repent or die. President Nimeiri confirmed the sentence and cut the deadline for repentance to 3 days. Mahmoud refused to repent and was hanged before a large crowd.

A kyrie is sung by all, during which a lighted candle is carried from the back and placed on the front table.

Voice 1:   Now the chief priests and the whole council were looking for false testimony against Jesus so that they might put him to death, but they found none, though many false witnesses came forward.

Voice 2:   Eighteen-year-old Edward Johnson was arrested in Mississippi in 1979 for the murder of a white police officer. Edward was black. The jury who tried him had ten white members but only two black in a county with a 45% black population. Edward had been put on an identity parade in front of the one eyewitness, a white woman. The woman said that she had known Edward all his life and he was not the murderer. She said the murderer was heavily built with a full beard. Edward was slim and had never had a beard. Two days later Edward was rearrested and taken by police to some woods. He later testified that they threatened to shoot him unless he confessed to the murder. So he signed the confession. He didn't see a lawyer until he had been brought to court to be charged. Edward recanted his confession at the first chance. However, the eyewitness changed her story on hearing of his confession and identified him as the killer. Edward was convicted and sentenced to death. Before his trial Edward had been offered a life sentence in exchange for a guilty plea. Edward refused. He was executed in a gas chamber in 1986. A week after the execution his lawyer located a woman whom Edward had always claimed he had been with in a pool hall when the crime was committed. She said that she had gone to the courthouse to testify for him during the trial but was told by a police officer to go home and mind her own business.

A kyrie is sung by all, during which a lighted candle is carried from the back and placed on the front table.

Voice 1: The high priest stood up and said, 'Have you no answer? What is it that they testify against you?' But Jesus was silent. Then the high priest said to him, 'I put you under oath before the living God, tell us if you are the Messiah, the Son of God.' Jesus said to him, 'You have said so.' Then the high priest tore his clothes and said, 'He has blasphemed! Why do we still need witnesses? You have now heard his blasphemy. What is your verdict?' They answered, 'He deserves death.' Then they spat in his face and struck him; and some slapped him, saying, 'Prophesy to us, you Messiah! Who is it that struck you?'

Voice 2: Dante Piandong, Archie Buian and Jesus Morallos were arrested in the Philippines in 1994, accused of shooting a policeman. They maintained their innocence. In police custody they were beaten, given electric shocks and forced to lie with towels over their faces, which were then doused with water. They testified about their torture during the trial but the judge made only passing reference to it – and then sentenced them to death. They were executed by lethal injection in 1999, when the use of the death penalty was recommenced in the Philippines after 23 years of absence.

A kyrie is sung by all, during which a lighted candle is carried from the back and placed on the front table.

Voice 1: Then they took Jesus from Caiaphas to Pilate's headquarters. Pilate went out to them and said, 'What accusation do you bring against this man?' They answered, 'If this man were not a criminal, we would not have handed him over to you.' Pilate said to them, 'Take him yourselves and judge him according to your law.' The Jews replied, 'We are not permitted to put anyone to death.' Then Pilate entered the headquarters again, summoned Jesus, and asked him, 'Are you the King of the Jews?' Jesus answered, 'Do you ask this on your own, or did others tell you about me?' Pilate replied, 'I am not a Jew, am I? Your own nation and the chief priests have handed you over to me. What have you done?' Jesus answered, 'My kingdom is not from this world. If my kingdom were from this world, my followers would be fighting to keep me from being handed over to the Jews. But as it is, my kingdom is not from here.' Pilate asked him, 'So you are a king?' Jesus answered, 'You say that I am a king. For this I was born, and for this I came into the world, to testify to the truth. Everyone who belongs to the truth listens to my voice.' Pilate asked him, 'What is truth?' After he had said this he went out to the Jews again and told them, 'I find no case against him. But you have a custom that I release someone for you at the Passover. Do you want me to release for you the King of the Jews?' They shouted in reply: 'Not this man, but Barabbas!' Now Barabbas was a bandit.

Voice 2: Mukobo Putu was arrested in the Democratic Republic of the Congo in connection with killings in Kinshasa in July 1998. Less than 3 weeks later he was sentenced to death by the Military Order Court on charges of murder and plotting to overthrow the president. Facing imminent execution his only recourse was to presidential grace, which was refused. However, Amnesty International organised a worldwide appeal, and due to the huge volume of letters his life was spared.

A kyrie is sung by all, during which a lighted candle is carried from the back and placed on the front table.

Voice 1: Then Pilate took Jesus and had him flogged. And the soldiers wove a crown of thorns and put it on his head, and they dressed him in a purple robe. They kept coming up to him, saying, 'Hail, King of the Jews!' and striking him on the face. Pilate went out again and said to them, 'Look, I am bringing him out to you to let you know that I find no case against him.' So Jesus came out, wearing the crown of thorns and the purple robe. Pilate said to them, 'Here is the man!' When the chief priests and the police saw him, they shouted, 'Crucify him! Crucify him!' He said to the Jews, 'Here is your King!' They cried out, 'Away with him! Away with him! Crucify him!'

Voice 2: In 1979 John Spenkelink was executed in Florida's electric chair. Twenty-four hours before his execution these words began a morning radio show in Florida: 'Hey, Spenkelink, you listening this morning? Spenkelink? Just think, in just over twenty-four hours, Spenkelink, you're going to fry, maggot!

You're going to fry! And there's nothing those bleeding hearts can do to save you. Get used to the sound, Spenkelink, think of yourself convulsing.'

A kyrie is sung by all, during which a lighted candle is carried from the back and placed on the front table.

Voice 1:   Pilate said to them, 'Take him yourselves and crucify him; I find no case against him.' So they took Jesus; and carrying the cross by himself, he went out to what is called the Place of the Skull, which in Hebrew is called Golgotha. There they crucified him, and with him two criminals, one on either side, with Jesus between them.

Voice 2:   In country after country it is the most vulnerable members of society, the poorest or otherwise disadvantaged, the least able to defend themselves, who are executed. In 1988 Amnesty International analysed the circumstances of more than 120 prisoners on death row in Jamaica. Most of them came from the very poorest sectors of the community. In the United States, 82 per cent of prisoners executed between 1977 and the end of 1998 were convicted of the murder of a white person, even though black and white people are the victims of homicide in almost equal numbers nationwide. A black person convicted of killing a white person in the United States is eleven times more likely to be condemned to death than a white person convicted of killing a black person.

A kyrie is sung by all, during which a lighted candle is carried from the back and placed on the front table.

Voice 1:   Pilate also had an inscription written and put on the cross. It read 'Jesus of Nazareth, the King of the Jews'. Many of the Jews read this inscription, because the place where Jesus was crucified was near the city; and it was written in Hebrew, in Latin, and in Greek.

Voice 2:   In September 1983 there was a mass public execution in Zhengzhou, China. About a million people were crowded along the pavements to watch the parade of the condemned. Forty-five flatbed trucks, one after another, rolled along the roads at no more than five miles an hour. At the front of each truck bed, just behind the cab, stood a condemned man bound with heavy rope holding in place a tall narrow sign. On the top half of each sign was an accusation: 'Thief' 'Murderer' 'Rapist'. On the bottom half was the accused's name, marked through with a large red X.

A kyrie is sung by all, during which a lighted candle is carried from the back and placed on the front table.

Voice 1:   From noon on, darkness came over the whole land until three in the after-
            noon. And about three o'clock Jesus cried with a loud voice, 'Eli, Eli, lema
            sabachthani?' that is, 'My God, my God, why have you forsaken me?'
            When some of the bystanders heard it, they said, 'This man is calling for
            Elijah.' At once one of them ran and got a sponge, filled it with sour wine,
            put it on a stick, and gave it to him to drink. But the others said, 'Wait, let
            us see whether Elijah will come to save him.' Then Jesus cried again with
            a loud voice and breathed his last.

The words 'Eli, Eli, lema sabachthani?' are sung solo at the point they appear in this read-ing. At the end of this reading the same soloist sings a final commendation, such as is sung towards the end of a requiem mass.

Voice 2:   A Thai construction worker hanged in Kuwait in 1981 took more than
            nine minutes to die because his slight weight did not suffice to break his
            neck. He died of strangulation. As he stood on the gallows beforehand
            facing the crowd, the Arab Times reported: 'For a moment his face
            expressed all the incomprehension, anguish and desperation.'

A kyrie is sung by all, during which a lighted candle is carried from the back and placed on the front table.

Voice 1:   Since it was the day of Preparation, the Jews did not want the bodies left
            on the cross during the Sabbath, especially because that Sabbath was a
            day of great solemnity. So they asked Pilate to have the legs of the cruci-
            fied men broken and the bodies removed. Then the soldiers came and
            broke the legs of the first and of the other who had been crucified with
            him. But when they came to Jesus and saw that he was already dead, they
            did not break his legs. Instead, one of the soldiers pierced his side with a
            spear, and at once blood and water came out.

Voice 2:   Stoning to death is one of the methods of execution practised in Iran. The
            procedure is designed to ensure that death is lingering. An eyewitness to
            a stoning reported: 'The lorry deposited a large number of stones and
            pebbles beside the waste ground, and then two women were led to the
            spot wearing white and with sacks over their heads. They were enveloped
            in a shower of stones and transformed into two red sacks. The wounded

women fell to the ground and Revolutionary Guards smashed their heads in with a shovel to make sure that they were dead.'

A kyrie is sung by all, during which a lighted candle is carried from the back and placed on the front table.

Solo: Were you there when they crucified my Lord? (verses 1–3, SOGP)

Peter's denial: A litany of responsibility *(based on Matthew 26:69–75)*

The tune of 'Were you there when they crucified my Lord?' continues to be played while the litany of responsibility is read slowly.

Voice 1:   I've got enough to think about in my own life. I don't want to know.
Voice 2:   And Peter said, 'I don't know what you are talking about.'
Voice 1:   I think the death penalty is a bad thing but it doesn't happen in Britain any more – so it's not my responsibility.
Voice 2:   'I don't know the man.'
Voice 1:   There's nothing I can do to influence governments in other countries to abolish the death penalty.
Voice 2:   'I don't know the man!'

Solo: Were you there when they crucified my Lord? (verse 4, SOGP)

Reflection: Taking action

There is something we can do to help bring about the abolition of the death penalty worldwide. Amnesty International campaigns tirelessly for worldwide abolition and petitions governments on specific cases.

Amnesty International needs new members both to give financial support and to write letters on individual cases and on the issue of abolition. You are invited to consider joining them if you are not already a member. *(The attention of the congregation is drawn to display materials and contact details for Amnesty International: Amnesty International UK, The Human Rights Action Centre, 17-25 New Inn Yard, London EC2A 3EA. Tel. 020 7033 1500. www.amnesty.org.uk)*

Invitation to gather

The congregation are invited to gather around the lighted candles as all again sing repeatedly the chant 'Goodness is stronger than evil'. They bring with them the small candle that they found on their seat at the beginning of the service. The first people to reach the front table light their candles from the candles burning there. The light is then passed from neigh-

bour to neighbour until all hold a lit candle. Attention is drawn to the similarity of this gath-ering to vigils held outside prisons in the United States each time an execution takes place.

The case for abolition

Voice 1:   The worldwide movement for abolition is growing. In recent years, an average of three countries a year have abolished the death penalty. But it is still retained in more than 80 countries. Well over a thousand executions are documented by Amnesty International each year; the true figures are certainly higher.

Voice 2:   There is no evidence that the death penalty has any special effect in reducing crime or violence. It is used unequally against the poor and minority groups. It is often used as a tool of political repression. It cannot be reversed. Many innocent people have been executed. Mistakes can never be corrected. It is cruel, calculated, cold-blooded killing.

Voice 1:   In 2000 the United Nations Secretary General Kofi Annan received a petition for a moratorium on the death penalty signed by more than three million people around the world. In accepting it he said: 'The forfeiture of life is too absolute, too irreversible, for one human being to inflict on another, even when backed by legal process. Let the states that still use the death penalty stay their hand lest in time to come they look back with remorse knowing it is too late to redeem their grievous mistake.'

Voice 2:   Hearts and minds can be changed. Governor George Ryan in declar-ing a moratorium in Illinois, USA, in 2000 said: 'I supported the death penalty, I voted for the death penalty. But when I was the last person between the prisoner and his execution, I might as well have been pulling the switch, and no human being should be asked to do that.' The day before he ended his term as governor, George Ryan gave clemency to all 142 people on death row. He now travels all over the world campaigning for a moratorium on the death penalty.

A prayer for change and absolution

Thus is our God –
blessed may he be –
who has given us to know how he calls at every moment
and at every moment is ready to receive us,
no matter the crimes we have committed.

And so, brothers and sisters …
    … those who have brought tears to so many homes,
those who have stained themselves
with the blood of so many murders,
those who have hands soiled with tortures,
those who have calloused their consciences,
who are unmoved
to see under their boots a person abased,
suffering, perhaps ready to die.
To all of them I say:
No matter your crimes.
They are ugly and horrible,
and you have abased the highest dignity
of a human person,
but God calls you and forgives you …
… in heaven there are no criminals.
The greatest criminal, once he has repented of his sins,
is now a child of God.

Archbishop Oscar Romero

Closing affirmation *(said by all)*

God, giver of all life
We believe that no person has the right to take away
your gift of life from another person,
that you do not give such authority
to any government or judge.

We believe in a God of compassion
not a God of blood.
A God of love and mercy
not a God who metes out hurt for hurt, pain for pain,
torture for torture, death for death.

We believe in Jesus Christ
and that the message of Christ
is a message of compassion.
A message to disarm our enemies without
humiliating and destroying them.

We believe that the movement to abolish the death penalty
needs the help of religious communities everywhere
because the heart of religion is about
compassion, human rights
and the inherent dignity of each person
made in the image of God.

We affirm our part in that movement.
We will seek for the worldwide abolition of the death penalty.

Chant: Goodness is stronger than evil

Sung repeatedly as the congregation process out carrying their lighted candles.

TWENTIETH CENTURY CRUCIFIXION:

A dramatic communion liturgy

John Smith

The liturgy is enacted round a central table covered with a white cloth and empty except for the communion elements and five lighted candles, four red and one white.[1] An additional large white candle is placed in a central position in the worship space, and remains lit throughout the service.[2]

Five people play the characters of Dietrich Bonhoeffer (DB), Martin Luther King (MLK), Oscar Romero (OR), Simone Weil (SW), and Jesus Christ (JC). The latter role is taken by the communion celebrant. All wear similar dark clothes.

Introduction *(Leader)*

Some words of Dom Helder Camara, former Archbishop of Recife, spoken during the military dictatorship in Brazil:

'In the last thirty years there have been more martyrs than there were during the first centuries of the church. People, young and old alike, are being murdered for the crime of encouraging, without hatred or violence, the promotion of human rights for the children of God living in destitution. What a wonderful light of hope; the martyrs, the numerous martyrs of today. And to think there were people who considered Christ incapable of creating martyrs any more.'

This act of worship celebrates four of those martyrs who offered their lives for others. There are many, many more, such as Charles de Foucauld, killed at Tamanrasset; Maximillian Kolbe, who gave his life to save another in Auschwitz; Mahatma Gandhi, victim of the violence and sectarianism that he had stood against all his life; and Ita Ford, murdered in San Salvador. Yet in the four martyrs in this service we honour the many, including those still being martyred in this twenty-first century, and celebrate their exemplar Jesus Christ, who offered himself for us and in whose atoning love we believe.

Opening prayer *(said by all)*

Lord make us instruments of your peace.
Where there is hatred, let us sow love.
Where there is injury, pardon.
Where there is doubt, faith.
Where there is despair, hope.
Where there is sadness, joy.
O divine Master,

Grant that we may not so much seek
To be consoled as to console.
To be understood as to understand.
To be loved as to love.
For it is in giving that we receive,
It is in pardoning that we are pardoned,
It is in dying that we are born again
To everlasting life. Amen.

Scripture readings:

1. Luke 1:68–79 (Zechariah's Song. The Benedictus)
(Read by the whole congregation. Verse 79 is repeated by the leader of the service for added emphasis.)

2. Luke 4:16–19
(A dramatised reading with verses 18 and 19 being read by JC.)

DB picks up one of the red lighted candles and moves to an appropriate place to speak.

Leader: Born in 1906, Dietrich Bonhoeffer was the son of a professor of psychiatry. He grew up in academic surroundings and in 1930 was appointed a lecturer in systematic theology at Berlin University. In 1933 he denounced Hitler and Nazi ideology on German radio. Two years later he was forbidden to teach and banned from Berlin by the Nazi authorities. At the outbreak of war in 1939, against the advice of his friends, he gave up the security of the USA, where he had been lecturing, and returned to Germany to work for the newly founded Confessing Church and the political opposition to Hitler. He chose violent opposition to the regime: a personal sacrifice of both his pacifism and his privileged position as a priest. The day after the attempt to assassinate Hitler, in which he was deeply involved, Bonhoeffer wrote about how Christianity is very much of this world and entails watching with Christ in Gethsemane.

Dietrich Bonhoeffer was arrested in April 1943 and two years later was moved to Flossenberg concentration camp. Soon afterwards the SS guards came for him just as he was finishing leading a service for his fellow prisoners in Flossenberg. They hanged him with a piano wire.

Bonhoeffer's letters and papers, smuggled out of prison, show what he might have become had he lived. His understanding of the world, balanced by humour, compassion, faith and a constant struggling with real world decisions and dilemmas, made up a character that was, in the fullest sense of the word, saintly. Captain Payne Best, a fellow prisoner at Flossenberg, described how Bonhoeffer brought hope to the other prisoners by his continuing joy in life, and marvelled that God was obviously real and very close for Bonhoeffer. As he left with the guards Bonhoeffer knew he was going to his execution and asked Payne Best to pass the word to Bishop Bell of Chichester. He spoke of his imminent death as 'the beginning of life'.

Among Dietrich Bonhoeffer's many writings was this confession:

DB: I am guilty of hypocrisy and untruthfulness in the face of force. I have been lacking in compassion and I have denied the poorest of my brethren.

***

[The Church] has often denied to the outcast and to the despised the compassion which she owes them. She was silent when she should have cried out because the blood of the innocent was crying aloud to heaven.

***

She has stood by while violence and wrong were being committed under cover of [the name of Christ].

***

The Church confesses that she has witnessed the lawless application of brutal force, the physical and spiritual suffering of countless innocent people, oppression, hatred and murder, and that she has not raised her voice on behalf of the victims and has not found ways to hasten their aid. She is guilty of the deaths of the weakest and most defenceless brothers of Jesus Christ.

***

The Church confesses that she has witnessed in silence the spoliation and exploitation of the poor and the enrichment and corruption of the strong. The Church confesses herself guilty towards the countless victims of calumny, denunciation and defamation.
[The Church] has rendered herself guilty of the decline in responsible action, in bravery in the defence of a cause and in willingness to suffer for what is known to be right.

DB snuffs out his candle and places it on the table.

Leader: In the confusion of the end of the war, Bonhoeffer's parents waited anxiously for news of their son. One day they tuned into the BBC. The broadcast was a service from Chichester Cathedral. They heard the hymn

'For All the Saints'. Then they heard Bishop Bell giving thanks for the life, death and martyrdom of Dietrich. Thus they learned of their son's death, in the realisation that they were listening to a memorial service for him.

Hymn: For all the saints who from their labours rest

Scripture reading: Matthew 5:1–12
(*A dramatised reading with the beatitudes being read by JC.*)

MLK picks up one of the red lighted candles and moves to an appropriate place to speak.

Leader: Martin Luther King was the grandson of a slave. He grew up in the American South, where all blacks were regarded as second-class citizens. There was segregation on buses, in schools, in cafes and in most public places. As a minister serving his congregation he sought to change this and bring freedom to the black people of America. He decided that the only way to create this change was by non-violent methods, following the ideals of Mahatma Gandhi. He found that he could combine his Christian principles with those of non-violent political action – the peaceful demonstration, the sit-in and the march. He inspired a movement for freedom that was to revolutionise race relations throughout the United States. He gave hope to those who were despised and freedom to those who were imprisoned by the bigotry of American society. Eventually federal law made discrimination illegal.

In 1968 Martin Luther King gave the following sermon, which was later played to the crowds at his funeral.

MLK: Every now and then I guess we all think realistically about that day when we will be victimised with what is life's common denominator – that something we call death.

We all think about it and every now and then I think about my own death, and I think about my own funeral. And I don't think of it in a morbid sense. Every now and then I ask myself what is it I would want said? …

If any of you are around when I have to meet my day, I don't want a long funeral. And if you get someone to deliver the eulogy, tell them not to talk too long.

Every now and then I wonder what I want them to say.

Tell them not to mention that I have a Nobel Peace Prize, that isn't important. Tell them not to mention that I have three or four hundred other awards, that's not important.

Tell them not to mention where I went to school.

I'd like somebody to mention on that day that … Martin Luther King Junior tried to give his life serving others … I'd like for somebody to say that day that … Martin Luther King Junior tried to love somebody.

I want you to say that day that I tried to be right on the war question.

I want you to be able to say that day that I did try to feed the hungry. And I want you to be able to say that day that I did try in my life to clothe those who were naked.

I want you to say that day that I did try in my life to visit those who were in prison.

I want you to say that I tried to love and serve humanity.

Yes if you want to say that I was a drum major, say that I was a drum major for justice.

Say that I was a drum major for peace.

I was a drum major for righteousness.

And all of the other shallow things will not matter.

I won't have any money to leave behind.

I won't have the fine and luxurious things of life to leave behind.

But I just want to leave a committed life behind.

And that's all I want to say:

If I can help somebody as I pass along

If I can cheer somebody with a smile or song

If I can show somebody that he's travelling wrong

Then my living will not be in vain.

If I can do my duty as a Christian ought

If I can bring salvation to a world once wrought

If I can spread the message as the master taught,

Then my living will not be in vain.

Song: If I can help somebody

Sung as a solo from the back of the room with the opening line coming in immediately after the reading ends.

Leader: On 3rd April 1968 Dr Martin Luther King preached in Memphis, Tennessee. His sermon ended:

MLK: I don't know what will happen now. We've got some difficult days ahead. But it really doesn't matter to me now because I've been to the mountain-top. I won't mind. Like anybody else I would like to lead a long life.

Longevity has its place. But I'm not concerned about that now. I just want to do God's will. And He's allowed me to go up to the mountain. And I've looked over, and I have seen the promised land.

I may not get there with you, but I want you to know tonight that we as a people will get to the promised land. So I'm happy tonight. I'm not worried about anything. I'm not fearing any man. Mine eyes have seen the glory of the coming of the Lord.

Leader: On the evening of 4th April Martin Luther King was standing on his hotel balcony. A shot rang out. The bullet hit Dr King in the neck. One hour later he was dead.

MLK snuffs out his candle and places it on the table.

Hymn: Mine eyes have seen the glory of the coming of the Lord

JC picks up the small white lighted candle and moves to an appropriate place to speak.

Scripture reading: Luke 23:32–46
(*A dramatised reading with JC reading the words spoken by Jesus.*)

JC snuffs out his candle and places it on the table.

Hymn: There is a green hill far away

OR picks up one of the red lighted candles and moves to an appropriate place to speak.

Leader: El Salvador in the late 1970s and 1980s was a country of terror. Army and paramilitary death squads carried out the torture and mass killing of thousands of peasants. Every peaceful demonstration and protest march was fired upon.

Monsignor Oscar Arnulfo Romero was appointed Archbishop of San Salvador in 1977. He was regarded as a conservative priest, and the military government did not believe he would cause them any problems. But Archbishop Romero was increasingly troubled by the actions of the government. In his weekly sermons in San Salvador Cathedral, regularly broadcast by the Catholic radio station, he denounced the brutality and repression of the armed forces and advocated social change. In his sermon on the Sunday before he was martyred Archbishop Romero addressed the Salvadoran military.

OR: Brothers, you are from our same pueblo, you kill our brother campesinos; and before an order to kill given by a man you ought to reflect on the law of God which says: do not kill. No soldier is obliged to obey an order that is contrary to the will of God. Nobody has to fulfil an immoral law. Now it is time that you recover your consciences and that you first obey your conscience rather than an order to sin. The Church, defender of the rights of God, of the law of God, of the human dignity of the person, cannot remain shut up before such an abomination. We want the government to take seriously that reforms achieved with so much blood serve no one. In the name of God, then, and in the name of this suffering pueblo, whose cries rise to the heavens, every day more clamouringly, I beg, I ask, I order you in the name of God: stop the repression.

Leader: Archbishop Romero was shot dead on 24th March 1980 by an army gunman while saying mass in the chapel of the Divine Providence Hospital for the terminally ill poor.

OR snuffs out his candle and places it on the table.

Song: Señor, tempiedade de nos (Lord have mercy on us) Kyrie from South America (MAG)

Scripture reading: John 19:40–42; 20:1–18a
(A dramatised reading, with a narrator, JC reading Jesus' words and a third voice, or SW, reading the words of Mary Magdalene.)

SW picks up the last of the red lighted candles and moves to an appropriate place to speak.

Leader: Simone Weil was born in Paris into a secular Jewish family. She suffered repeated ill-health as both a child and an adult, and was particularly prone to violent headaches. Weil became a distinguished philosophy student and teacher. She was an intellectual, but wanted to stand in solidarity with the working class. Between teaching posts in universities and schools she worked at the Renault car factory and served on the Catalonian front of the Spanish Civil War. Weil found these experiences incredibly hard. She described working in the factory as degrading and exhausting. She dreaded going into work, was constantly tired and was disappointed at the lack of solidarity among the workers. The experience in Spain provided further disappointment, particularly the division and inequality between the Republican army and the peasants for whom they were supposed to be fighting.

In her disillusion, Simone Weil began a quest in search of truth and God, and recorded in her diary a number of mystical experiences that led her to Christian faith. She wrote that she was always inspired by the post-communion radiance of a young English Catholic. This man told Simone about the seventeenth-century 'metaphysical' poets. She began to read their work and discovered the poem 'Love' by George Herbert.

SW: Love bade me welcome: yet my soul drew back,
     Guilty of dust and sin.
     But quick-eyed Love, observing me grow slack
     From my first entrance in,
     Drew nearer to me, sweetly questioning
     If I lacked anything.

     'A guest', I answered, 'worthy to be here.'
     Love said, 'You shall be she.'
     'I, the unkind, ungrateful? Ah my dear,
     I cannot look on thee.'
     Love took my hand, and smiling did reply,
     'Who made the eyes but I?'

     'Truth, Lord, but I have marred them; let my shame
     Go where it doth deserve.'
     'And know you not', says Love, 'who bore the blame?'
     'My dear, then I will serve.'
     'You must sit down', says Love, 'and taste my meat.'
     So I did sit and eat.

Leader: Simone learnt this poem by heart. Often at the culminating point of a violent headache she made herself say it repeatedly, focusing all her attention on the tenderness it offers. She began to realise that she was reciting it as a prayer, and wrote in her diary that during one of her recitations Christ himself came down and took possession of her. Up to then she had always considered the question of God as an intellectual one, never believing in real contact in this life between a human being and God until she experienced it so dramatically for herself. She recorded feeling, in the midst of her suffering, the powerful presence of a love that she described as being like the smile on the face of a loved one. Despite these experiences Simone Weil refused to join the Church officially, but her love for Christ continued to grow and deepen.

War broke out in Europe, and in 1941 Simone went to live in the South of France where she worked in the fields and studied Greek and

Hindu philosophy. She went to America in 1942 and then to England to work for the Free French Movement.

In January 1943 Simone Weil was diagnosed with tuberculosis. She refused to eat any more than her compatriots living in occupied France, despite her severe illness. She died in August 1943 at the early age of 34 from a combination of malnutrition and tuberculosis.

SW: 'And know you not', says Love, 'who bore the blame?'
'My dear, then I will serve.'
'You must sit down', says Love, 'and taste my meat.'
So I did sit and eat.

SW snuffs out her candle and places it on the table.

Communion

All who took the roles of the martyrs stand. JC lifts the chalice and paten in the air and they all say together:

Our bodies and our blood we give to you. Do this in remembrance.

These five people pass the bread and the wine between themselves and then to all assembled.

After communion, JC relights the five extinguished candles on the table then all those who played the characters of the martyrs leave the room together.

Song: Jesus Christ is waiting (CG)

Blessing *(given from the back of the worship space)*

Be poor, go down to the far end of society, take the last place, live with those who are despised, love others and serve them instead of making them serve you.
Do not fight them when they push you around, but pray for those that hurt you.
Do not look for pleasure, but turn away from things that satisfy your senses and your mind and look for God in hunger, thirst and darkness, through the deserts of the spirit in which it seems to be madness to travel.
Take upon yourself the burden of Christ's cross, that is Christ's humility and poverty, obedience and renunciation, and you will find peace for your souls.

Charles de Foucauld

Solo: Make me a channel of your peace (SOGP)

Notes

[1] The four red candles represent the four twentieth century martyrs highlighted in this liturgy. The white candle represents the person of Jesus Christ.

[2] This candle represents the continuing presence of God, even in the darkest times.

IN AN UNJUST WORLD

IN AN UNJUST WORLD

Peter Millar

A phrase that has stuck in my consciousness for many years is this: 'It is so easy to tame the gospel.' It certainly is! Taming the gospel of Christ means removing its radical edge so that it becomes only a vehicle of spiritual comfort, rather than one of challenge. That is not to say that the gospel does not also carry comfort and healing, but the dimension of challenge is much needed in our time.

Bishop Helder Camara, whom I regard as a modern saint because of his long and courageous commitment to the poor in his native Brazil, invited us, in one of his beautiful prayers, to experience what he called the 'uncomfortable peace of God'. That peace which propels us to work and struggle for justice – even against all the odds. He himself was motivated by that kind of peace, and the most marginalised families in his poverty-stricken diocese in Recife knew that he walked with them, both in solidarity and in deep compassion.

And what this chapter helps us to understand is that amazingly powerful linkage of concern for injustice with a heart propelled by compassion. By love. A Christian commitment to work for lasting justice in our world begins (and ends) in the heart of God. For God is justice – a fact from which we cannot escape. And that means that work for justice and listening to God are always interconnected.

This radical engagement is never going to be a particularly comfortable expression of Christianity in the modern world for it involves sacrificial living, or – to put it another way – costly discipleship. And to live sacrificially is, in many ways, a counter-cultural witness.

As I know from my own experience of living for many years in the south world, there are no quick fixes to global and local injustice. Yet it is also a marker of our times that those women and men who are engaged in this struggle for justice are, through their lives, renewing and transforming us all, whether we are conscious of it or not. That is a remarkable truth in our globalised world. Almost a miracle, I would suggest!

It is also a moment of great possibility for the world community. The world can become a more compassionate place. People everywhere do care. There is hope. I love the idea that angels are nudging us all to open our hearts, hands, baskets and pockets. God is writing a message on our hearts, and in love we can respond. And we need not be afraid.

FROM SLAVERY TO FREEDOM:
A liturgy of repentance, commemoration and commitment
Iain Whyte

Iain Whyte, a Church of Scotland minister and member of the Iona Community, has recently completed a doctorate on the Anti-Slavery Movement in Scotland in the 18th and 19th centuries.

Slavery was part of the 'great' ancient civilisations of Greece, Rome, Babylon and Egypt. In the 15th century, European powers captured or bought men, women and children as slaves from the west coast of Africa and, until the late 19th century, transported ten million of them across the Atlantic in what has been termed 'Africa's holocaust'. The sugar colonies of the West Indies and the cotton states of America were built on slave labour and provided a platform for the prosperity of the industrialised West today. Slave owners and their governments resisted any changes with violence, and the Southern States fought a war to protect their interests in slavery. Few provided any challenge to the system until the late 18th century when, in response to this shame on Christendom, there developed a great movement of men and women who dedicated their lives to bringing about the destruction of the slave trade and of slavery. The names of William Wilberforce and David Livingstone are well known. Alongside them were many unsung heroes: politicians, church figures, local organisers, and, above all, slaves themselves, who contributed to the ending of slavery in the British Colonies in 1834 and to emancipation in the United States in 1863. Yet today, in the 21st century, millions of people remain enslaved around the world.

Before the service, construct a long paper chain and wrap it around, for example, a cross, the communion table of the church, the font, the pews, chairs …

Prepare action sheets using information from campaigning organisations suggesting actions (e.g. letter writing campaigns, use of consumer power – FAIRTRADE Mark, Rug Mark …) that can be taken to help end 21st-century slavery.

Introduction

In this service we will remember with penitence the evils of the Atlantic slave trade and celebrate the lives of those many unsung people who contributed to emancipation.

Tragically, slavery is not a story from history. There are 27 million slaves in the world today – more than ever before. We will be invited to commit ourselves to be 21st-century abolitionists, working for freedom from slavery in our time.

In this place we are hopefully all agreed that slavery is incompatible with the Christian Gospel of love, which values every human being as God's child. But those Christians who worked to overthrow slavery in the 18th and 19th centuries did not always find the Bible an automatic ally and their opponents would often challenge them with scripture passages to justify their position.[1] Imagine the following conversation between *James Tobin*, a West Indian sugar planter, and *James Stephen*, an abolitionist, around the end of the 18th century.[2]

Dramatic dialogue

Tobin: Mr Stephen, I see that you are one of the Clapham 'Saints'.[3] I take it that you know your Bible well. You cannot deny that God permitted the Israelites to take slaves of other races. The book of Leviticus makes that very clear.

Stephen: There is no comparison between the domestic slaves kept by the Hebrews and the conditions being endured by field slaves on the plantations. You should read Exodus 5. It was from this same situation of cruel working conditions and repeated floggings that God delivered the people of Israel from slavery in Egypt. That's the real parallel.

Tobin: Even Abraham was permitted to use his wife's Egyptian slave Hagar, and God told her to return to her mistress and submit to her. *(Genesis 16)* The word of God sanctions taking slaves from other nations, yet you object to us buying heathen slaves from Africa.

Stephen: To quote my good friend Rev. James Ramsay[4]: 'Was Hagar taken in chains on a slave-ship and imprisoned in the hold for weeks on end, emerging starved and sick to be sold on the block?' Once again your analogy doesn't stand up.

Tobin: Ramsay was a menace. He stirred up the slaves by his fancy notions of their conversion and improvement. He should have minded his own business and simply preached the gospel instead of getting involved in matters that are nothing to do with priests. Jesus didn't condemn slavery – he even healed the slave of a centurion.

Stephen: That is exactly what Ramsay did for Caribbean slaves. Until your friends drove him out. Jesus taught that the Law and the Prophets depended on love of God and love of neighbour as ourselves. And the neighbour in his best known parable was of another race. If slavery is so beneficial why don't *you* take a trip on the Middle Passage and then spend seven years toiling in the fields?[5]

Tobin: Paul made it clear that slaves should obey their masters *(Colossians 3:22)* and he returned a runaway slave to Philemon. What do you say to that?

Stephen: Paul also wrote that in Christ there is no distinction of slave and free *(1 Corinthians 12:13)* and encouraged the Corinthians to seek freedom rather than bondage. He instructed Philemon to receive Onesimus back as a brother. That's rather a contrast to the hunting of runaway slaves from your estates with dogs, and the lashes and chains you subject them to when they're caught.

Tobin: The Bible is quite clear about God allowing slavery, and permits discipline to control them, which you wish to deny to us.

Stephen: If you follow the instructions of scripture in the Old Testament I suggest you read Exodus 21:26. It says that if a slave's eye or tooth is destroyed by the master's violence they must be released. If that were followed in the West Indies there would be hardly any slaves left.

Tobin: It's all very well for you and your pious friends in Clapham to quote bits of scripture at me. But I'm a businessman. I live in the real world. I can't afford the luxury of idealism. All this petitioning of Parliament and boycott of sugar is dangerous nonsense. Our sugar plantations create the wealth that keeps this country advancing and if slavery were abolished we would all suffer. Ask any merchant; they'll back me up.

Stephen: Not so! In March **1788** the Edinburgh Chamber of Commerce declared in a petition to the House of Commons that they do not believe that the slave trade is as necessary or profitable as has been represented. And they went on 'even if this were not so much the case, the feelings of your petitioners as men would overbear their opinion as merchants and lead them to sacrifice somewhat of the convenience and profit of commerce to the rights and principles of humanity.'

Hymn: Amazing grace[6]

Scripture reading: Exodus 5:1–18

Reflection: Slavery today

Today up to 200,000 people are held in conditions of slavery in the United States, and perhaps one quarter of that number in Britain. Many people live next door to a family which has a domestic from the Philippines; thousands of these women work long hours without pay or holiday, trapped by their immigration status or the withholding of their passport by those they work for. Women from impoverished Eastern Europe are 'recruited' for employment in cities such as London and Paris and find themselves trapped as slaves in the sex industry.

There are millions more slaves around the world. Much of the chocolate we buy may be made from cocoa harvested by young boys enslaved on plantations in the Ivory Coast, our wood may come from a 'debt camp' in Brazil's rainforest, many of our domestic carpets are made by children forced to work as bonded labourers in India.

Prayer of confession

Leader: We confess that so much of our standard of living lies on the foundations of a system of slavery. A system that held human life cheap, destroyed families, transported human beings as cargo, and condemned millions to a shortened life of hopeless misery.

ALL: GOD FORGIVE, AND HELP US TO ACKNOWLEDGE OUR PAST.

Leader: We confess that this system was conveniently accepted as commercial necessity and justified for centuries by religion; that it corrupted and brutalised our fellow citizens as sailors on slave ships or plantation overseers.

ALL: GOD FORGIVE, AND ENABLE US TO FIND A NEW SOLIDARITY WITH OTHERS.

Leader: We confess that our standard of living still rests on the slavery to debt endured by so many in our world. Poor people denied medical, educational and social facilities in order that their governments may repay interest to the rich world.

ALL: GOD FORGIVE, AND INSPIRE US TO POLITICAL ACTIVITY FOR A JUST WORLD.

Leader: We confess that we shop or bank uncritically, enabling profits to be made from children enslaved on cocoa farms or in rug-making factories, and men and women imprisoned in labour camps.

ALL: GOD FORGIVE, AND HELP US TO USE OUR PURCHASING POWER RIGHTLY.

Leader: We confess that all too often we close our ears to the cries of women exploited in sexual slavery or domestic servitude because we don't want to believe that this happens in our society.

ALL: GOD FORGIVE, AND LEAD US TO OPEN OUR EARS AND RAISE OUR VOICES. AMEN

Hymn: Let us break bread together[7]

Scripture reading: Exodus 6:2; 6–8

Prayer of thanksgiving

Leader: For the pioneers who first led the struggle against slavery.
Granville Sharp who studied law to rescue slaves in England through the courts,
Thomas Clarkson who collected evidence on the slave trade in the pubs of Bristol and Liverpool, and
William Dickson who persuaded people in Scotland to send 176 petitions to Parliament for the abolition of the slave trade.

ALL: GOD BE PRAISED.

Leader: For the courage of countless slaves who resisted the system.
Olaudah Equinano, Ottabah Cugoano and Ignatio Sancho who had experienced the slave trade and tirelessly campaigned against it, and women such as Mary Prince in the West Indies and Sojourner Truth in the United States who wrote and spoke for the destruction of the slave system.

ALL: GOD BE PRAISED.

Leader: For the faith of those who saw the total inconsistency between Christianity and slavery and spoke out boldly.
John Wesley in England,
Andrew Thomson in Scotland, and
Anthony Benezet and the Quakers in America.

ALL: GOD BE PRAISED.

Leader: For all who today risk their lives to seek the truth and expose the reality of modern slavery.
Investigative journalists, welfare officers and social workers,
those who campaign for and organise release,
and those who contribute money and time to the cause of abolition.

ALL: GOD BE PRAISED.

Leader   For all who work or volunteer for organisations concerned about those in bondage.
Anti-Slavery International,
Free the Slaves,
and for their members and supporters.

ALL: GOD BE PRAISED.
AMEN

A litany of celebration[8]

Reader 1:   *David Spens* was a slave bought from a Scottish planter in Grenada and brought to Fife by his master Dr David Dalrymple, who named him 'Black Tom'. David Spens was baptised in Wemyss Parish Church in 1769 and the next day left Dalrymple's house. He returned with a local farmer and declared that as a Christian he was no longer under his master's 'tyrannous power', he was a good subject of the king, and he had friends who would support him to remain a free man. Despite arrest and brief imprisonment, he secured widespread and varied support. Lawyers represented him without a fee, several churches held collections for him, and the local miners and salters contributed to his costs. Dalrymple died before the case went to court and David Spens was free.

ALL: GOD OF THE COURAGEOUS, WE CELEBRATE THOSE WHO REFUSE TO ACCEPT THE STATUS OF SLAVES BUT AFFIRM IN FAITH THEIR BIRTHRIGHT AS MEMBERS OF THE HUMAN FAMILY.

Reader 2:   *James Ramsay* was an Episcopalian priest from Aberdeenshire who trained in medicine. After being invalided out of the navy, where he had risked his life in treating an epidemic on a slave-ship, he held a church-living in the West Indies and gave medical treatment to plantation slaves. Forced out of St Christopher's by the slave owners, he dedicated the rest of his life to destroying the slave trade. His evidence to William Wilberforce was crucial to the campaign in Parliament, but attacks on his character by the powerful West Indian planters' party in the House of Commons led to his early death in 1789. His Nigerian biographer Folarin Shyllon called him 'the unknown abolitionist', saying that he was the first person to 'lift the veil from plantation slavery' and expose its true horrors.

ALL: GOD OF JUSTICE, WE CELEBRATE THOSE WHO TAKE THE LONELY ROAD FOR CONSCIENCE'S SAKE AND WHO SPEAK THE TRUTH AT GREAT PERSONAL COST.

Reader 3:   *Hannah More* was a playwright, novelist and poet from Bristol, one of the principal ports in England from which the slave trade was conducted. Although Wilberforce and the male abolitionists were unwilling to allow women even to sign petitions on slavery until the 1800s, More became a key figure amongst their circle, offering personal support and political advice. She wrote a highly influential poem on the slave trade in 1788, commended the cause to society women, and made her home a centre from which many anti-slavery campaigns were organised. She was prominent in the Bristol and Clifton Female Anti-Slavery Society, which promoted a boycott of West Indian sugar in 1827 in the teeth of strong counter-measures from the city's merchants.

ALL: GOD WHO RAISED UP UNLIKELY PROPHETS, WE CELEBRATE THOSE WHO REFUSE TO ACCEPT THEIR 'GIVEN' ROLE BUT BRING NEW AND CREATIVE GIFTS TO GREAT CAUSES.

Reader 4: *Zachary Macaulay* was born in 1768 in Inveraray where his father was the parish minister. As a young man he worked as an overseer in Jamaica and the experience haunted him all his life. Macaulay served as governor of the new colony established in Sierra Leone for free slaves. In 1795 he sailed on a slave-ship to Barbados, keeping a diary in code that detailed the facts of the slave trade and slavery. For nearly forty years he collected data that gave ammunition to abolitionists in Parliament. From 1824 until slavery was abolished in the British Empire he edited the campaign's newspaper, *The Anti-Slavery Monthly Reporter*, which at its peak ran to twenty thousand copies. His single-minded and effective dedication despite increasing ill-health led many to see him as the most feared opponent of slave-owning interests in Britain.

ALL: GOD OF CONSTANCY, WE CELEBRATE THOSE WHOSE PAINSTAKING WORK PROVIDES THE RESOURCES FOR OTHERS TO BRING ABOUT FREEDOM.

Reader 5: *Harriet Tubman* spent twenty-five years as a slave in Maryland. After her escape to the Northern Free States she became a key figure in the 'underground railway', a network of both black and white people who provided food and shelter for runaway slaves from the South and guided them on their next journey to safer havens. In the 1850s a thousand slaves a year managed to reach freedom, despite the professional 'slave-catchers' who returned many more to their masters. Despite the severe risks and the horrific penalties of being caught, Harriet made nineteen trips to the eastern shore of Maryland to shepherd over three hundred slaves to freedom. She was nicknamed the 'Moses of her people', and, before her death at the age of 93, Queen Victoria awarded her a silver medal.

ALL: GOD OF COMMUNITY, WE CELEBRATE THOSE WHO DO NOT SIMPLY REST IN THEIR OWN FREEDOM BUT RISK IT TO ENABLE OTHERS TO GAIN LIBERATION.

Reader 6: *Sam Sharpe*, a Jamaican Baptist preacher, led a rebellion of his fellow slaves in 1831, when the planters in the West Indies were resisting every attempt to advance the abolition of colonial slavery. Sharpe preached that he had learnt from the Bible that whites had no more right to keep blacks in slavery than the other way round, and he encouraged his followers to use non-violent resistance by refusing to work and claiming their freedom. The revolt was brutally suppressed by the military with great loss of life, and Sharpe was quickly executed. His final words were 'I would rather die upon yonder gallows than live in slavery'. Sharpe's death led to increased and urgent calls in Britain to hasten abolition.

ALL: GOD IN WHOM DEATH BRINGS LIFE, WE CELEBRATE FAITHFUL MARTYRS FROM WHOSE BLOOD COMES THE SEEDS OF LIBERATION FOR US ALL.

Reader 7: *Kevin Bales* is the first Director of Free the Slaves, founded in 2000 as a sister organisation in America to the British-based Anti-Slavery International. Kevin's extensive work researching slavery in the global economy today, from prostitution in Thailand to the debt-bondage logging camps in Brazil, has made him an international expert. He has travelled to remote parts of India and the Ivory Coast to investigate children held in slavery to make carpets and produce cocoa for rich-world consumption. Kevin has published several books, and acted as consultant to the United Nations on trafficking in people. His passion to publicise the plight of the forgotten 27 million slaves who fuel our economies has been warmly commended by Archbishop Desmond Tutu.

ALL: GOD OF THE FORGOTTEN PEOPLE, WE CELEBRATE THOSE WHO RISK THEMSELVES TO BRING EVIL TO LIGHT, AND WHO CHALLENGE US TO ACTION.

Action

The congregation are invited to go to the paper chain and to break one or more of its links, as a symbol of their commitment to work for the abolition of all forms of slavery. They are also invited to pick up an action sheet and to undertake one or more of the suggested actions subsequent to the service.

Song: Freedom is coming (from South Africa) (FIC) *or* If you believe and I believe (from Zimbabwe) (CG)

Closing responses (based on Psalm 30)

Leader: Sing praise to God all you faithful people!
ALL: GIVE THANKS TO THE HOLY NAME OF GOD
Leader: For the tears of night have turned to joy with the dawn.
ALL: AND YOU HAVE CHANGED OUR SADNESS TO A JOYFUL DANCE.
Leader: We will sing of your praise and never be silent.
ALL: O GOD, OUR GOD, WE WILL GIVE YOU THANKS FOR EVER.

Notes

[1] A modern equivalent of this would be the Dutch Reformed Church in South Africa, whose justification of apartheid cited the inferiority of the sons of Ham as 'hewers of wood and drawers of water', and the Tower of Babel as supposedly showing divine disapproval of racial mixing. South African church leaders such as Desmond Tutu and Alan Boesak challenged these arguments on theological grounds in the same way as did the abolitionists two centuries earlier.

[2] **James Tobin** was a leading planter in Nevis. He returned to England and became a spokesperson in the 1790s for business interests in the West Indies. **James Stephen** had worked as a lawyer in the neighbouring island of St Kitts. He returned to Britain, married Wilberforce's sister, entered Parliament and drafted legislation against the slave trade and slavery.

[3] A group of evangelical abolitionists who lived near to Wilberforce.

[4] **James Ramsay** – *James Ramsay: The Unknown Abolitionist* by Folarin Shyllon, Canongate, Edinburgh, 1977.

[5] Most West Indian slaves on the plantations survived less than seven years.

[6] This famous hymn was written by **John Newton** (1725–1820), the former captain of a slave ship, who experienced a dramatic conversion during a storm at sea. At first he tried to reconcile his new-found faith with the slave trade as 'God's providence', but later had a further change of heart and became an effective preacher and advocate for abolition.

[7] There are several versions of this hymn, which was one of the many sung by American slaves containing code words. For example, 'Steal away to Jesus' had the double meaning of a call to escape. In this hymn, 'Let us fall on our knees with our face to the rising sun' indicated prayer before the journey on the 'underground railway' to Canada and freedom.

[8] This litany involves seven readers, representing six significant figures in the movement against slavery in past centuries, and one in our own time.

Alternative hymns

Dear Lord and Father of mankind – The author of this hymn, John Greenleaf Whittier (1807–1892), was a friend of the abolitionist William Lloyd Garrison and, through him, became passionately involved in American anti-slavery, editing *The Pennsylvania Freeman.*

Put thou thy trust in God –This hymn was written by the founder of Methodism, John Wesley (1703–1791), who was a strong opponent of slavery. Wesley's pamphlet 'Thoughts on Slavery', published in 1774, was one of the first against the slave trade. His last letter before he died was to William Wilberforce, encouraging him in the cause.

Ye gates lift up your heads – Andrew Thomson (1778–1831), who wrote the familiar tune St Georges, Edinburgh to this Scottish Psalter version of Psalm 24, was a leading member of the Edinburgh Committee for the abolition of slavery. In 1831 his speech in the Assembly Rooms turned public opinion in favour of an immediate rather than a gradual approach to abolition.

AIDS/HIV:

A liturgy of solidarity and justice

Helen Boothroyd, Elizabeth Paterson, Neil Paynter

This liturgy addresses the tragedy of AIDS/HIV as a justice issue, particularly on the continent of Africa, where AIDS is pandemic in many countries yet the vast majority of those infected cannot afford life-saving medication. The assertion of patent rights by large rich-world pharmaceutical companies has severely exacerbated this injustice by keeping drug prices high.

We compiled the liturgy using an idea and material from Elizabeth Paterson, a member of the Iona Community who worked for many years in Uganda and witnessed the tragedy of AIDS/HIV.

Before the service begins, a world globe is placed in the centre of the worship space and is surrounded by candles. A Peters Projection map of the world is placed on a table or on the floor in front of the globe and candles. Countries of the world where a high proportion of the population suffer from AIDS/HIV, or where infection rates are growing very rapidly, are highlighted on the map by a colour or symbol (a red ribbon).

The following are placed near the central tableau:

- *A supply of small unlit hand-held candles[1] and night lights, sufficient for one candle and one night light for each member of the congregation;*
- *A pile of action sheets containing information about the assertion of patent rights by pharmaceutical companies and rich countries and the impact this has on those suffering from AIDS/HIV in poorer countries. The action sheet should include case studies, actions needed to overcome the unjust distribution of life-saving drugs, and addresses to which letters or emails should be sent, including, for example: large multinational pharmaceutical companies, rich-world governments and the World Trade Organisation.*

The candles surrounding the globe are lit before the congregation arrives for the service.

Introduction

We come together in solidarity with those affected by AIDS and HIV throughout the world.

Opening responses *(based on Psalm 121)*

Leader: We come searching for help,
            raising our eyes to the hills and heaven.

ALL: GOD, LOVING MAKER OF EVERYTHING AND EVERYONE,
            COME, HELP US.

Leader: We come with our anxieties and fears,
            our doubts and pain –
            with all the things that keep us awake in the dark night.

ALL: GOD, WHO NEVER SLEEPS OR TURNS AWAY,
            STAY WITH US; COMFORT US NOW AND IN THE LONG LONELY HOURS.

Leader: We come needing to feel safe and accepted,
            fearful of all that judges, hurts and excludes.

ALL: GOD, WHO KEEPS OUR LIVES, ENFOLD US IN YOUR LOVE;
            BE WITH US NOW AND FOR EVERMORE.

Gathering song

A personal story from Africa: *A story is read, from a newspaper or magazine, concerning the experience of a person, family or community affected by AIDS/HIV.*

Scripture reading: Psalm 22:1–11

Reflection

Voice 1:   HIV and AIDS cut across all boundaries.
            Parents, aunts, uncles, brothers, sisters, children.
            Members of communities and congregations.

Voice 2:   36 million people in the world are HIV positive.
            75% of these people live in poor countries.
            25 million people in Africa alone.
            2.3 million people in Sub-Saharan Africa die of AIDS each year[2].
            (Pause)

Voice 1:   Young, mobile people are often most at risk –
            those working away from home, students, long distance lorry drivers, members of the armed forces.
            Women are more easily infected – and teenage girls are particularly vulnerable.

Voice 2:   At present rates of infection and mortality,
a 15-year-old in Botswana has a 9 in 10 chance of dying of AIDS. Already 35% of the adult population of Botswana is infected.
(Pause)

Voice 1:   Young couples die,
leaving children to be brought up by aged grandparents,
or to be shared among relatives –
or to fend for themselves.

Voice 2:   There are already 12 million children orphaned by AIDS in Sub-Saharan Africa, about the same number of children as live in the whole United Kingdom.

Scripture reading: Luke 16:19–31

Prayer of confession

Voice 1:   Lord, we live in a world that is divided.
A world of obscene wealth and
a world of scandalous poverty.
A world of greed and conspicuous consumption,
and a world of hunger and famine.
A world where some live in the lap of luxury,
and where many live in hell.

Voice 2:   Lord, we live in a world where the gulf between rich and poor people is widening by the minute:

A world obsessed with the lifestyles of the 'chosen few',
and a world of people who are completely left out of the picture.
A world hungry to consume more and more resources,
and a world of advancing deserts and increasing debt.
A world witnessing great medical and technological breakthroughs,
and a world that is being pushed back into the stone age.
A world where people expect to live for ever,
and a world where millions won't live to see their fortieth birthday.

A world of seemingly infinite choice.
And a world where people have no choice.

Voice 1:   Lord, forgive us for creating divisions in your world.

For erecting barriers that shut out the poor and hungry
and that safeguard us and the many things we own;

barriers that keep us insulated and in a state of unreality;
barriers that separate us from those we see as different, strange, alien –
from those we view as dangerous and unclean and want to keep from
entering our lives, our neighbourhoods, our world.

Barriers that stop us from reaching out to our sisters and brothers
and building your Kingdom of justice and peace.

Voice 2:   Lord, we are grateful for all of the good things we have received.
We remember those gifts for a moment now:
the people who love and accept us,
the security of home and healthcare …

Lord, we remember the many, in our divided world, who do not have
these things:

(silence)

Lord, open our hearts;
come close to us.

Help us to stop dividing up your world into first world, second world
third world, fourth world –
to stop creating more and more barriers.
Help us to see your world as One World,
and all people on this beautiful planet as our sisters and brothers.

Lift our eyes to those
in torment and anguish.
Help us to bring them comfort.

Lord, the starving are at our gates and we offer them crumbs!

Lord, have mercy.
Christ, free us.

Help us to open gates,
break down walls,
roll away stones,
lift heavy conditions,
heal divisions,
to share with our sisters and brothers the bread of life –
food, water, medicine, love.
Amen

Reading: A person of hope

There are some images that stay in the mind for ever. Even as I watched Dr Sandy Logie holding the hands of a young African man, dying of AIDS, in the middle of the Zambian bush, I knew I would always remember the moment.

Sandy had none of the West's expensive antiretroviral wonder-drugs, or strong painkillers, to offer the weak, emaciated man sitting under a tree by his dilapidated shack on that sweltering, uncomfortable day. That he was armed only with rehydration salts and vitamins made his tenderness all the more poignant. Patients back in his native Scotland had grown used to his gentle personal style, but it was accentuated that day by shared personal experience, for Sandy was, by then, himself a very ill man, also infected with the HIV virus.

He became infected with HIV in a Zambian hospital some years ago during what he hoped would be the first of a series of placements in Africa. There were several incidents that might have allowed infected blood into his system during his five-week stay at St Francis' Hospital in Katete, a rural backwater on the Malawi border, but his fate was probably sealed by an accidental prick with an infected needle.

I had the privilege of speaking at his funeral service. As we planned for that event I remember his widow, Dorothy, saying to me: 'I am sure Sandy would want us to concentrate more on the AIDS situation in Africa than on himself.'

Sandy wrote in *The British Medical Journal*:

'Any momentary relapse into self-pity responds to a comparison of my position with that of many patients with AIDS, who suffer severe, unsupported illness and die lonely, distressing deaths at less than half my age. During my time in Zambia I was often upset by my therapeutic impotence and inability to provide more than the simplest palliation to terminally ill young men and women, many of whom, especially women, had been cruelly rejected by their families and communities, and even separated from their children. In contrast I know that I can continue to rely on excellent medical care and all the necessary support to help me through whatever may lie ahead.'

As his own body became weaker and weaker, Sandy saw with clarity that AIDS in sub-Saharan Africa was not only a medical problem but was also having major socio-economic effects. He became more determined than ever to plead with his own government and aid agencies on the issue of international debt, which was only bringing further burdens to AIDS-stricken countries like Zambia.

Through it all he remained a person of hope. His lack of self-pity was nothing short of inspiring, and Dorothy now continues their international work, despite the sorrow which she carries after Sandy's death. As a tireless campaigner for the provision of really significant AIDS prevention and treatment services worldwide, she is herself a courageous and compassionate hope-bearer in our time.

Peter Millar

Introduction to action

There is increasing knowledge of how to slow and control AIDS with antiretroviral drugs. In the richer countries this is bringing hope to many who are HIV positive.

But in most poor countries AIDS/HIV sufferers are being denied access to the necessary medication. Patent rights on antiretrovirals and other drugs are owned by large rich-world pharmaceutical companies, who keep the market price far too high for poor people to afford. They fight to protect the patents on their products and to prevent the manufacture or import of cheaper generic copies by poor nations. These powerful multinational corporations are supported by western governments and by the World Trade Organisation.

Meanwhile, the poorest people in the world are left to die of AIDS. Up to 20 million Africans have died already.

Action

Members of the congregation are invited to come forward to the central area and pick up one night light, one hand-held candle and an action sheet.

They light the night light and place it on the world map, on a country or area where many people are suffering from HIV/AIDS.

They then light the candle, as a sign of their commitment to use the action sheet to write letters seeking justice for those suffering from HIV/AIDS in poorer countries, and return to their seats with the candle and their action sheet.

A chant is sung during the action.

Scriptural affirmation *(based on 1 Corinthians 12:12–27)*

FOR JUST AS THE BODY IS ONE AND HAS MANY MEMBERS,
AND ALL THE MEMBERS OF THE BODY, THOUGH MANY, ARE ONE BODY,
SO IT IS WITH CHRIST.
IF ONE MEMBER SUFFERS, ALL SUFFER TOGETHER WITH IT;
IF ONE MEMBER IS HONOURED, ALL REJOICE TOGETHER WITH IT.
WE ARE THE BODY OF CHRIST AND INDIVIDUALLY MEMBERS OF IT.
AMEN

Prayer of intercession

Voice 1:   God of love, we pray for all who are HIV positive or suffering from AIDS throughout the world.
For children left orphaned by the disease.
For all who are bereaved or who must watch their loved ones suffer.
May your arms, opened wide in compassion, surround and embrace them, this day and always.

Lord in your mercy,
ALL: HEAR OUR PRAYER.

Voice 2:   God of mercy, we thank you for the tremendous work done in hospitals,
by health care workers and by traditional healers.
We bring before you all who are involved in the work of caring:
pastors and elders; many thousands of ordinary women and men.
Bless and guide their work of love and care,
as they baptise, marry, counsel, visit, comfort, bury, console.
Lord in your mercy,
ALL: HEAR OUR PRAYER.

Voice 1:   God of service, we pray for your Church throughout the world.
May it give compassionate moral leadership, earning the trust and confi-
dence of those whom it seeks to serve.
Empower its leaders to be open, non-judgemental and truthful in
discussing AIDS, and to work with others to promote awareness.
May your Church be always a place of caring and healing, a grassroots
organisation concerned for the poor, the widowed, the orphaned, the
sick, those outcast; a passionate advocate for all who are disadvantaged.
Lord in your mercy,
ALL: HEAR OUR PRAYER.

Voice 2:   God of justice, we pray for those who make decisions
in pharmaceutical companies, governments and the
World Trade Organisation.
May they begin to put people before profit.
May the drugs available in the rich world be made affordable and avail-
able to all with HIV/AIDS.
Lord in your mercy,
ALL: HEAR OUR PRAYER.

Voice 1:   God of life, we pray for ourselves.
May we grow in compassion;
May we work for justice;
May we be bearers of light and hope.
Lord in your mercy,
ALL: HEAR OUR PRAYER. AMEN

The Lord's Prayer (said together)

Song: A touching place (CG)

Closing responses (Affirmation from South Africa)

Leader: It is not true that this world and its inhabitants are doomed to die
and be lost;

ALL: THIS IS TRUE: FOR GOD SO LOVED THE WORLD THAT HE GAVE HIS ONLY SON SO THAT EVERYONE WHO BELIEVES IN HIM SHALL NOT DIE BUT HAVE EVERLASTING LIFE.

Leader: It is not true that we must accept inhumanity and discrimination, hunger and poverty, death and destruction;

ALL: THIS IS TRUE: I HAVE COME THAT THEY MAY HAVE LIFE, AND HAVE IT ABUNDANTLY.

Leader: It is not true that violence and hatred shall have the last word, and that war and destruction have come to stay for ever;

ALL: THIS IS TRUE: FOR TO US A CHILD IS BORN, TO US A SON IS GIVEN, IN WHOM AUTHORITY WILL REST, AND WHOSE NAME WILL BE PRINCE OF PEACE.

Leader: It is not true that we are simply victims of the powers of evil that seek to rule the world;

ALL: THIS IS TRUE: TO ME IS GIVEN AUTHORITY IN HEAVEN AND ON EARTH, AND LO, I AM WITH YOU ALWAYS, TO THE END OF THE WORLD.

Leader: It is not true that we have to wait for those who are specially gifted, who are the prophets of the church, before we can do anything;

ALL: THIS IS TRUE: I WILL POUR OUT MY SPIRIT ON ALL PEOPLE, AND YOUR SONS AND DAUGHTERS SHALL PROPHESY, YOUR YOUNG PEOPLE SHALL SEE VISIONS, AND YOUR OLD FOLK SHALL DREAM DREAMS.

Leader: It is not true that our dreams of liberation of humankind, our dreams of justice, of human dignity, of peace, are not meant for this earth and its history;

ALL: THIS IS TRUE: THE HOUR COMES, AND IT IS NOW, THAT TRUE WORSHIP-PERS SHALL WORSHIP GOD IN SPIRIT AND IN TRUTH.

Alan Boesak

Closing prayer and blessing

Watch now, dear Lord,
with those who wake or watch or weep tonight,
and give your angels charge over those who sleep.
Tend your sick ones, O Lord Christ,
rest your weary ones,

bless your dying ones, soothe your suffering ones,
pity your afflicted ones, shield your joyous ones,
and all for your love's sake. Amen

And now may the God of hope
fill us with all joy and peace in believing,
that we may abound in hope
in the power of the Holy Spirit. Amen

Recessional chant

The chant used during the action is sung as the congregation process out carrying their lighted candles.

Suggested chants

Behold the Lamb of God (CG)
Kindle a flame to lighten the dark (WWB)
A Kyrie eleison
Lord, to whom shall we go? (CAYP)
Stay with me, remain here with me (CG)

Suggested songs

Brother, sister let me serve you (CG)
Christ be beside me (SGP)
Gather us in (CG)
God give us life (CG)
Humbly in your sight (SOGP)
Inspired by love and anger (LAA)
When our Lord walked the earth (Gifts of the Spirit) (WWB)

Notes

[1] A circle of cardboard should be placed around the middle of each candle for safe handling.

[2] '2.3 million people in Sub-Saharan Africa are dying of AIDS each year' – 2003 figure from Hansard 21.1.04.

LIVING WATER:
A liturgy from Iona Abbey, 2002

Katrina Crosby

Katrina Crosby was a member of the Iona Community's resident group from 2002 to 2005. When she first arrived on Iona she was inspired by the calm beauty of the island and the wildness of the sea; soon, though, she discovered a deeper passion: a personal commitment to justice and peace.

Katrina comes from British Columbia, a region of Canada characterised by mountains, rivers, lakes, the ocean, and lots of rain. The more Katrina learned about the need for a fair distribution of life-giving water in other parts of the world, the more she recognised the advantages she enjoys and felt the need to change some of her bad habits.

Wanting to share these concerns, she composed this liturgy, which she led in Iona Abbey in May 2002.

Opening responses

Leader: Creator Spirit, wellspring of our lives,
            as the refreshing rain falls on the just and unjust alike
ALL: REFRESH US WITH YOUR MERCY,
            WHO KNOWS OUR OWN INJUSTICE.
Leader: As the stream flows steadily on,
            defying all the odds of stone and water
ALL: FLOW OVER EVERY BOUNDARY AND BORDER
            THAT SEPARATES US FROM EACH OTHER.
Leader: As the waters of our baptism washed us and welcomed us
ALL: RENEW US NOW IN NEWNESS OF LIFE
            AND UNITY OF LOVE.
Leader: As we were once held
            in the waters of our mother's womb
ALL: HOLD US IN THE POWER AND PEACE
            OF YOUR ABIDING PRESENCE.

Song: As the deer longs (CG)

Scripture reading: John 4:5–15

Voice 1:   I live by the ocean, but can't drink the water.
Voice 2:   I live by a lake, but it's full of parasites.
Voice 3:   I live by a river, but it's polluted by industry.
Voice 4:   *(slowly)* I turn the tap … and clear, clean, fresh water pours out.

Leader: That last voice was our voice. But we are the lucky few. When we turn the tap, clear, clean, fresh water pours out. Most of the world's population are not so fortunate. As competition for access to water resources increases, the most vulnerable have the least influence. Water allocation and management favours the rich and powerful. Over a billion people have no safe water supply and over two billion people lack sanitation services[8]. Poor communities in both rural and urban areas lack these basic facilities. In many shanty towns poor people are forced to pay exorbitant prices for low quality, dirty water from small-scale private vendors.

Voice 1:   Like Hawa Amadu, who lives in one of the poorest parts of Accra, the capital of Ghana. Hawa's family and thirty-one others live clustered around a small courtyard. The tiny compound has no mains water supply and the nearest source of drinking water is a mile away. Every day Hawa has to pay forty pence when she collects the water. That may not sound much but it is more than half of the average daily wage in Ghana – for the most basic necessity for human life.

A rain stick is upturned slowly, its sound amplified throughout the worship space by a microphone.

Scripture reading: Psalm 42:1–2

Voice 4:   I brushed my teeth this morning.
             I do it twice every day.
             I know I shouldn't let the tap run.
             But I'm just not awake enough to remember.

Leader: Millions of people have no choice but to drink water that could kill them. Water-related diseases are the single largest cause of sickness and death in the world as a whole. Every 15 seconds a child dies from such diseases[2]. The lack of safe sanitation is a major contributor to this dirty water.

A rain stick is upturned slowly.

Scripture reading: Proverbs 11:25

Voice 4:   I had the best shower last night.
I just stood there for ages …
It felt soooo good,
just letting the water beat down.

Leader: Every day each person in the UK uses 150 litres of water, while at the same time some of the world's poorest people survive on the equivalent of a shower lasting just 90 seconds as their entire day's water supply. The United Nations has predicted that two out of three people will be living with water shortages in 2005[3].

A rain stick is upturned slowly.

Scripture reading: Psalm 24:1–2

Voice 4:   I just bought a new car.
I'm so in love with it.
So, of course I keep washing it …
nice and shiny; buff and wax and polish.
I suppose some of those cleaners aren't too good going down the drain.
But it's not for long; I know the novelty will soon wear off.

Leader: Last century global water consumption rose six-fold; more than twice the rate of population growth. The rate of consumption is still accelerating. It is the rich countries who are the big consumers.
Agriculture accounts for 70% of global water use. Growing consumption of meat and dairy products adds to this usage. A greater demand for animal feedstuffs means more water is needed for irrigation.
The industrial sector also consumes a huge amount of water: for example nearly 40,000 gallons for every new car manufactured.
The expansion of tourism for the rich in many poor countries swallows up valuable water resources from local communities for conspicuous consumption in hotel complexes and golf courses.[4]

A rain stick is upturned slowly.

Scripture reading: Genesis 24:17–20

Voice 4:   OK, I'll try and do better.
Use less water.
But it won't make much difference will it?

It's policy that's got to change.
But that's not down to me.

Scripture reading: Matthew 27:24b

Introduction to action

We cannot wash our hands of the injustice surrounding water management. We need to make our voices heard politically. Campaigning agencies are calling for governments to agree an action plan that will halve the number of people without sanitation by 2015 and secure adequate sanitation for all by 2025, and to give more aid to provide safe, accessible water supplies for all. If enough of us speak out, our government will have to listen. Let us commit ourselves to press the case for justice.

Action

Members of the congregation are invited to gather in the centre of the church to be sprinkled with water as a sign of their commitment to work for the provision of clean, safe water for all. The service leaders may use a branch or greenery to sprinkle the water.[5] During the sprinkling a chant is sung, e.g. Behold I make all things new (CAYP)

On the way back to their seats members of the congregation are asked to pick up an action sheet containing: information about the issues raised in this service, suggestions as to how they can conserve water, and government addresses they can write to supporting the demands of the campaigning agencies for access to water and sanitation for all.

Affirmation of faith

ALL:　　　WE AFFIRM OUR FAITH IN
　　　　　GOD THE CREATOR,
　　　　　JESUS, THE LIVING WATER,
　　　　　AND THE HOLY SPIRIT, FOUNT OF LOVE.

Leader:　God who created heaven and earth,
ALL:　　　AND FOUNDED THE LAND ON DEEP WATERS.
Leader:　God who flooded the earth
ALL:　　　AND GAVE US A PROMISE.
Leader:　God who divided the water
ALL:　　　AND SET THE PEOPLE FREE.
Leader:　God who leads us beside still waters
ALL:　　　AND GIVES US NEW STRENGTH.
　　　　　WE AFFIRM OUR FAITH IN YOU.

Leader:　Jesus who walked on water

ALL:	AND CALMED THE RAGING SEA.
Leader:	Jesus who turned water into wine
ALL:	AND BAPTISES US WITH WATER, SPIRIT, LOVE.
Leader:	Jesus who washed his disciples' feet
ALL:	AND WASHES OUR SOULS CLEAN.
	WE AFFIRM OUR FAITH IN YOU.
Leader:	Holy Spirit who is poured out
ALL:	AND COMES TO US AS WATER AND FIRE.
Leader:	Holy Spirit who is strength and power
ALL:	AND FILLS US WITH YOUR LIVING WATER.
Leader:	Holy Spirit who is gentleness and love
ALL:	AND IS GOD'S GIFT TO EACH OF US.
	WE AFFIRM OUR FAITH IN YOU.

Prayer: The water of life

O God,
pour out on us the water of life
that we may quench our thirst
and draw our strength from you.
Help us to stand alongside those
who struggle daily for clean water
so that all may be
refreshed and renewed by your love.

Christian Aid

Song: Mallaig sprinkling song (CG)

Scripture reading: Isaiah 55:1; 10–13

Closing responses

Leader:	A blessing on you who are poor,
ALL:	YOURS IS THE KINGDOM OF GOD.
Leader:	A blessing on you who mourn,
ALL:	YOU SHALL BE COMFORTED.
Leader:	A blessing on you who hunger and thirst for justice,
ALL:	YOU SHALL BE SATISFIED.
Leader:	A blessing on you who make peace,
ALL:	YOU SHALL BE CALLED THE CHILDREN OF GOD.
	AMEN

Notes

[1] 'Over a billion people have no safe water supply and over two billion people lack sanitation services' – statistic from Christian Aid, 2003

[2] 'Every 15 seconds a child dies from such diseases' – information from Water Aid website: www.wateraid.co.uk

[3] 'Two out of three people will be living with water shortages in 2005' – information from Water Aid website: www.wateraid.co.uk

[4] 'Last century global water consumption ...' – all information from Water Aid website: www.wateraid.co.uk

[5] This action is not necessarily intended to refer to Christian baptism. However, a sprinkling rite is used in some denominations as a reminder of baptism and baptismal promises. If appropriate, this renewal of baptismal commitment could also be referenced here.

IN THE BEGINNING ...
A liturgy about justice, food and sharing
Joy Mead

This liturgy would be particularly appropriate on Harvest Festival or on any occasion when food is to be shared.

Before the service, prepare a selection of seeds and fruit of as many shapes, sizes and colours as possible and place them at the front of the worship space.

Leader: For centuries, majority-world farmers have evolved crops and given us the diversity of plants that provide us our food – over centuries, Indian farmers have evolved 200,000 varieties of rice! Today, multinational corporations are stealing from poor farmers to secure patents on life forms, claiming seeds and plants as their own inventions and property.

Small farms are much more productive by land area than large farms. Yet in many poor countries exports of food crops by agri-businesses have boomed, as large rich companies use their wealth to acquire and exploit the best land, squeezing out small-scale food production for local consumption. Hunger is not about lack of food, but lack of rights

THE PROMISE OF LIFE

Opening responses

Leader: God, the promise of life in little bodies and tiny seeds,
ALL: WE SEEK EYES THAT WONDER AT THE MYSTERY OF THE EARTH.
Leader: God, the promise of life in the fragile wings of a butterfly,
ALL: WE SEEK TO KNOW OUR PART IN THE INTRICATE PATTERN OF BEING.
Leader: God, the promise of life in a child's trusting hands,
ALL: WE SEEK TO MAKE THE WAY OF WHOLENESS AND PEACE.
Leader: God, the promise of life in friendship and companionship,
ALL: WE SEEK TO UNDERSTAND THE MIRACLE OF EVERY SHARED MEAL.

Song: Imagination is a tree (TOEWK)

Litany of wonder

Reader 1:   Then God said: 'Let the earth produce growing things; let there be on the earth plants that bear seed, and trees bearing fruit each with its own kind of seed.' So it was; the earth produced growing things; plants bearing their own kind of seed and trees bearing fruit, each with its own kind of seed; and God saw that it was good. *(Genesis 1:11–12)*

Reader 2:   Give us seed corn to keep us alive or we shall die and our land will become a desert. (*Genesis 47:19b)*

Leader: Sustainability begins with wonder – the wonder of beginnings, of all life and means of life in tiny seeds, each holding secrets necessary to bear its own kind of fruit.

Reader 3:   The given beauty of it –
inert in my palm
tender, fragile thing
quietly holding
good for all people,
complex and intricate
storing life and the means
of life.
The silent wonder of it –
Jack in the beanstalk story:
always ready to sprout
while the sower is away;
fairy story; or miracle
seed, soil, labour, love;
life, death, rebirth,
earth's best gift,
seed of freedom.

Leader: Continuing life on earth may depend upon rekindling our sense of wonder and understanding fragile connections. Seed is not commodity. It is gift to be exchanged freely amongst people. Hope comes in such little things, little acts.

Reader 4:   In Bangladesh, over a hundred thousand farming families are part of the Bangladeshi Nayakrishi Andolan or 'New Agriculture Movement'. They have set up seed banks of traditional varieties that they call 'community seed wealth centres', and by swapping seeds they bypass commercial seed entirely. This maintains not only their self-reliance but also the biodiversity of the world's agricultural resources. They have over one thousand varieties of rice and thirty-seven vegetable varieties. Diversity is not just interesting – it is essential for continuing life. The slogan of the women in Nayakrishi Andolan is 'Keep the seed in your hand, sister'. They resist the trend of modern agriculture towards high yields and fashion foods. Their agri-*culture* is about nurturing the seed and depending more on local farmers' knowledge than cash investment.

Reader 5:   All beans have their own Jack in the Beanstalk story. They are magic in many different ways. The Happiness Co-operative on the edge of the Peten Rainforest in Northern Guatemala uses the macuna bean as a free fertiliser. These magic beans are planted in between rows of maize and allowed to decompose, making bean manure, which leaves the soil visibly richer and increases cereal yields, naturally and sustainably.

Leader: Hope is in the God of small things.

(Let us pray)

God of life's littleness,
give us
sensibility:
that we may learn to think fragility
and feel the wonder of the earth

understanding:
that we may know our part
in the intricate pattern of being

compassion:
that we may truly see
the small things of our earth,
and live gently and simply
alongside all living things.

Or:

Leader: We have need of awe and wonder:
that we may see the beauty of the earth as a finite whole; eternity in a tiny seed that seems to die; the understanding of all in the fall of a sparrow.

ALL: GOD OF ALL LOVE AND EVERY TRUTH,
HELP US TO LOOK WITH OPEN EYES,
TO SEE WITH OPEN HEARTS.

Leader: We have need of vision and imagination:
that we may see how waste and greed in one place diminish life in another; that we may rediscover the significance of surprise and sharing.

ALL: GOD OF ALL LOVE AND EVERY TRUTH,
HELP US TO LOOK WITH OPEN EYES,
TO SEE WITH OPEN HEARTS.

Leader: We have need of compassion and understanding:
that we listen to hidden people who know the value of diversity; whose long and earthy memories and ancient wisdom for survival could even now be our hope and our salvation.

ALL: GOD OF ALL LOVE AND EVERY TRUTH,
HELP US TO LOOK WITH OPEN EYES,
TO SEE WITH OPEN HEARTS.

Leader: We have need of fire and vigour:
that we may be angry at short-term policies, cold-blooded economics and heartless trading;
that we may protest at greed and the misuse of the earth's resources and the theft of nature's harvest by those who seek to patent life forms, who claim seeds to be their invention and property;
that we may desire justice with all our being and seek passionately the use of our abundant knowledge, skills and resources to cherish all life.

ALL: GOD OF ALL LOVE AND EVERY TRUTH,
HELP US TO LOOK WITH OPEN EYES
TO SEE WITH OPEN HEARTS.

Song: The greatness of the small (LFB)

CELEBRATING ABUNDANCE

Leader: Understanding seed, growth and culture also means having the wisdom and knowledge to celebrate abundance.

Listen to these verses from Psalm 104. People sang this psalm on pilgrimage to the temple. They walked through valleys filled with grain, saw the year crowned with good gifts and were filled with wonder and thankfulness not only for food and continuing life but also for the sheer beauty and wonder of it all.

If you have ever watched the morning light playing on rain-washed apples; looked at sun-lit strawberries, red as a trumpet sound, or broad beans and cabbages as green as tomorrow; tasted brown crusty bread, soft at its heart, cheese that crumbles on the tongue and tastes of dew-damp fields, the sweet floweriness of honey or the wonderful harmony of herbs, you will know that these things are magical.

That is what abundance is about – not about harnessing, enslaving or even storing, but about celebrating the sheer magic and beauty of food to be shared by all creation.

Scripture reading: Psalm 104:1–15

Leader: The psalm is clear about abundance – there is enough food for all to share. Hunger in a world of plenty is not caused by lack of food. There is enough food to make most people in the world fat! It is caused by lack of compassion and justice. Inequality is not just about economics; it's about moral choice. It's about compassion, community and getting personal. 'The personal is always political – but the political only becomes real, not theoretical, when it is grounded in the personal,' wrote Kathy Galloway, leader of the Iona Community. Food is creation's gift to all and becomes real in the sharing. George MacLeod, the founder of the Iona Community, wrote: 'The greatest community problem of our modern world is how to share bread.'

Song: Inspired by love and anger (CG)

Litany of change

Huge farms, genetic engineering, 'green revolutions' may make more food but they will not on their own feed the hungry. What is needed is attention to small things and the political will to make the food go around.

Voice 1:   Reforming global food trade:
            End dumping ... No subsidies for intensive agriculture ... Fair prices for farmers ... Protect local markets ... Domestic food crops before export crops ... Regulate trade.

Voice 2:   Giving farmers control:
            Access to land ... Access to markets ... End women's exclusion ... No patents on life ... Give farmers control over seed.

Voice 3:   Farming sustainably:
            Ecological techniques and stewardship ... Agricultural biodiversity ... Use farmers' knowledge ... Move away from intensive agriculture ... Encourage rural employment ... Diversify food cultures.

Leader: To make all this happen we need to feel and think and imagine – to see how things could be different. Food, in all its ordinariness and concreteness, calls us to enter the mystery of our relationship with the earth and our interconnectedness with all life. Our food is sacred; our eating together a holy act, a miracle, not to be taken for granted. We need to recapture the wonder and spontaneity of food sharing.

SHARING BREAD

Scripture reading: John 6:1–13

An ordinary miracle

The first to come out of the crowd
as the sun goes down
and touches the hillside
with expectancy: a small guardian
of the future
with trust in his eyes
and hope in his hands.

In him, Andrew sees something
of himself; meets a memory:
a shadow of long ago when he was a boy,
his energy unsullied and his vision clear;
a whisper from the depths of his being
about fairness and sharing
and simple answers.

A disciple in an impossible position,
reminded of his first care –
to feed others,
wondering about miracles;
a boy bearing food, risking ridicule,
trusting the bread of life:
here, now, late in the day
they make their gentle way
to one whose work
is in such small but costly acts;

who sees in each hungry face
an undying melody, an essential fragility,
a childlike joy not wholly lost
to a bigger future.

And so …
in this once upon a time moment …
the story begins.
Outrageous hope, outspoken love,
justice and joy are released
like nudging angels
amongst people
longing for comfort and community,
sensing the beginnings of friendships,
wanting touch and affirmation.

Child, disciple and the one who understands
about just and equal sharing:
know there will be enough
to go round;
refuse to say, 'It can't be done.'

So it happens – the great feast:
hearts and hands, baskets and pockets,
open;
neighbour gives bread
and peace to neighbour
each makes a place for another
and in this most ordinary of miracles
all are fed.

Leader: Our sharing, our stumbling generosity, our simple actions are good enough to prepare a feast for all people, good enough to change the world. Maybe it's naïve to think that small groups of people gathered to share ordinary food – to value the food and the sharing – can make a difference; but in the end it's probably the only thing that will.

The miracle of sharing

God of our open futures,
help us:

to explore
once upon a time moments
where stories begin
and outrageous hope
outspoken love
justice and joy
are released;

to see
where the nudging angels
move amongst people
longing for comfort and community
sensing beginnings of friendship
wanting touch and affirmation;

to enable
life's great feast to happen,
hearts and hands, baskets and pockets
to open,
neighbour to share bread
and peace with neighbour,
to make a place for another;

so that in the most ordinary of miracles
all are fed.

Closing responses:

ALL: GOD OF OPEN HANDS AND ONCE-UPON-A-TIME MOMENTS,
          HELP US TO EXTEND THE BOUNDARIES OF THE POSSIBLE
          AND TO CONTINUALLY RE-DREAM THE WORLD. AMEN

Closing song: Hands shaped like a cradle (TOEWK)

Blessing

Spirit of lightness and life
be with all makers and dreamers:
all who make bread
and long to share it;
all who make music
and long to dance;
all who make words
and long for poetry;
all who are born in flesh
and long to be human;
all who make love
and trust their longing
for life.
Amen

On the way out of the service, each person is given a seed to take away and plant.

BALANCING THE SCALES:
A liturgy for justice in the global marketplace
Helen Boothroyd

For this service you will need:

- *A large set of kitchen scales, placed on a central table. These scales need to be of the type with a scale pan on one side and a platform for a set of weights on the other. This set of weights is initially piled beside the scales, and the weights are gradually placed on to the scales during the litany of trade injustice.*

- *Counter weights: to be placed by members of the congregation in the scale pan during the symbolic action. To make the counterweights:*
  - *Cut out rough circles of cloth or plastic (e.g. from a bin bag).*
  - *Put a little sand or soil in the middle of each circle.*
  - *Fold the cloth or plastic in over the filling, scrunch the top and tie it firmly with an elastic band, piece of string or rubbish bag tie.*
  The combined weight of all the counterweights should be slightly less than or equal to the total of the set of weights that come with the scales. (It is important that they are not heavier.) The bags are placed in a pile by the kitchen scales.

- *A large drawing of the international FAIRTRADE Mark, which is hung centrally.*

- *An information sheet for each member of the congregation listing the full range of available Fairtrade products and contact details for the Trade Justice Movement. It would be good to leave these information sheets on each seat before the service or to have them given out at the door as people leave the service.*

Opening responses *(based on Isaiah 40 & 43)*

Leader:	Creator God, who made the sea and sky, who measured the waters in the hollow of your hand,
ALL:	YOU ARE A GOD OF JUSTICE.
Leader:	Great God, who weighed the mountains in a scale and the hills in a balance,
ALL:	YOU ARE A GOD OF JUSTICE.
Leader:	Righteous God, who accounts the power of nations as but dust, and brings corrupt rulers to nothing,
ALL:	YOU ARE A GOD OF JUSTICE.
Leader:	Loving God, in whose sight all people are precious and valued, honoured and redeemed,

ALL: YOU ARE A GOD OF JUSTICE.
Leader: God, who calls us each by name,
            come among us, give us understanding.
ALL: TEACH US THE WAY OF JUSTICE.

Song: Singing, we gladly worship (CG)

Scripture reading: Amos 8:4–7

Trampling the poor: A litany of trade injustice

Voice 1:   World trade is unfair. Very unfair. It favours the rich and powerful. Rich
            countries, rich companies, rich individuals. The poor are trampled, the
            needy pushed aside.

Voice 2:   It didn't start fair. There is no level playing field. The poor are weighed
            down by the policies of colonialism. The scales are tipped by the legacy
            of the past. Colonised countries were used by their conquerors as giant
            specialised farms, growing one or two primary products for export to
            the coloniser. Cheap labour, cheap materials. A huge profit for the
            manufacturer.

A weight is placed on the scale platform.[1]

Voice 1:   When colonialism ended, rich countries used their financial power to
            continue dictating what poor countries should produce. Encouraged
            monoculture. Encouraged oversupply. They knew the laws of supply and
            demand would keep prices low. Very low. Coffee. Cocoa. Sugar. Tea. The
            main export products of poor countries. Our cheap food.
            Low prices falling lower. So low that many poor producers cannot
            feed their families, educate their children, afford even the most basic
            health care. A cycle of poverty. No money to diversify business or develop
            new products. No money for seeds, tools, transport. Poor farmers unable
            to compete in home markets or export abroad.
            Malnutrition. Illness. Death.

Another weight is placed on the scale platform.

Voice 2:   Poor people took action. Began to manufacture finished products to earn
            more through trade. But rich countries didn't want competition. So we
            tax manufactured imports from poor countries four times higher than we
            tax other rich countries. [2]
            Rich countries pay their farmers big subsidies. So they can export
            cheap goods to poor countries. Subsidies mean UK sugar beet is sold in
            poor countries at a quarter of its production cost. Local farmers who grow

sugar cane go out of business.
Malnutrition. Illness. Death.

Another weight is placed on the scale platform.

Voice 1:   The World Trade Organisation was set up to bring in some rules to trade by. But many poor countries cannot afford representatives to negotiate there. Rich countries have many high-powered negotiators. So the rules favour the rich. They are aimed at free trade. Poor countries want fair trade. But rich countries won't allow poor countries to use taxes and subsidies to build up their trade. Even though we have built our trade on these things for centuries.

Another weight is placed on the scale platform.

Voice 2:   By 'free trade' rich countries mean multinational companies operating without restriction, taking over public services, such as water supply; charging more than the poor can afford. Patenting traditional crops and life-saving medicines. Poor people priced out of the essentials of life.
Malnutrition. Illness. Death.

Another weight is placed on the scale platform.

Voice 1:   World trade is unfair. Very unfair. Poor countries lose 440 billion pounds a year from unfair trade rules.[3] 14 times what they receive in aid. 30 times the amount they pay in debt repayments.
The scales are grossly unbalanced.

Prayer of confession *(based on Amos 5 & 8)*

Leader: For a system of trade that weighs on the scales of injustice
to increase our wealth, while keeping others in poverty:
ALL: GOD OF JUSTICE, WE COME BEFORE YOU IN SORROW AND CONFESSION.
Leader: For a system of trade that tramples on the poor,
so we can eat cheap food, while they go hungry:
ALL: GOD OF JUSTICE, WE COME BEFORE YOU IN SORROW AND CONFESSION.
Leader: For a system of trade that pushes aside the needy
to sell our subsidised goods in their markets,
while their crops rot in the fields:
ALL: GOD OF JUSTICE, WE COME BEFORE YOU IN SORROW AND CONFESSION.

Kyrie eleison or another song of penitence

Leader: The system of world trade does not have to be this way. We do not have to accept an unfair system. We are part of the problem but we can also be part of the solution. We can choose another way.

Scripture reading: Luke 19:1–10

Reflection: Being part of the solution

We are not powerless in the face of an unjust trading system. We have power as both electors and consumers.

There is an international movement for trade justice. We can join one or more of the organisations involved in this movement, and become involved in active campaigning for a fair system of international trade.

We can use our power as consumers to support fair trade. An increasing number of small companies are now committed to paying a fair price for the goods they buy from poor-country producers. Brands of an expanding range of products, including coffee, tea, chocolate, sugar, fruit juice, wine, bananas, pineapples, oranges and mangoes, now carry the international FAIRTRADE Mark, which certifies that the producer has received a fair price for their product *(point out the FAIRTRADE Mark, which is hanging prominently)*.

Fairtrade agreements set a base price with producers, so that, even if the world market price falls lower, the producer will continue to be paid the agreed fair price and will have enough money for their family to live on. We can all buy Fairtrade goods. As demand increases from the consumer, more and more companies will start to trade fairly. The future is in our hands.[4]

At this point, the congregation's attention is drawn to the information sheet.

Symbolic action *(during which music is played or a solo sung)*

The congregation are invited to come to the scales in the centre of the church, and take it in turns to place one of the small bags in the scale pan, symbolising their commitment to take campaigning action for trade justice and/or buy Fairtrade goods in the future.[5]

Song: Sent by the Lord am I (CG)

Closing responses *(based on Isaiah 40)*

Leader: A voice cries:
ALL: IN THE WILDERNESS PREPARE THE WAY OF THE LORD,
MAKE STRAIGHT IN THE DESERT A HIGHWAY FOR OUR GOD.
<u>Women:</u> Every valley shall be lifted up,
and every mountain and hill be made low.

Men: The uneven ground shall become level,
            and the rough places a plain.
ALL: THEN THE GLORY OF GOD SHALL BE REVEALED,
            AND ALL PEOPLE SHALL SEE IT TOGETHER.

Leader: Let us go out and prepare the way of the Lord.
ALL: LET US GO OUT AND BUILD GOD'S HIGHWAY.
            AMEN

Alternative songs:
Christ be our light (CG)
Heaven shall not wait (CG)
How can we stand together (LAA)
I, the Lord of sea and sky (CG)
Inspired by love and anger (CG)
Jesus Christ is waiting (CG)
Oh the earth is the Lord's (CG)
The God who sings (CG)
Till all the jails are empty (CG)
Travelling the road to freedom (EOA)
We lay our broken world (CG)
Who can sound the depths of sorrow

Notes

[1] This will immediately create imbalance. Consequently the subsequent adding of weights to this side will not cause the scales to move further. This does not matter. The symbolism is in an initial heavy burden that is gradually made harder and harder to counterbalance.

[2] Information from the Trade Justice Movement. Contact details for the Trade Justice Movement – www.tjm.org.uk

[3] Information from *The Economist* 23.9.99, cited by CAFOD campaigns, Feb 2001.

[4] A full range of available Fairtrade products is detailed on the website of the Fairtrade Foundation: www.fairtrade.org.uk

[5] The result of the action will be that the scales become more balanced. The service leaders will need to ensure that a sufficient number of bags are placed on the scales to get some movement to occur. However, it does not matter if the scales are not perfectly balanced at the end of the action. The idea is not to suggest that a solution will be easy, but that it is possible for the action each one of us takes to make a positive difference. This can be pointed out to the congregation, encouraging them to persist in real world action even when change seems to come only in small increments!

LIVING LETTERS:

A liturgy of solidarity from Iona Abbey, 2000

Neil Paynter

During the time I lived and worked on Iona, two women from an African country suffering civil war came to volunteer in the centres' kitchens. They were generous, warm, amazingly life-filled people who taught us all so much about what is truly important in life. One day they expressed their need to lead a service in the Abbey concerning the troubles in their country. They were desperate for more people in the West to know and understand the plight of their people, and to find some help for their community back home. We created the following service together. I've re-created it from memory and have fleshed out some sections.

After the service, many members of the congregation expressed their desire to give some kind of offering and, the next day, a bank account was set up in the name of a village co-operative. The co-operative sold local arts and crafts, and the money it earned was used to buy food for the entire village.

After leaving Iona, the volunteers went on a tour of Britain, not to sightsee but to spread wider word of the situation in their country.

A 'liturgy of letters' would be particularly appropriate when, like here, folk from another country are visiting a church or community.

Before the service the following materials needed for the action are set out on the communion table or other central table: a long sheet of brown paper (the letter); coloured markers and pens; campaign information from a human rights organisation (e.g. Amnesty International, Human Rights Watch, Christian Aid, Pax Christi, CAFOD, Oxfam).

Opening responses

Leader:	In the beginning was the Word.
ALL:	AND THE WORD WAS WITH GOD,
	AND THE WORD WAS GOD.
Leader:	He was in the beginning with God;
ALL:	ALL THINGS WERE MADE THROUGH HIM,
	AND WITHOUT HIM NOT A SINGLE THING WAS MADE.
Leader:	In him was life,
ALL:	AND THE LIFE WAS THE LIGHT OF THE WORLD.
	THE LIGHT SHINES IN THE DARKNESS
	AND THE DARKNESS WILL NEVER PUT IT OUT.

Or:

Scripture reading: John 1:1–5. *First read in an appropriate foreign language or dialect (e.g. Swahili, Akan, Fon, Somali ...) and then in English.*

Song: Before the world began (SOGP)

Prayer of confession

God, we confess that we often close our ears to your Word,
to the messages of your prophets,
and to the cries of the poor.

We confess that we often pay far more attention
to the life-in-all-its-fullness promise of advertisers
and the announcements of the rich and famous,
to the pronouncements of pop idols and
the predictions of sports stars.

We confess that we seek to be entertained and comforted
and not disturbed and challenged;
that we would rather retreat into fantasy worlds
than engage with reality, and the tortured earth's suffering people;
that we prefer sound bites and sensationalism
to long, difficult stories of everyday pain and struggle,
faith and courage, great sacrifice and
precious, hard-won gains.

God, we confess that, close to home, we are often gossipy
and talk about our neighbours without any real understanding or compassion.

We confess that we take our freedom of expression for granted,
and loudly voice a great many strong views and opinions
concerning matters which seem important,
while, at other times, we are afraid to speak out about the slightest thing
that might single us out, bring trouble or cause offence.
Meantime, our sisters and brothers across the world are silenced with bullets,
or are shut up in dark prisons for voicing opposition and calling for change –
for demanding that basic human rights be respected.

God, open our ears to the cries of your people,
to the warnings of your prophets,
and to your good news.

Open our hearts to our neighbours
and help us to love them as Jesus taught us.

God, help us to hear your voice through the babble of this busy world
where words are used to confuse, distract, manipulate, sell illusion, buy power;
help us to be still and receptive to your healing, encouraging, inspiring, enduring,
life-giving Word.

Scripture reading *(A reading from one of the letters to the churches, one which fits with
the particular situation.)*

Before the reading:
Leader: Listen now for the Word of God.

Following the reading:
Leader: For the Word of God in scripture,
             for the Word of God among us,
             for the Word of God within us.
             Thanks be to God.
ALL: AMEN

Readings from letters, e-mails, faxes ...

*In the Abbey, this section of the service included a letter from the volunteers' minister –
writing from a battle zone just as helicopter gunships were strafing his village; an e-mail
from the volunteers to their minister; and a letter from an aid worker sending word of the
present situation and calling for the immediate delivery of food and medicine. The excerpts
from the letters were short, direct and very moving. (The idea here is to include readings
that give an impression of the political/social situation in a country; bear witness to the
struggles, courage and spirit of God's people; and highlight our global connections.)*

Testimony: *If someone is visiting from another country or church and they wish to address
the congregation.*

Song: Abundant life (CG)

Action: Writing a letter to another church or community

*Folk are invited to come to the table to write a message to a church or group in another
country. It is good to suggest that people write simple, encouraging messages, keeping in
mind that in many places, as in St Paul's time, Christians and activists and people struggling to live from day to day are harassed and persecuted by the powers that be. Messages
like 'Greetings from (e.g. the Isle of Iona)', 'We are thinking of you', 'You are not forgotten',*

'Grace to you and peace' (Thessalonians 1:1), 'Peace be with you', 'We send our love and are with you in spirit'. (At the end of the service on Iona, the volunteers were presented with a beautiful, six-foot-long letter to bring back to their village church. Several children in the congregation decorated the letter with colourful drawings of friendly suns and rainbows, birds and flowers.)

After doing this, people take campaign information away with them, and later send letters, e-mails or faxes, e.g. to their Member of Parliament, Prime Minister, friends … (In the Iona service, the information for further action focused on a letter-writing campaign concerning the role of Western companies in civil wars in Africa.)

During the action a chant is sung by a small group or a single voice.[1]

Prayers of intercession

For concerns in the country that the service centres upon, and for concerns at home.[2]

Song

Closing responses[3]

Leader :	Christ has no hands but our hands;
ALL:	NO HANDS BUT OUR HANDS
	TO DO GOD'S WORK IN THE WORLD.
Leader:	Christ has no lips but our lips;
ALL:	NO LIPS BUT OUR LIPS
	TO PROCLAIM THE GOOD NEWS.
Leader:	Christ has no love but our love;
ALL:	NO LOVE BUT OUR LOVE TO SHARE
	WITH THE IMPRISONED, THE SILENCED, THE PERSECUTED,
	THE MARGINALISED.
	AMEN

Blessing

May God write a message upon your heart,
bless and direct you,
then send you out
living letters of the Word.
Amen

Or simply:

May the grace of the Lord Jesus Christ and the love of God and the fellowship of the Holy Spirit be with you all. *(2 Corinthians 13:14)*

Notes

[1] One of the volunteers sang a chant their home country. Because of the size of the congregation, the action took some time. The chant was sung repeatedly. This became powerfully symbolic of the incredible patience of the people of Africa. When will we listen to the voices of the poor? Who is crying now?

[2] In the Iona service, prayers were said for concerns such as tribal relations, dialogue between different faiths, violence against women and children, and all victims of civil wars.

[3] In the original service the Beatitudes were used as closing responses.

CHOOSING GOD OR CHOOSING MAMMON:
A liturgy for a globalised world

Helen Boothroyd

Before worship a table is set up, in a central and visible area of the worship space, on which modern symbols of wealth are placed, e.g. imitation bank notes, coins, lists of currency exchange rates, the financial pages of a newspaper, stock exchange listings.

A store of spiritual symbols and symbols of a more just economic order is placed in a less visible area, e.g. crosses, candles, prayer cards, Fairtrade goods, campaigning posters, etc.

Three sets of action cards are placed on another central table, one set for each of the main themes of the service (land ownership, trade and debt), suggesting campaigning actions relating to the theme and providing relevant contact details. Examples of suggested actions might be:

- *Support campaigns for a more just land distribution, e.g. the Landless Workers' Movement in Brazil who ask for financial support and letter-writing campaigners.*
- *Buy Fairtrade goods.*
- *Support the Trade Justice Movement.*
- *Join the Jubilee Debt Campaign to get all unpayable poor-country debt cancelled.*
- *Be part of the Make Poverty History campaign for debt cancellation, trade justice, and more and better aid.*

Gathering song: Oh the Earth is the Lord's (CG)

Introduction

Leader: There is a prevalent myth that poverty and hunger are due to climate and overpopulation. But in fact they are consequences of a world economic system dominated by multinational companies, backed by rich-country governments, and underpinned by the goals and ethos of capitalism, making profit for the few at the expense of the many.

This service focuses on three main issues that keep so many people in desperate poverty in this age of globalisation: land ownership, trade injustice and unpayable poor-country debt.

The world economic system keeps land ownership overwhelmingly in the hands of a few, perpetuates an unfair system of trade, and insists that poor countries continue to try to pay vast sums in interest on debts that did not benefit those who are now suffering from the attempts at repayment. It ensures that the majority of the world's population continues to live on the margins, without secure access to the basic necessities of food, water, education and health care.

Reader: Jesus said: 'No one can serve two masters; for they will either hate one and love the other, or be devoted to one and despise the other. You cannot serve God and wealth.' *(Luke 16:13)*

Leader: The present world economic order is unjust, unbiblical and contrary to the way of Jesus. As his followers we should seek new ways of organising our world, based on justice for all not wealth for the few, community not competition, the values of God's Kingdom not the value of the dollar.

Did Jesus ask the moneychangers if they could behave a little fairer? No! He upturned their tables and drove them out. We too need to be angry at injustice and active in working for real change in the way God's world is run.

Reader: In 1999 Nelson Mandela asked the Davos World Economic Forum: 'Is globalisation only to benefit the powerful and the financiers, speculators, investors and traders? Does it offer nothing to men, women and children ravaged by the violence of poverty?'

Song: Oh the Earth is the Lord's *(repeat)*

Prayer of confession *(based on Psalm 10)*

Leader: In arrogance the wicked persecute the poor –
            let them be caught in the schemes they have devised.
ALL: GOD, FORGIVE US THE ARROGANCE
            THAT LEADS US TO GROW RICHER
            AND MAKE OTHERS POORER.
Leader: They think in their heart, 'We shall not be moved;
            throughout all generations we shall not meet adversity.'
ALL: GOD, FORGIVE US THE COMPLACENCY
            THAT CAUSES US TO ACCEPT WEALTH AS OUR RIGHT
            AND DISMISS THE POVERTY OF OTHERS AS A NECESSARY EVIL.
Leader: Their eyes stealthily watch for the helpless;
            they lurk that they may seize the poor.
ALL: GOD, FORGIVE US OUR WORLD ECONOMIC SYSTEM
            THAT DAMAGES THE VULNERABLE
            AND KILLS THE WEAK.
            SHOW US HOW TO CHALLENGE AND CHANGE IT.
Leader: Rise up, O Lord; do not forget the oppressed.
            Seek out the wickedness of evildoers until there is no more to be found.
            O Lord, you will hear the desire of the meek;

you will strengthen their hearts, you will incline your ear
to do justice for the orphan and the oppressed,
so that those who live upon the earth may strike terror no more.

Voice 1:   My name is Paulo. I work on a sugar cane plantation in Brazil. I am paid very little and often my family go hungry. If only I had some land of my own to grow food. But it's all owned by the big landlords. My landlord used to let us grow a bit of food on small plots. But he's taken all the land back. He says he needs to grow sugar cane on it now. Quite a lot of the big landlords just leave land empty. It's a status symbol for them to own land. I knew a man called Antonio da Silva who joined a group of 1500 other landless workers last year and started to grow food crops on the Sao José farm. But when the landlord heard about it he hired a gang to evict them. They came with guns and fired many shots. Antonio was killed and ten other workers were wounded. One of them was a fourteen-year-old girl.

Song: Oh the Earth is the Lord's *(verses 1, 3 and 4 with refrains)*

Voice 2:   I am Miguel. I am a maize farmer in the south of Mexico. I have always been poor, but in the last few years things have got much worse. Since the free trade agreement was signed between my country and the United States, the market here has been flooded with cheap American maize. The US farmers get $20,000 a year each in subsidies. We used to get a guaranteed price for our maize and some financial support. But we don't get this any more, and the price I'm paid for my maize is a third less than it was.

Song: Oh the Earth is the Lord's *(verse 2 with refrain)*

Voice 3:   My name is Men. I am campaigning for the cancellation of debt owed by my country, the Philippines, which was incurred under the Marcos dictatorship. My people did not get any benefit from these loans. Instead the money was used to suppress people, abuse human rights and line the pockets of the dictator and his family. Why should we continue to suffer in order to pay back these debts and all the interest that has built up on them?

Song: Inspired by love and anger (CG)

Scripture reading: John 2:13–16

During this reading the table with the symbols of wealth is overturned suddenly, vigorously, angrily. The action should surprise and shock the congregation with its suddenness and starkness.

Congregational action

The overturned table is slowly and deliberately righted again, while the symbols of wealth are left where they fell. Then the congregation is invited to come forward and to place on the table the spiritual symbols and symbols of economic justice. In sharing in this symbolic action, the congregation are asked to commit themselves to take real action in the world for global justice. They are invited to select one of the action cards on their way back to their seats and to pursue the suggested action after the service.[1]

Prayer of commitment

Leader: Christ, who turned the tables of the moneychangers;
ALL: TURN GREED TO JUSTICE, PROFIT TO PRINCIPLE.
Leader: Let the land be shared fairly,
ALL: AND ALL YOUR CHILDREN EAT AND BE SATISFIED.
Leader: Rebalance the scales
ALL: UNTIL ALL TRADE IS FAIR TRADE.
Leader: Lead us to Jubilee;
ALL: BREAK THE CHAINS OF DEBT.

Leader: Christ, in this age of globalisation, we hear you calling us
            to turn upside down the present unjust world order
            so that your kingdom may come.
ALL: WE WILL ANSWER YOUR CALL.
            WE CHOOSE TO SERVE YOU.
            WE COMMIT OURSELVES TO PUT GOD BEFORE WEALTH
            AND TO TAKE ACTION FOR JUSTICE IN YOUR NAME.
            AMEN

Song: Heaven shall not wait (CG)

Closing responses

Leader: Christ has come to turn the world upside down:
ALL: TO HUMBLE THE POWERFUL AND TO LIFT UP THE LOWLY.
Leader: Christ has come to turn the tables:
ALL: TO TOPPLE VAIN IDOLS AND TO STAND WITH THE POOR.
Leader: Christ has come to proclaim God's kingdom:
Men: to feed the hungry,
Women: to liberate the oppressed,

Men:	to strengthen the weary,
Women:	to set the prisoners free.
Leader:	Christ has come to turn the world upside down:
ALL:	TO OVERTHROW THE PRESENT ORDER WITH A REVOLUTION OF LOVE.

Notes

[1]For examples of suggested actions
- Landless Workers' Movement in Brazil: www.mstbrazil.org
- Fairtrade: www.fairtrade.org.uk
- Trade Justice Movement: www.tjm.org.uk
- Jubilee Debt Campaign: www.jubileedebtcampaign.org.uk
- Make Poverty History: www.makepovertyhistory.org

IN OUR OWN BACKYARD

IN OUR OWN BACKYARD

Norman Shanks

Perhaps I am deluding myself, but I hope not! I believe that within mainstream church life there is evidence of increasing acceptance that a concern for justice is a fundamental part of Christian faith. Of course there are still some who will maintain that religious convictions are a private matter, and that it is really only our personal relationship with God that is important. Yes, it is accepted that we are also to love our neighbour as ourselves, but to stray beyond that into seeking and working for social justice takes us into the complicated and messy world of political priorities and processes – territory which, if not explicitly forbidden, is not sufficiently warranted in scripture or tradition to be appropriate for faithful Christians to enter.

However, across the spectrum of theological leanings and church traditions, we find a recognition that a commitment to pursue justice issues is not an optional extra of the life of faith; that the Gospel is 'good news' precisely because the promise of 'saving grace' embraces the transformation of the world as well as individual salvation; that we cannot separate doing justice from loving mercy and walking humbly with God. So there is broad support within the churches for campaigns like 'Making Poverty History', for initiatives to reform the rules that govern world trade, for organisations and projects relating to such issues as homelessness, environmental pollution, racism, immigration and asylum, and so much more.

In our work on Iona and at Camas, and on the mainland too, the Iona Community has for some years now had direct experience of the widespread contemporary interest in spirituality. Our understanding of spirituality, however, is a far cry from the fanciful self-indulgent approach that is too often to be found (not least in some perceptions of 'Celtic spirituality'). We advocate and seek to express in our lives a spirituality not of escape but of engagement, that affirms a 'with-us' God, present in 'every blessed thing', that is essentially social rather than self-absorbed. This is to be seen above all in the seam-lessness of the elements of our five-fold Rule, in which we cannot separate our commitment to action for justice and peace from our devotional discipline, our prayers and worship from our social and political priorities and how we spend our money and time.

With this integrated, grounded approach to spirituality there is a continuing challenge to find and develop material for worship that is relevant to the concerns and circumstances of our lives. The familiar hymn books and standard liturgical resources do not contain much that has any bearing on justice issues. In worship, however, it is important not only to have the space and opportunity to reflect on our lives 'apart' from the noise and preoccupied bustle of our everyday lives and to be inspired and encouraged on our continuing journey. Worship is to be seen also as 'a part' of our lives, in and through which, trusting in God's grace and affirming our hope in God's loving purpose for all, we offer our concerns and commitment to God, expressing our solidarity with victims of injustice and those who are suffering.

The material in this section thus is thoroughly specific: it is rooted in and comes out of particular events and occasions, and reflects concern about issues that are immediate and down-to-earth. It has theological and intellectual integrity, but it is not at all abstract or detached; it is participative and, in the scope it provides for symbolic action, it engages the body as well as the mind; it is both reassuring, expressing the confidence and hope that come from faith, and challenging – encouraging and propelling towards sharing in God's work for justice, community-building and renewal. But the context is all-important; and when these liturgies are used elsewhere (in a different 'backyard'!), almost inevitably a measure of adaptation will be necessary: creativity is to be encouraged.

Above all, in our worship and work for justice, in keeping our vision, our commitment, our hope alive, we must recognise our limitations – our need for one another; especially our reliance on the grace of God. In February 2006 thousands of church representatives from all over the world will be gathering in Porto Alegre, Brazil for the Ninth Assembly of the World Council of Churches. The Assembly theme – 'God, in your grace, transform the world' – reflects both a concern for justice and the hope that the present order of things can change; it is modest, even tentative, deliberately couched in the form of a prayer – expressing our engagement in the process of transformation but also acknowledging our dependence on God.

GIVE US THIS DAY OUR DAILY BREAD:
A communion liturgy
Oliver Fernandes of Church Action on Poverty

This liturgy was prepared for Unemployment Sunday 2003 as part of resource material distributed by Church Action on Poverty. The theme for Unemployment Sunday 2003 was 'Give us this day our daily bread', which asks us to make sense of these familiar words of Jesus in a world where many struggle to make ends meet. Although the Minimum Wage has improved basic living standards for some, many people on low incomes still struggle greatly.

Before the service, bread dough is prepared, kneaded and proved once, for the children to complete during the service, and to be used for communion.[1]

The congregation is seated in a circle for this service, preferably around a central table.

Scripture reading: Leviticus 25:35–38 (loans to the poor)

Hymn: Lead me O thou great Jehovah

Tape/video or dramatisation: John 6:1–13 (feeding the five thousand). This could be taken from *The Miracle Man*.

Children's address *(notes)*

Bread, the staple diet.
Bread-making used to be a regular sight in our kitchens! But now we buy it at the shops.
How bread is made: using yeast; kneading and proving.
You are going to finish making the bread for communion today.
The bread dough prepared earlier is brought out for the children to knead and shape.

Children's hymn: Jesus the Lord said …'I am the Bread'

Prayer of dismissal

Lord, be with us now as we go to our various groups. Remind us daily that we are fortunate to have you as our friend and that there are others less fortunate than ourselves. Help us to help each other and be friendly with everyone we meet. Amen

Departure of the children who take the bread to the kitchen to be baked before sharing in their own activities.[1]

Scripture reading: John 6:25–59 (The Bread of life)

Lord's Prayer (said or sung)

Sermon *(notes)*

Give us today *our* daily bread.
Poverty in our land.
You only have to look around you to see families or an older person living on benefits. For many it is an 'existence', rather than 'living', with no money for the little luxuries most of us take for granted.
Imagine:

– Going to the cupboard for tea and it's almost empty – pay day is still several days away.
– Having to consistently say 'No' to school trips because you haven't the money to let the children go.
– Having to hide when the debt collector calls (again).
– Constantly feeling cold because your gas (or other source of heating) has been cut off.

For some this is *not* imagination – it is reality. And many in our own neighbourhoods will identify with at least one of these. Many people are lucky they have families and friends they can call on for support or the odd meal, but some people don't have anyone and get 'lost'.

Why does it happen? Try this quiz:[2]

1. What is the Minimum Wage per hour?   £4.10   £4.85   £5.85   £6.50

2. What would a single person on benefits receive per week?
   £50-59   £60-69   £70-79   £80-89

3. If you receive Incapacity Benefit, do you have to pay any rent?   Yes   No

4. Can everyone on low income get help with prescription charges?   Yes   No

5. Where do people on benefits go for a quick loan?
   Bank   Provident   Building Society

A lot of poverty is hidden. We see and recognise the 'scroungers', but do we really see those genuinely poor people? They tend to hide the fact that they are poor because their pride will not let them admit it. For many, they see it as 'failure'.

What can we do as a church?

Get to know people around you. Watch out for that young mum or elderly person. Offer the hand of friendship (not interference). Have an open door policy here at church. Jesus welcomed the poor – do we? Could we start collecting and have food parcels available (all year round) for families who need them (for the minister to give out when asked)? Become known as a 'friendly' church. But, most of all, don't bury your head in the sand and pretend poverty isn't there – it is!

Hymn: What a friend we have in Jesus (*during which a collection is taken and the children return, bringing the bread forward.*)

Prayer of intercession

Leader: Father, we come before you, aware of our shortcomings, aware that we don't always see what is going on around us.
           Help us to be aware of other people and offer the hand of friendship whenever we can.
ALL: IN YOUR MERCY, HEAR OUR PRAYER.
Leader: Father, we recognise the hard job the professionals, the peacemakers, the politicians and our own church leaders have to do, and we ask you to give them wisdom and encouragement.
           We pray that they may all work together to ease poverty in our nation.
ALL: IN YOUR MERCY, HEAR OUR PRAYER.
Leader: Father, help us to begin to understand and identify ways we can help as a church.
           Help us not to bury our heads in the sand, but to have the courage to stand up and be counted.
ALL: IN YOUR MERCY, HEAR OUR PRAYER.

Communion (*using the bread that the children have made*)

Hymn: Great is Thy faithfulness

Blessing

Notes

[1] It is wise for a spare loaf to be prepared and baked in advance in case the bread made in the service is a disaster!

[2] Answers: 1. £4.85 per hour from October 2004 – even less if you are under 18 years of age. 2. It is in fact about £56. Not a lot is it? 3. Yes. You have to pay a contribution out of £76 per week. 4. No. Those on Disability and Incapacity Benefits have to pay for their prescriptions. 5. Provident – who charge something like 160% interest.

HOLY GROUND:
Praying for our cities, Iona Abbey, 2002

Sandra Fox

The service was compiled and led by Sandra Fox, who is from London and had come to work on Iona for three years. Sandra was shortly to return to city life following this service.

For use elsewhere, the responses and reflection of this liturgy could be adapted.

Opening responses

Leader: In the peace and the bustle of island life:
          the sounds of creation.
ALL: RUNNING WAVE AND RESTLESS EARTH,
          FLOWING AIR AND SPINNING STARS
          DECLARE THE SON OF PEACE.
          (Silence)
Leader: In the activity and stillness of an ancient church:
          the cries of a broken world.
ALL: ANGRY AND HOPEFUL CRIES,
          HUNGRY UNENDING CRIES
          PROCLAIM THE CROSS OF CHRIST.
          (Silence)
Leader: In the silence and turmoil of our hearts:
          the voice of the Risen One.
ALL: COMFORT TO THE SUFFERER,
          CHALLENGE TO THE FOLLOWER,
          THE CALL OF CHRIST TO ALL.

(Silence)

Song: The God of heaven (IAMB)

Scripture reading: Exodus 3:1–8a

Holy ground litany

This litany works well if the four readers (denoted A,B,C and D) are unseen, their voices coming from different parts of the worship space. Variations in rhythm and pace are important; the intention is to create a cacophony, suggestive of sounds as well as images of the city.

A: city streets

B: city centre

C: outskirts, edges, margins

A: concrete jungle

B: cardboard city

A: wasteland

C: urban wilderness

D: Remove the sandals from your feet, for the place on which you are standing is holy ground.

B: housing estate

C: slum

A: shanty town

B: bed-sit, penthouse

C: dockside development, silent shipyard

A: high rise, tower block, tenement, prison

B: shop doorway, park bench, street corner

C: railway arches, under bridges, underground stations

A: ghettos

B: (of poverty)

C: ghettos

B: (of privilege)

D: Remove the sandals from your feet, for the place on which you are standing is holy ground.

A: fences, walls, barbed wire

B: noise, din

C: clamour, chaos

A: rubbish, heat, stench

B: fast cars, traffic jams, exhaust fumes, gridlock

C: shopping malls

A: multiplex cinemas

B: parks

C: playgrounds

A: back yards

B: allotments

C: rooftop gardens

A: Church

B: Cathedral

C: Mosque

A: Gurdwara

B: Synagogue
C: Temple
D: Remove the sandals from your feet, for the place on which you are standing
   is holy ground.

C: carnival
A: procession
B: Orange parade
A: street theatre, street preacher
B: busker, pavement artist, street vendor
C: 'Big Issue, Sir? Big Issue, Madam?'
B: vagrants, beggars
A: users and junkies
C: (wheelers and) dealers
D: Turn aside and look; do not hide your face from God.

C: civil unrest
A: racial tension
B: rioting
C: petrol bombs, Molotov cocktails
A: burned out cars
B: roadblocks, barricades
C: riot shields, water cannon, plastic bullets
D: Turn aside and look; do not hide your face from God.

A: neighbours
B: strangers
C: young
A: old
B: black
C: white
A: women
C: men
B: gay, straight, transgender
C: lost
B: found
A: lonely in a crowd
B: homeless
A: on the streets
B: kerb crawlers
C: pimps
A: street workers

B: soup runs

C: night shelters

A: credit unions

B: dole queues

A: needle exchanges

B: pain

C: healing

B: poverty

C: wealth

D: I have seen the misery of my people …
   I have heard their cry …
   indeed I know their sufferings.

B: city hall

C: parliament buildings

A: red light districts

B: community gardens, colourful murals

C: sheltered housing

A: peaceful protest

B: picket line

A: pavement vigil

B: demonstration

C: blockade

A: non-violence

B: revolution

D: I have come to deliver them …
   to bring them up to a good and broad land,
   a land flowing with milk and honey.

Song: Our cities cry to You, O God

Our cities cry to you, O God, from out their pain and strife;
you made us for yourself alone, but we choose an alien life.
Our goals are pleasure, gold and power; injustice stalks our earth;
in vain we seek for rest, for joy, for sense of human worth.

Yet still you walk our streets, O Christ! We know your presence here
where humble Christians love and serve in godly grace and fear.
O Word made flesh, be seen in us! May all we say and do
affirm you God Incarnate still and turn sad hearts to you!

Your people are your hands and feet to serve your world today,
our lives the book our cities read to help them find your way.
O pour your sovereign Spirit out on heart and will and brain:
inspire your church with love and power to ease our cities' pain!

O healing Saviour, Prince of Peace, salvation's Source and Sum,
for you our broken cities cry: O come, Lord Jesus, come!
With truth your royal diadem, with righteousness your rod,
O come, Lord Jesus, bring to earth the City of our God!

Margaret Clarkson

Reflection

I was speaking to a guest in the dining room of the MacLeod Centre a while ago. We were at that familiar stage where we had exchanged names and established that I had been here on Iona for nearly three years, and that she had visited Iona every year, without fail, for many years.

'What is it that keeps bringing you back?' I asked her. 'Oh,' she said, 'the beauty of the island, the peace and tranquillity, the worship in the Abbey, the escape from the city.' That conversation has stayed in my mind ever since, partly, I guess, because I came to Iona from the city, and to the city I shall soon return. But what about that bit in the middle? Where does the city figure there?

My mind eventually came to rest on the passage from Exodus which was read, where Moses led his flock 'beyond the wilderness' to Horeb, the mountain of God. I have come to think of Iona as a place 'beyond the wilderness', a place where God is worshipped and where God calls to us and challenges us in sometimes startling ways. A place where God shows us the pain and suffering in the places we have left behind and we turn our eyes to see; a place from which we go, refreshed, inspired and challenged to work for justice, wherever we find ourselves. God said to Moses: 'Remove the sandals from your feet, for the place on which you are standing is holy ground.' We can be sure that this place where we stand together now is indeed holy ground. And holy also is every inch of the ground in our cities. My invitation to you this evening is to pray for our cities.

Reading: Weeping for cities and working for justice

The pain of the cities is complex. The suffering that cripples our inner cities is often the pain of lifetimes and generations. The pain of individuals is bound up with the pain of the whole community ... I cannot pray for the healing of others with integrity without also acting on my prayers. If I am blind to the sources of injustice around me, and divorce the needs of an individual from the pain of a whole community, my prayers for healing are non-sense and bear no resemblance to the good news of the gospel ... Weeping for cities and working for justice is rarely dramatic or sensational. It is not an activity that brings instantaneous results. The suffering of a dispossessed community, in Britain or anywhere else in the world, has no easy solutions. For healing and justice to occur there needs to be change – change in values and attitudes; change in political policies and social conditions. And change for those in need means change for everyone, and none of us change easily. When we pray for the healing of those around us, are we willing to live out the implications of our prayers? Jesus, teach us how to pray.

Ruth Burgess

Prayers of intercession

Leader: Remove the sandals from your feet, for the place on which you are standing is holy ground.

As a prayerful and symbolic action, the congregation are invited to take off their shoes and, if able, to stand for the prayers of intercession. Prayers may be included, as appropriate, for neighbourhood projects and specific local needs and concerns.

Leader: O God, who knows all the struggles and sufferings of your people, hear us as we pray for city communities near to us and far away; cities where hope seems hard to find, self-worth so easily crushed, and where so many live with fear and loneliness, suspicion and rejection. Help us as we work to heal the pain of our cities.
In the place beyond the wilderness, call to us from the flames;

ALL: LET THE STREETS OF OUR CITIES BE THE HOLY GROUND UNDER OUR FEET.

Leader: O God, who has promised to your people a good and broad land, we pray that our cities may become places where all people can live in freedom and dignity; where shelter, food, warmth and friendship are in abundance and where all have a sense of worth and belonging.
In the place beyond the wilderness, call to us from the flames;

ALL: LET THE STREETS OF OUR CITIES BE THE HOLY GROUND UNDER OUR FEET.

Leader: O God, who cares for each one of your people, we pray for all who work to build community in the streets of our cities; through youth work, night shelters, day centres, lunch clubs, community projects, training programmes, soup kitchens. Give courage to all who work together for your kingdom of justice, peace and love.

	In the place beyond the wilderness, call to us from the flames;
ALL:	LET THE STREETS OF OUR CITIES BE THE HOLY GROUND UNDER OUR FEET.
Leader:	O God, who through your Son brings light to the darkest places, hear us as we pray for the dark places of our cities; the poorest communities, the ghettos, the no-go areas, the derelict and desolate places, the painful places.
	In the place beyond the wilderness, call to us from the flames;
ALL:	LET THE STREETS OF OUR CITIES BE THE HOLY GROUND UNDER OUR FEET.
Leader:	O God, who in Jesus suffered humiliation and violence and yet who over-came even death, hear our prayer for those who struggle daily against racism, violence, poverty and homelessness, yet still retain their dignity and continue to live with hope.
	In the place beyond the wilderness, call to us from the flames;
ALL:	LET THE STREETS OF OUR CITIES BE THE HOLY GROUND UNDER OUR FEET.
Leader:	O Christ, who wept for the city you loved, you ministered and preached in cities, and you walk the streets of our cities today. Open our eyes to see you. Give us words to speak of healing and renewal. Give us the tools to build cities of joy and communities of hope. Send us into the streets in witness, in praise, in protest and – dare we ask it – in revolution.
	In the place beyond the wilderness, call to us from the flames;
ALL:	LET THE STREETS OF OUR CITIES BE THE HOLY GROUND UNDER OUR FEET.
Leader:	Holy God, in the streets of our cities Your people walk in faith and hope. Come, walk with us. Lead us in paths of righteousness; Come, create holy ground beneath our feet.
ALL:	AMEN

(Silence)

Song: Sing we a song of high revolt (SOGP)

Affirmation *(said together)*

We believe that God is present
In the darkness before dawn;
In the waiting and uncertainty

Where fear and courage join hands,
Conflict and caring link arms,
And the sun rises over barbed wire.
We believe in a with-us God
Who sits down in our midst
To share our humanity.
We affirm a faith
That takes us beyond the safe place:
Into action, into vulnerability
And into the streets.
We commit ourselves to work for change
And put ourselves on the line;
To bear responsibility, take risks,
Live powerfully and face humiliation;
To stand with those on the edge;
To choose life
And be used by the Spirit
For God's new community of hope.
Amen

Iona Community

Prayer

Visionary God, architect
of heaven and earth,
unless we build in partnership with you we labour in vain.

Help us work to create cities
modelled more faithfully
on the plan of your Kingdom –

Communities where children are respected and encouraged
where young people can express themselves creatively
where the experience of old people is called on
where the insights and gifts of all God's people are fully realised
where shared gardens and plots bloom in once derelict places
where all cultures and traditions are honoured and celebrated
on soulful, carnival streets
where gay couples can dance to the beat of their hearts
homeless people are received with loving arms and open borders

news vendors cry Hosanna!
All are fed and loved and set free …

O God, our maker, open our eyes to new possibilities and perspectives,
organisations and projects, structures and outlooks …

Help us to rebuild the walls of Jerusalem:

to break down the barriers within ourselves that
prevent us from reaching out to neighbours and making peace;
to rebuild communities based on understanding and justice,
illuminated with the true light of Christ.
Amen

Neil Paynter

Song: Jesus Christ is waiting (CG)

Closing responses

Leader:	Christ has come to turn the world upside down:
ALL:	TO HUMBLE THE POWERFUL AND TO LIFT UP THE LOWLY.
Leader:	Christ has come to turn the tables:
ALL:	TO TOPPLE VAIN IDOLS AND TO STAND WITH THE POOR.
Leader:	Christ has come to proclaim God's kingdom:
<u>Men:</u>	to feed the hungry,
<u>Women:</u>	to give sight to the blind,
<u>Men:</u>	to strengthen the weary,
<u>Women:</u>	to set the prisoners free.
Leader:	Christ has come to turn the world upside down:
ALL:	TO OVERTHROW THE PRESENT ORDER
	WITH A REVOLUTION OF LOVE.

Blessing

May the God who shakes heaven and earth,
whom death could not contain,
who lives to disturb and heal us,
bless you with power to go forth
and proclaim the Gospel. Amen

A RURAL LITURGY

Christian Maclean

Christian Maclean is a member of the Iona Community. This liturgy is based on a service that she led at the Iona Community's annual general meeting in the town of Biggar in Lanarkshire, Scotland in June 2002.

The liturgy could be adapted to another rural locale or situation.

Opening responses *(Psalm 36:5–9)*

Leader: Your love is as high as the heavens, O God;
            your faithfulness soars through the skies.
ALL: YOUR RIGHTEOUSNESS REACHES THE TOWERING PEAKS;
            YOUR JUSTICE THE DEPTHS OF THE SEA.
Leader: We shelter beneath your wings;
            we feast on the food you provide.
ALL: WE OPEN OUR EYES TO DRINK IN YOUR GOODNESS;
            FOR YOU ARE THE SOURCE OF ALL LIFE,
            AND BECAUSE OF YOUR LIGHT WE SEE LIGHT.

Song: The Lord's my shepherd (CG)

Prayer of thanksgiving

Leader: God, on this day of early summer we give thanks for warmth and light
            and new growth
            And we rejoice in:
Voice A: greening fields
Voice B: nets stretched out to dry
Voice A: drizzle and dreich days
Voice B: shelter from the storm
Voice A: shouts from the playground
Voice B: jokes over a pint
Voice A: internet and teleworking
Voice B: discos in village halls
Voice A: dogs, hens, cattle, lambs
Voice B: post offices, post buses
Voice A: daffodils in the wind
Voice B: tractors in ribbed fields
Voice A: village churches

Voice B:	hazels, birches, oaks
Voice A:	craft shops and B&Bs
Voice B:	new houses and old
Voice A:	bare branches against winter skies
Voice B:	kettles on the boil.
Leader:	For space and light and growth,
	For closeness and kindliness and willing hands,
	For continuity and for change,
	Challenges and hopes,
	We are thankful.

Prayer of confession

Leader:	O God, gladly we live and move and have our being in you.
	Yet always in the midst of this creation-glory,
	we see sin's shadow and feel death's darkness:
	around us in the earth, sea and sky, the abuse of matter;
	beside us in the broken, the hungry and the poor,
	the betrayal of one another;
	and often, deep within us, a striving against your Spirit.
ALL:	O TRINITY OF LOVE,
	FORGIVE US THAT WE MAY FORGIVE ONE ANOTHER,
	HEAL US THAT WE MAY BE PEOPLE OF HEALING,
	AND RENEW US THAT WE ALSO MAY BE MAKERS OF PEACE.

Scripture reading: Psalm 65:1a, 9–13

Reflection *(A sharing of a story by someone in the community or a discussion between members of the congregation.)*

I have always liked the fact that we take our name as a community not from an abstract concept but from a real place. Iona is a tiny dot on the map but it teems with life – animal and human. It gives us, as a community, a history, roots, and real issues to grapple with. Places have a deep resonance. The Iona Community has an incarnational faith, not disembodied but rooted in the day-to-day realities of where we live and the people we live with.

And land, the earth, has that resonance whether we live in the centre of a city or work and live on the land, in a rural community. Our sense of place shapes us – both personally and nationally – and is fundamental to our sense of who we are. This is true in Biggar or in Birmingham, and also in Iran, Palestine, and southern Africa, where millions face starvation. It's true for refugees, forced to leave their homes and communities; for migrant workers and share-croppers – and it's true for the rural dispossessed forced into urbanisation.

It's sometimes too easy for the *real* issues to be seen as urban, with the countryside being viewed as a place of escape, and concern for the environment as an evasion of the gritty issues. The concentration of people in cities – and the complexity of the factors shaping lives there – leads, of course, to a concentration of poverty, distress and social problems. But it's too easy to adopt the urban-dweller's romantic view of the countryside – viewing it as a playground, a place of recreation. This is to ignore the realities of limited or seasonal employment, the scarcity of affordable housing, poverty, isolation, limited opportunities and shrinking or greying populations. For every day of light-filled space and fresh growth, there's another of mud, darkness, worry and nowhere to go. To watch children grow up knowing that there can be no future for them in your community, to know that your livelihood and house are dependent on the whims of a landowner, to realise that your independence as a food-producer is not real but totally dependent on a fickle market and the demands of the supermarkets – this is poverty; this is injustice; this is a denial of abundant life.

There are as many tensions, difficulties and conflicts in rural areas as there are in any other way of life. In a recent broadcast, the American writer Annie Proulx suggested that a defining characteristic of rural life is marginalisation and a sense of being on the periphery. Power over the land – and the lives of those who dwell on it – lies far away, and is held by those who may have no understanding of the realities of rural life. You don't need to look far to see the issues: the differing conceptions of rural interests seen in the rise of the Countryside Alliance or of the fuel protesters; the conflicts between environmentalists and those whose livelihoods they appear to threaten; and, above all, the conflict between the vastly powerful forces of global capital and those who struggle to survive with dignity on the land. Somehow the forces for life – for social and ecological justice, for a more human and equitable economic system, for communities and people of faith – need to recognise their common ground. The concept of sustainability is a holistic vision. The Biblical vision is of a land overflowing and burgeoning with growth – crops and vines and animals – of the land itself singing for joy and the trees of the field clapping their hands. And it is equally of the City of God – the new Jerusalem – a place of dignity and space and right dealing. Together they form a whole, a vision of land and people living in rich harmony.

Prayer of intercession

Leader: God of place and of history,
            we pray for the broken and torn fabric of the earth as it yearns for healing.
ALL: JESUS, WHO WALKED WITH FARMERS AND FISHERS
            AND SAT IN VILLAGE KITCHENS,
            WALK WITH US NOW.

Leader: We hold before you those who have the privilege and responsibility of
           working on the land,
           and those who struggle to make a living.
ALL: JESUS, WHO WALKED WITH FARMERS AND FISHERS
           AND SAT IN VILLAGE KITCHENS,
           WALK WITH US NOW.
Leader: We hold before you those whose relationship with the earth is ruptured;
           through conflict, poverty, stunted opportunities, and environmental
           degradation.
ALL: JESUS, WHO WALKED WITH FARMERS AND FISHERS
           AND SAT IN VILLAGE KITCHENS,
           WALK WITH US NOW.
Leader   We hold before you rural communities where people feel isolated, margin-
           alised and powerless in the face of distant economic and political forces;
           and we remember especially those who have lost all hope.
ALL: JESUS, WHO WALKED WITH FARMERS AND FISHERS
           AND SAT IN VILLAGE KITCHENS,
           WALK WITH US NOW.
Leader: We hold before you those whose policies affect the land, the earth and all
           of our lives;
           and we pray that those in positions of power,
           in particular the leaders of wealthy nations,
           will have the courage and vision to make hard decisions.
ALL: JESUS, WHO WALKED WITH FARMERS AND FISHERS
           AND SAT IN VILLAGE KITCHENS,
           WALK WITH US NOW.
Leader: God of the sheltering wings, hear these prayers today
           and fill us with your Spirit.
           That we may live in peace with the earth
           and with each other.
           That your Kingdom may come.
           Amen

Song: The peace of the earth be with you (CG)

Symbolic action

Leader: As new growth springs from the dark and cold,
           and trusting in our brother Jesus whom death could not destroy,
           let us now commit ourselves as people of hope
           to listen to each other's truth in love,

to seek justice for all,
and to walk gently on the earth as stewards of God's creation.

(Silence)

Leader: As a sign of your commitment I invite you now to ...

This act of commitment could involve the planting of seeds or seedlings (getting hands dirty being an important part of this), or the weaving of prayers of concern for rural issues into a piece of willow hurdling. There might be a sharing of local, seasonal food and drink during this time.

Closing prayer

God of all the earth,
you share our joys and our fears.
You hear the cries of the despairing,
you set free the oppressed,
and you yearn for fullness of life for all.
We pray for the end of all injustice.
Open our eyes to the wonder of life.
Strengthen us to keep going, even when the way is hard.
Inspire us with your vision of land and people in joyful harmony.
In the name of the Trinity of love. Amen

Song: To Christ the seed (CG)

Closing responses

Leader: O God, star kindler
ALL: KINDLE A FLAME OF LOVE WITHIN US
                 TO LIGHT OUR PATH IN DAYS OF DARKNESS.
Leader: O God, sun warmer
ALL: WARM US WITH YOUR LOVE
                 TO MELT THE FROZEN HAND OF GUILT.
Leader: O God, moon burnisher
ALL: BURNISH THE SHIELD OF FAITH
                 THAT WE MAY SEEK JUSTICE
                 AND FOLLOW THE WAYS OF PEACE.

Blessing

Leader: And now may the God of hope bring you
such joy and peace in believing
that you may overflow with hope
in the power of the Holy Spirit.

ALL AMEN

Song: You shall go out with joy (CG)

Alternative scripture readings

Genesis 8:22
Isaiah 24:4–6

Alternative songs

Almighty God (Indian traditional) (LAA)
As the deer longs (CG)
For the fruits of all creation (CG)
How can we stand together (LAA)
Many and great (First Nation traditional) (MAG)
Now the green blade rises
Oh the earth is the Lord's (CG)
Oh the life of the world (CG)
Touch the earth lightly (CG)
Sara shriste (You are author and Lord of creation) (Nepal) (MAG)

THEN SHALL THE LIGHT SHINE FORTH:
A liturgy about poverty and the environment
Rachel McCann

Rachel McCann lives in Glasgow and is a member of the Iona Community. This liturgy grew out of her experience of local environmental and social justice projects. Often the most economically deprived areas are those that suffer most from environmental injustices such as pollution, poor housing, lack of green spaces, lack of fresh food, and traffic dangers. For example, children in areas of poverty in the UK are more likely to have poor health conditions such as asthma and restricted growth. The liturgy asks forgiveness for these injustices, celebrates the courage and creativity of those who fight from the grassroots for change, and asks God's help in all work for justice.

A version of this liturgy was used in Iona Abbey by Rachel and the Camas staff team.

Before worship, a spiral of recyclable rubbish is arranged in the centre of the worship space. A supply of unlit candles is also placed centrally.

Opening responses

Leader: Creator God,
             in Jesus we see you:
             born with no place to call home,
             making friends amongst the poor and rejected,
             living your life with no place to lay your head,
             challenging unjust ways and teaching us to share.
ALL: CREATOR GOD, BE AMONG US AS WE OFFER YOU OUR STORIES AND PRAYERS.

Sharing of a story: *A story from someone who lives with the effects of poverty is shared. Alternatively, a short video may be shown (e.g. a Church Action on Poverty video).*

Prayer of confession

Leader: We are interconnected;
ALL: WE ARE BROTHERS AND SISTERS, SHAPED BY THE SAME CREATOR.
Leader: When we have plenty and our neighbour has none:
ALL: FORGIVE US, CREATOR GOD.
Leader: When our gain causes our neighbour's pain:
ALL: FORGIVE US, CREATOR GOD.

Leader: When we do not listen
            and our hearts become hardened;
            when in our comfort we cannot see the truth
            and spin and headlines feed our lives,
ALL: FORGIVE US, CREATOR GOD.
            HELP US TO LIVE OUR LIVES WITH LOVE.

Song: Abundant life (CG)

Scripture reading: Isaiah 58:6–11

Litany of hope

Leader: When politics and policies are biased to the poor,
ALL: THEN SHALL THE LIGHT SHINE FORTH LIKE THE DAWN.
Leader: When none go hungry and good food is for all,
ALL: THEN SHALL THE LIGHT SHINE FORTH LIKE THE DAWN.
Leader: When all have a safe place to call home and feel welcome,
ALL: THEN SHALL THE LIGHT SHINE FORTH LIKE THE DAWN.

Thanksgiving and celebration

We give thanks for all through whom the Light shines,
for men, women and children who stand up for change with dignity and creativity.
We honour the people and projects that go on quietly, unseen and uncelebrated.
A time of quiet during which members of the congregation are invited to call out the names
of those known to them who work for change and justice.
For credit unions and food co-ops,
For collective action and courageous campaigns,
For community gardens and youth clubs,
For neighbours who care for and support one another …
For all through whom the Light shines, we give thanks.

Action

All are invited to come to the centre of the worship space and to clear up a piece of rubbish
from the spiral, replacing it with a candle, which they light as a prayer for a place or for
people who face, or work to overcome, environmental injustice in a situation of poverty.[1]

Song: Heaven shall not wait (CG)

Closing prayer *(said together)*

Creator God,
as we leave this place we commit ourselves
to try to see the world with your eyes,
to share and celebrate all our gifts,
to work together for change,
and to care for one another, your people and your Earth.

Alternative songs

Here I am, Lord (CG)
Inspired by love and anger (CG)
Jesus Christ is waiting (CG)
Oh the life of the world (CG)
Touch the earth lightly (CG)

Notes

[1]At the start of the action it should be pointed out that all the rubbish that will be picked up is recyclable, and details given of local recycling facilities. Separate bins should be provided for each type of item.

IN A MOMENT'S SILENCE:
Prayers from a soupie

Louise Glen-Lee

I was under the impression, when I began my job at the Salvation Army soup kitchen in Falkirk, that I would be ministering to the needy and downtrodden; in actual fact, the ministry, care and wisdom *I* received were amazing.

The people who used the soup kitchen were most often women and men addicted to alcohol, heroin, glue, self-harm, shoplifting ... They were treated appallingly by the outside community (bad reputations stick). In time, it became known that the soupie was one escape from being treated like a criminal. At the soupie, folks were invited to receive a full measure of life in spirit and sustenance, in which they could choose, or not choose, to participate. The majority of folks participated.

The prayers that follow brought angry people, worn people, hurt people, abused people, drunk people, drugged people to silence and reflection; they brought some discipline and loads of discussion about life and the nature of God and the universe. The Spirit thrived and transformed my first sanctimonious prayers into prayers that spoke to people – prayers that resulted from getting alongside people and listening to them.

The biggest thing that I learned in our prayer life together was not to be afraid to mention the unmentionable, or to leave silence for people to mention their own unmentionable.

MONDAY

Prayers for ourselves

Let us pray:

Lord God, we are good people who do bad things at times, we are good people who get ourselves into trouble and situations that no one would wish for us.

But accept us are we are, Lord, for, at the moment, we come no other way.

We have hurt other people and we cannot forgive ourselves; the pain and agony of what we have done takes us away from each other, takes us away from our families and true friends.

Accept us, Lord.

We have shouted and cursed and hated those people who have tried to help us, we are so far away from Love that we cannot remember what it is like to be loved. Show us

Love again, Lord; let love and hope and joy flow through our bodies that we might want something different than what we have today.

Accept us, Lord

We have simple medical problems that we have not dealt with because we are too busy trying to escape from our everyday lives; help us deal with the simple things that we may have the courage to deal with our bigger problems.

Accept us, Lord.

In a moment's silence, we think of those things that harm us most …

Accept us as we are, Lord, for we come no other way.

You love us God, truly love us, whoever, whatever we are; let us feel that love so that we may have a new life, built upon that foundation.

Amen

TUESDAY

Prayers for healing

In connection with people in Iona Abbey, and with people all over the world, we pray for healing for each person here tonight.[1]

Jesus, listen to our prayers:

We are a people everybody forgets, folks who are often passed over, or who are treated as if they are the worst people in Falkirk – and yet we have good hearts. We are in bad situations: we are often in trouble with the police, or with the courts, or with our families and friends, and yet we wish to be healed of all that harms us.

Some of us are addicted to heroin, or valium, or other drugs that make us escape from all that is painful in our lives. Some of us are addicted to alcohol, or painkillers to allow us a release from the daily pointlessness of life. Some of us are sex workers, some of us have mental health problems, some of us are lonely, some of us are abused, and yet we are the people, Jesus, if you were here on earth today, with whom you would be sitting at this table.

You offer us healing through the Holy Spirit, touching the most painful places of our lives. These are not just words; we need only ask you and our healing will begin.

So come, Lord, come into the painful places in our lives and let healing begin; we think of all the things in our hearts that we want your healing to touch …

(Silence)

Lord, you came to set us free through your healing touch; we have asked for healing for ourselves, and now we ask for healing for those people we are worried about …

(Silence)

We pray for our brothers and sisters who have died, we pray for our families and friends who have died – we especially pray for those who have died from the same addictions that we have and we remember (*names*). We are made new in you, let the healing of our bodies, minds and spirits begin.

We say the words that Jesus taught us:

Our Father …

Amen

WEDNESDAY

Prayers for families and children

Lord God, on this day we always remember our families and children. This is painful for us as we have good and bad memories of things we have done that have separated us from them.

We pray for ourselves as your children, loved and accepted, truly loved and accepted, and we ask that this love and acceptance will spill over into our relationships with those we are separated from.

We think of our parents, and the last time that we saw them; if that was a difficult situation, we ask that we may be able to put things right with them.

We are aware that they may have damaged or hurt us, and yet we have damaged and hurt them by our lifestyles; we never set out to hurt them intentionally.

We just want things to be right.

And we think of our children, many of them in foster care, many of them adopted. May they have unending love, Lord God; may they know what it is to be accepted and loved; and may they know that we love them deeply. Although we cannot see them at the moment, let them feel love from us.

We think of those of us who are pregnant at the moment and all we would want for our new babies. Lord, let us think about the way we treat our bodies while we are pregnant so that our children may have the best start in life.

In a moment's silence, we think of our families and our children and what we would wish to say to them ...

Your love for us is a mystery but you do love us, and you love our families, so be with us, Lord, as we begin to rebuild our lives.

Amen

THURSDAY

Prayers for new life

In you, God, we are promised new life.

These are not just words – the volunteers here, the workers here, have been changed by the love you have had for us; none of us have ever been perfect, and yet we are offered new life because we have accepted your love for us into our hearts.

Let each of us make a new space to accept that love for the first time, for the first time in a long time, or for more love to overcome the difficulties we have encountered on this day, because in you, God, we are promised new life.

There are things from our pasts that we know we carry with us because we have not forgiven ourselves, and we bring them before you now ...

(Silence)

There are things we have done that we are ashamed of, that we have never confessed and we bring them to you now ...

(Silence)

There are things that other people have done to us and we are unable to understand why, but we lay them at your feet now ...

(Silence)

Lord Jesus, you hung on a cross to bring us new life; you came and sat with people just like us to offer us new life; you healed people like us everyday; your death was not the end, just the simple beginning of our freedom from all that harms us.

Bring us new life, let this moment be the beginning of change, let us accept your love for us into our hearts.

We only need to say the words that we want new life and our journey will begin.

Amen

FRIDAY

Prayers for peace and justice

Every Friday we pray for peace and justice, and, Lord God, we ask that you bow down to listen to our prayers this night.

Some of us are people on the wrong side of the justice system; some of us have been in court this week; some of us missed our court appointments this week; some of us have warrants out for our arrest; some of us have been cautioned for crimes this week; some of us have been housebreaking; some of us have been shop-lifting; some of us have been violent, or aggressive or angry; some of us have done crimes that we dare not think about, and yet if we bring these things to you and confess them before you, our healing can begin. Peace can begin to settle in our hearts.

We pray for the justice system in our town: we pray for the fairness of the police, the wisdom of the procurator fiscal's office, the loyalty and honesty of our lawyers, we pray for our local sheriffs – that they will know how best to deal with all we have done to harm other people, and, for those of us at a higher court, we pray for fairness in our trials and the skills of the jury.

Lord you are the fairest, wisest, most honest person we know, and we wish that you may touch the hearts of those who make judgements over us.

We ask that your fairness will touch us that we will not commit crimes any more; that we see that our crimes hurt and harm other people, make other people scared and vulnerable. Keep us from harming other people, Lord; let us have peace between each other.

We pray for peace and justice in our lives and the lives of others around us, and, in a moment's silence, we think about how we can make peace in our own hearts.

(Silence)

Wise and wonderful God, restore us and renew us with love and joy and hope in our hearts that life does not need to go on like this; that we can find peace and justice in our hearts and in this world.

Amen

Notes

[1]The Tuesday evening service in Iona Abbey is a service of prayers for healing and the laying-on of hands. Members of the Iona Community Prayer Circle, living all around the world, also join in prayer on Tuesday evenings for specific people or situations for whose needs prayer has been requested.

WORLD AIDS DAY SERVICE, GLASGOW
Suet-Lin Teo

The Glasgow World AIDS Day Service was formed in the early 1990s by a group of Glasgow women who had lost their children to HIV/AIDS. It started as a vigil of a few and now approximately 300 people attend annually. Over the years it has been held in a variety of locations, from spiritual to secular, and now takes place in St Mary's Episcopal Cathedral on 1st December each year.

The service, although held in a church, is inclusive. It is spiritual rather than religious. There is no mention of God, of Jesus or of the Holy Spirit. This is a time and space for people of faith and of no faith to gather together to remember, reflect and celebrate.

Outline of the service

The service is divided into three sections: *Remember, Reflect* and *Celebrate*. Live or recorded music might be played during the symbolic actions.

Remember

During this section of the service we remember those we know who have died of HIV/AIDS. We remember them by standing in silence as their names are projected onto a screen. (To maintain confidentiality, we use people's first names only.)

There is a sculpture of a ribbon to which approximately 340 numbered red ribbons are attached. Each ribbon represents a person somewhere in the world who will die in the hour the service is held.

Vigil candles are lit to mark the lives of those we know and don't know.

Reflect

During this part of the service we reflect on both the local and global impact of HIV/AIDS.

In the first part of this section we reflect on the local impact by hearing personal stories from those who are brave enough to stand and speak of their experiences to a 300-strong crowd. (If you can't find anyone to tell their story, then there are a number of websites where positive people have published their stories, or you could read out an appropriate poem.)

We then pass round aromatherapy oils and ask people to introduce themselves to the person next to them, and to take some oil and rub it into the back of their neighbour's hand.

In the second half of this reflection we focus on the global issues and situation and incorporate some of the basic facts and figures to put HIV/AIDS into a wider context.

At the end of this section we exchange a red ribbon with someone around us, to show that we support each other and that we stand in solidarity with those near and far.

Celebrate

This is an opportunity to get together, meet new people and catch up with friends we haven't seen for a while over a glass of mulled wine or soft drink and some nibbles. It is not all doom and gloom in the world of HIV/AIDS. The people who are affected/infected are valued people who all have brought joy and smiles to the people around them and this is what we celebrate.

Words for the service

Below, you will find some words that can be said by whomever is leading the service to introduce the symbolic actions, or which can be included on the service sheet.

Lighting the vigil candles

The lighting of candles is a significant and powerful symbol used by many cultures which transcends many barriers.

These candles we light this evening are

- In memory of those who have died of HIV/AIDS
- To celebrate the lives of those who are affected by HIV/AIDS, be they brother, sister, friend, lover, partner, mother, father or carer.
- To remember our brothers and sisters affected by HIV/AIDS in distant countries.
- As a symbol of the light needed to overcome prejudice and stigma.
- As a sign of hope for the future that a cure may be found.

We invite you to light a candle in memory of someone, in celebration of life, to show support and unity with others, and as a sign of hope.

Exchange of red ribbons

The red ribbon is an internationally recognised symbol.

We wear the ribbon as a sign of solidarity. It is a public statement of our support of those living with or affected by HIV/AIDS. It is a visual sign that we stand in solidarity with them and that we remember, support and celebrate their lives.

We wear it to show others that we will not be hidden, we will not be cast aside, we will not be silenced and that we stand for justice and equality.

We reach out and exchange ribbons with someone we do not know in remembrance of all those strangers who are living with or are affected by HIV/AIDS. We remember all those from Africa, to China, to Russia, adults and children, and offer to them our solidarity and support.

Please use this time to reflect on the global situation: How can we support those living and affected by HIV/AIDS not only in Glasgow but in other countries? What can we do for them? How can we change society's perceptions and combat prejudice?

At this point in the service, red ribbons will be passed around. Please take one and give it to someone you do not know.

The red ribbon sculpture

We remember those we knew and loved …

Those who have died were friends, acquaintances, partners, parents – they are people whom we now remember.

We also remember the estimated 340 people in the world who will die of AIDS over the next hour. The red ribbon sculpture has 340 red ribbons pinned to it, one for each of these people.

The sharing of oils

As babies our senses of smell and touch are powerful tools which help us to learn about the world and to identify those we need and depend upon. As a child or adult, touch is soothing. It communicates many things – sympathy, love, jubilation, solidarity …

Aromatherapy oils will be passed around. We invite you to turn to the person next to you and introduce yourself, then take some of the oil and gently rub it into the back of their hand.

This is our way of showing to those around us that we are not scared to touch, to feel …

IN ALL GENERATIONS

IN ALL GENERATIONS

Ruth Harvey

God of all life, our Creator and Sustainer,
you support and love each one of us.
Your love surrounds us from cradle to grave,
and beyond the grave.

Jane Rogers

When I was seven I was asked what I wanted to be when I grew up. I knew very little then about careers, jobs, vocations or calling, so my response was based on what I had overheard respected adults talking very happily about: I said, 'I want to retire.' The hilarity which greeted my answer was a little confusing, given that adults had raved so wildly about this status. The fact that I was surrounded by lots of adults who were working beyond the regular pattern of nine to five, who could only dream about this 'glory status', made my reply and the laughter all the more poignant. At the same stage in my life, I believed that every child my age worshipped ecumenically at least twice each day. By the age of 10, when I slowly and painfully learned about Protestants and Catholics, and the horror of division, cynicism not just about retirement but about corporate integrated worship had fully set in. I'm not sure that I have ever recovered.

'In All Generations' is a collection of liturgies and resources overflowing with healing words and actions for corporate and personal worship, which goes a long way to recover some of the wisdom and innocence found in all ages. These liturgies model for us fresh forms of a contextual liberation theology that integrates pain and confusion with hope and light. The simplicity of the form and the words found in Ruth Burgess's 'Playful God', blending powerful symbolic actions with words that any three-year-old would relate to, takes us to a style of 'all-age worship' that is neither patronising nor tokenistic. The model adopted by Bridget Hewitt with the young people of Hexham in 'Help us make a difference', where the voices of young people themselves shine through, putting to rest any notions of apathy among mainstream youth, reminds us that a 'children's address' is usually a missed opportunity for young people, and children, to address the whole worshipping congregation. The translucent poems and reflections by Tom Gordon take everyday experiences of living with the reality of ageing and youth to a divine depth of laughter and tears. And Jane Rogers' moving and profound resources give a voice to the many who live in the sometimes indignity of poverty and judging that can co-exist with old age. This is a rare collection.

'All-age worship' at its worst can be a patronising attempt *by* adults to find and fit together songs and prayers *for* children. At its best it can be a collaboration *between* children and adults, all generations, each listening to the wisdom, insights, humour and longings of the others, brought together and shared before God in an act of corporate and public worship. This kind of contextual, or liberation theology is not new. It has transformed the way we are invited to read the Bible alongside women, people of colour, those living with disability, those discriminated against in our churches because of their sexual orientation and many others. The process of applying such a radical, justice-filled theology to inter-generational worship is long overdue. To get it right takes time, energy, patience and wisdom. In the liturgies and resources that follow, skilled writers have crafted the words, raw emotions, longings and physical needs of small children, teenagers, and those approaching and beyond retirement, with the radical liberating message of the Gospels to unlock for us the faith story once more.

As I await the imminent arrival of my third child, noticing all the while the deepening wrinkles on my own face and hands, while watching my parents grow old with grace, I sometimes come upon myself dwelling on life not so much as a two-dimensional time line, but more as an organic cycle of birth, life, death, new life, new birth … And I am reminded that as children of God we are called not to wish away our linear time on this earth, but to dwell fully in the kairos moment in which we are blessed to exist, 're-attiring' ourselves at all stages in our lives (getting ready, dressed, attired) and working together for the peace and justice of all on our planet.

PLAYFUL GOD:
A liturgy for children and adults together
Ruth Burgess

Opening responses

Leader: Playful God
Starshaper
ALL: WE WELCOME YOU
Leader: Playful God
Storyteller
ALL: WE WELCOME YOU
Leader: Playful God
Firedancer
ALL: WE WELCOME YOU
Leader: Joyful and welcoming God
ALL: WE ARE GLAD TO BE HERE WITH YOU

Song of approach[1]

Prayer of approach

The younger children (perhaps aged 3–8) might act out some of the phrases in the first part of this prayer as the adults say the words. This will work best if the children are gathered centrally and practise the actions first.[2] Some words and phrases that might be acted out or mimed are, for example, 'daisies and dandelions', ' hold out hands in friendship', 'dance in the wind' ...)

Leader: Creative and loving God,
your world is full of beauty and glory.
We rejoice in daisies and dandelions
even when they blossom in the middle of our lawns.
You call us to laughter and to dreaming.
ALL: WE ARE SAFE IN YOUR STRONG LOVE.
Leader: Just and generous God,
your world is full of questions and stories.
You make us smile and think.
You hold out your hands in friendship.
You call us to truth and to justice.
ALL: WE ARE SAFE IN YOUR STRONG LOVE.

Leader:	Holy and mysterious God,
	your world is full of wisdom and wonder.
	You dance in the wind.
	You are full of surprises.
	You call us to holiness and to glory.
ALL:	WE ARE SAFE IN YOUR STRONG LOVE.
Leader:	You call us, God.
	You ask us what kind of lives we are living.
	And now, in the silence, we share our stories with you:

(Silence)

For all the good things that have happened to us we thank you.
For the mistakes we have made and the people we have hurt we are sorry.
We ask for your help and your love.

(Silence)

Leader:	God says to all who ask:
	I love you, I forgive you, come and walk with me.
	Thank you, God.
ALL:	AMEN

Song

The Word of God

Leader: Let us listen to some words from the Bible and then to a story about a little boy named Alfie.

The reading that follows is a paraphrase of Zechariah 8:2–5, 12a, 15b–17a, 19b. Again, the younger children might act out or mime part of this.

God gave this message to Zechariah:
I have longed to help Jerusalem
because of my deep love for her people.
I will return to Jerusalem and live there;
it will be known as the faithful city.
Once again old men and women,
so old that they use a stick when they walk,
will be sitting in the city squares.
The streets will be full again of boys and girls playing.

People will sow their crops in peace,
the vines will bear grapes,
the earth will produce food,
there will be plenty of rain.

These are the things you must do:
Speak the truth to one another;
in the courts give real justice
the kind that brings peace;
do not plan ways to hurt each other;
do not tell lies about each other.
Have courage,
do not be afraid.
Love truth and love peace.

Alfie sang

Alfie was small, fat and four years old. Too small to go to school, too big to be kept safely in a pram. The flat Alfie lived in was small; on the 18th floor of a huge block of flats. He could only come down when his mother went shopping. And then there were only lift shafts, stone stairs, crowded streets, and if the lift was out of order there were 280 steps to climb.

Alfie liked noise – the shouting, stamping, banging kind. But the lady in the flat below did not like people stamping on her ceiling and the man next door did not like shouting. Alfie liked sand and water. But sand scratched the floors and water made a mess. Sometimes Alfie cried.

One day Alfie's mother took him downstairs; not to go shopping, but to a hall near the flats. There were children everywhere. Sitting at tables, climbing up ladders, shouting, laughing, banging. There were swings and see-saws, blocks and tins, books and papers. Alfie did not know where to begin.

That afternoon, all the way back to the little flat on the 18th floor, Alfie sang. All his mother heard was a solemn, tuneless chant, but actually Alfie was singing of the glory of noise, of the stamping of feet, the banging of hammers, the shouting out loud. He sang of climbing and running and rolling; of the roughness of sand, the wetness of water and the rainbow beauty of paints, and of the pleasure of friends; and he sang because he knew he could go again the next day.

From Save the Children

Song: Lord, I love to stamp and shout

(This would be another good opportunity for children, and adults, to act or mime – stamp and shout.)

Lord, I love to watch things fly
Whizzing, zooming, flashing by;
Engines, aircraft, speedboats, cars,
Spacecraft shooting to the stars.

Lord, I love to probe and pry
Seeking out the reason why;
Looking inside things and out,
Finding what they're all about.

Lord, I'm many things and one
Though my life's not long begun;
You alone my secret see
What I am cut out to be.

Leader: We listen to some words of Jesus and to some imagined thoughts of the children he spoke about.

The reading that follows is a paraphrase of Matthew 11:16–19.

Jesus was talking to the crowds about some of the people he met. He said, 'Now to what can I compare the people of this day? What are they like? They are like children sitting in the market place. One group shouts to the other: "We played wedding music for you, but you wouldn't dance! We sang funeral songs, but you wouldn't cry." When John the Baptist came, he starved himself, he drank no wine and you say, "He's mad! He has a demon in him." I come, I eat, I drink, I go out to dinner with all sorts of people, and you say: "Look at this man! He eats too much and he is a drunkard, a friend of tax collectors and scoundrels!" God's wisdom, however, is shown to be true by its results.'

Weddings and funerals conversation

All the readers in this conversation are children, perhaps of age 8–11. The reading could be dramatised, with additional parts (such as wee Davie) for non-readers.

Reader 1:   Watched us he did. I saw him.
             We were playing Weddings.
Reader 2:   We'd got a band together,
             and Miriam had borrowed her mum's shoes and shawl.
Reader 3:   And I'd got a glass to smash when it came to the right moment.
             I like that bit.

Reader 1:	And wee Davie wouldn't play because he couldn't be the bridegroom.
Reader 2:	It was his mam's chair and he'd borrowed it and he wanted to sit in it and be carried along the street and he said it wasn't fair.
Reader 3:	But he was too small be a bridegroom and we wouldn't let him.

(Pause)

Reader 4:	Watching us he was. I saw him.
	We were off down to the caves to play funerals.
Reader 5:	We'd all got our hankies ready,
	and Anna had borrowed some of her mum's perfume.
Reader 6:	And we'd got loads and loads of cloth,
Reader 4:	And we were going to wrap up wee Davie as the body,
	but he didn't want to play.
Reader 5:	Started bawling for his mam and ran away home.

(Pause)

Reader 1:	He was watching us all right.
Reader 2:	Great big grown-up.
Reader 3:	And he was smiling.
Reader 4:	Perhaps he wanted to play, to be the bridegroom.
Reader 5:	Perhaps he had a hankie and he wanted to cry with the mourners.
Reader 6:	We could have wrapped him up as the body, we had loads of cloth.

A game

A game is played by everyone. This could be a well-known game such as I-Spy or Pass the Parcel. Or the congregation could be invited to spend 10 minutes in small, mixed-aged groups playing weddings or funerals.

Song: Come and gather round (CG)

The rights of children

Everyone has human rights including children. Because they are young, however, children are more likely than adults to have their rights forgotten about or ignored or abused. To protect children's rights the United Nations has drawn up an international agreement called the United Nations Convention on the Rights of the Child. The UK agreed to be bound by the convention in 1991. This means that our Government has to make sure that our laws and the way we treat children in this country meet the standards laid down in the Convention. Let us affirm our belief in these rights of the child.

Leader: With the United Nations Convention on the Rights of the Child we affirm that:

Up to six of the following Articles of the United Nations Convention on the Rights of the Child are read by all as an affirmation:

When adults or organisations make decisions which affect children they must always think first about what would be best for the child. *(Article 3)*

Children have a right to life and to the best possible chance to develop fully. *(Article 6)*

All children have a right to a name when they are born and to be able to become a citizen of a particular country. *(Article 7)*

Children too have the right to say what they think about anything which affects them. What they say must be listened to carefully. *(Article 12)*

Parents have a duty to give guidance but children have the right to choose their own religion, and to have their own views as soon as they are able to decide for themselves. *(Article 14)*

Children have a right to personal privacy. *(Article 16)*

Children should be able to get hold of a wide range of information, especially any which would make life better for them. *(Article 17)*

Children have the right to be protected from all forms of violence. They must be kept safe from harm. *(Article 19)*

Children have the right to be as healthy as possible. Children have the right to live in a safe, healthy and unpolluted environment with good food and clean drinking water. *(Article 24)*

Every child has the right to an adequate standard of living. This is, in the main, for parents to provide, but in cases of need the Government should help parents reach this standard. *(Article 27)*

Every child is entitled to rest and play and to have the chance to join in a wide range of activities. *(Article 31)*

Children under 15 years old are not to be recruited into the armed forces. *(Article 38)*[3]

Prayer of intercession

We pray for all children growing up in our world.
(Pause)
We pray for children who grow up in places of danger, in places where there is fighting and fear especially …
(Pause)
We pray for children who are in trouble, who are bullied or abused, who are hungry.
(Pause)
We pray for children who are ill, for children whose life is a struggle, for children who are in pain.
(Pause)
We pray for children whose names we know and we ask God to help them.

All members of the congregation are invited to come and light a candle as a prayer for a child or children, themselves, someone they know, or children suffering in different parts of the world.[4]

Jesus, you called the children to you and you blessed them. We ask you to bless the children we have prayed for today and to help us all to grow in love. Amen

Song

Closing responses

Leader:	May God the Maker bless us.
	May we be brave and loving and cheerful.
ALL:	MAY GOD BLESS US WITH JOY.
Leader:	May Jesus the storyteller bless us.
	May we be full of questions and justice.
ALL:	MAY JESUS BLESS US WITH COURAGE.
Leader:	May the Holy Spirit bless us.
	May we be wise and creative and full of wonder.
ALL:	MAY GOD'S SPIRIT BLESS US WITH HOPE.
Leader:	May the saints and the angels dance in and out of our footsteps.
	May the little ones invite us to share in their play.
ALL:	MAY WE JOURNEY HOMEWARDS IN LOVE AND LAUGHTER.
	MAY WE BE SURPRISED AND SAFEGUARDED IN GOD.
	AMEN

Notes

[1]Choose songs the youngest children know or could easily learn.

[2] It is OK if the practising takes some time as this will enable the congregation to appreciate that the children are a full and active part of the service.

[3] Children and/or adults could make posters relating to the United Nations Convention prior to the service. These could then be placed in different locations around the room and used during the prayer of intercession.

[4] Most children can light candles under supervision. Younger ones may need discouraging from blowing them out! If posters on the United Nations Convention have been made for the service, groups of candles could be located at the foot of each poster.

HELP US MAKE A DIFFERENCE:
A liturgy prepared by young people for the whole people of God
The Hexham Abbey Youth Group and Bridget Hewitt

This liturgy was written in 2002 by a group of twelve young people aged 14–18, all of whom were linked with Hexham Abbey, and who participated together in the Iona Youth Festival 2001.

The group decided to focus on issues of justice and peace as they affected them in their own lives, rather than as abstract concepts. Some heartfelt discussions resulted during the preparation of the liturgy, as the issues became more real for them.

The group led a service based around this liturgy in Hexham Abbey in May 2002.

A supply of candles, cut out paper leaves, and pens, all sufficient for the anticipated size of congregation, are placed in a convenient place at the front or centre of the worship space before the service.

Introductory reflection

Read slowly from within the centre of the gathering

When the last dove of peace has flown.
When the last olive branch of peace been stretched out.
Will we realise what we have done?

When the last war is waged.
When the last terrorist act is carried out.
Will we hear the cry of the people?

When the last crime is committed.
When the last innocent person is imprisoned.
Will we be able to undo our wrongs?

When the last gun is fired.
When the last bomb has been set off.
Will we see the land we have left for children?

Lord, in your love help us always to seek justice and promote peace.

John Young, aged 18

Opening prayer *(said together)*

God, father and mother of all the human race;
God who lives within every human being, in every child, woman and man;
God, broken by our divisiveness,
hurt by our woundedness,
dying in every battlefield.
Vulnerable, holy God.
We offer to you ourselves as we come together here
and we ask you to transform us from within;
to heal our hurts and hates,
and to lead us to ways of peace and growth.
Amen

Song

Prayer of confession

God, we come to you to say sorry for our part in the wrongs of the world.
Often we do not welcome the stranger.
Often we do not open wide our arms to people who are different.
We put up barriers, we push others out, we want our own safety and security.
Help us, Lord God, to be less quick to make judgements;
to be more open-minded and willing to help others, to listen, and learn from them.
Help us to realise that we are not superior, that all are equal.
Help us to accept ourselves and to grow in self-awareness.
Amen

Scripture reading: Luke 24:13–24 (The Emmaus road)

Where are you, God?

Leader:	When, at school, we see people being bullied, we see pain and hurt, and we feel anger,
ALL:	WHERE ARE YOU, GOD?
Leader	When we see people being picked on, because of their race, sexual orientation, different accents, or clothes, and we feel powerless to stop it,
ALL:	WHERE ARE YOU, GOD?

Leader:	When teachers treat people unfairly, when they treat us unfairly, when we make a mistake and can't find a way to explain,
ALL:	WHERE ARE YOU, GOD?
Leader:	When we see on the news strong nations bully weak nations and hear of religions and cultures being prejudiced against each other,
ALL:	WHERE ARE YOU, GOD?
Leader:	When loneliness and fear is all around us, breeding suspicion and insecurity, and we need a sense of belonging,
ALL:	WHERE ARE YOU, GOD?
Leader:	There is so much that is hard to understand, and so much that feels wrong, and yet it is easier to do nothing about it.
ALL:	ARE YOU THERE, GOD? OR ARE YOU FAR FAR AWAY?

Reading

A Native American grandfather was talking to his grandson about how he felt after a tragedy. He said, 'I feel as if I have two wolves fighting in my heart. One wolf is the vengeful, angry, violent one. The other wolf is the loving, compassionate one.' The grandson asked him, 'Which wolf will win the fight in your heart?' The grandfather answered, 'The one I feed.'

Prayer for God's help

Sometimes, God, it seems so difficult to walk the path of justice, and to find peace.
Sometimes we really don't like people, don't get on with them.
Surely it must be OK to like some people more than others?
Sometimes we try to befriend the person being bullied,
only to find that makes things worse for us, and we resent it.
Sometimes, whichever action we take seems not to be the right one;
either we feel bad, or we feel used.

Lord God, help us when we feel powerless and helpless.
Help us to know that our grappling selves,
often seeming to walk in the dark and to take wrong turnings,
are greatly loved by you.
Help us somehow through the muddy waters of uncertainty,
to find ways that lead to peace. Amen

Song

Litany: If only ...

Voice 1:   Perhaps there would be justice ...

Voice 2:   If only all faiths could co-exist rather than fearing and competing with each other.

Voice 3:   If only the resources of the world could be equally shared between all people.

Voice 4:   If only people could feel OK about themselves, and respect each other.

Voice 5:   If only rich countries did not put their own interests first.

Voice 1:   And if there was justice, perhaps there would be peace.

Voice 6:   Is this Utopia? Or could it happen?

Scripture reading: Luke 24:25–31 (The Emmaus road)

Reflection

It would be nice and comfortable to have answers to all our questions. But life does not have easy answers. As Thomas Merton said, 'Life is not a problem to be solved, but a mystery to be lived'. When Jesus died his friends thought there were no answers at all. And yet ...

When two disciples on the road to Emmaus were despondent, not understanding and asking difficult questions – suddenly there was Jesus walking with them.

When Mary, not able to find the body of Jesus, turned desperately to the gardener – Jesus himself was there speaking to her.

When the disciples were debating with each other in the upper room, confused and frightened, not knowing what was going on – suddenly there was Jesus, asking for food.

Somehow it seems that by asking the questions, and embracing the pain and weakness of the human condition, and not running away from it or pretending it's not there, maybe, just maybe, we will find Jesus walking the road with us.

(Short silence)

Scripture reading: Revelation 22:1–2 (The leaves of healing)

Reflective action

How greatly the world needs those leaves of healing now. The river that feeds the trees flows from God. Can we allow ourselves to be like that river, sent by God to become agents of peace and reconciliation in our communities, our families, our schools, our places of work? Let us try to open ourselves to God's presence within us.

During the time of quiet that will follow in a moment, anyone who would like to is invited to light a candle. As we do so, let us try to allow God's presence to flow through us, change us, soften our hard edges and strengthen our weak edges, so that the light of that candle symbolises the love of God spreading out through us to the world around us. And after lighting a candle, each of us is invited to pick up a paper leaf and write something on it that we would like to change in ourselves, in order that we might become more a bearer of God's peace in the world. After you have written on your leaf, please take it away with you as a reminder of your prayer.

A quiet time follows with gentle background music or a quiet song by a soloist or small group. Towards the end of this time, a congregational chant might be sung, for example a Taizé chant.

Affirmative responses

Leader:	God says: I will judge with fairness.
ALL:	LET US NOT JUDGE OTHERS WITH OUR PRE-FORMED IDEAS.
Leader:	God says: I will hear the cries of the oppressed.
ALL:	LET US HEAR THEM TOO, AND ACT TO HELP THOSE WHO SUFFER.
Leader:	Jesus says: Happy are those who work for peace.
ALL:	LET US DO ALL WE CAN TO BE CHANNELS OF PEACE IN OUR FAMILIES, COMMUNITIES, AND THE WORLD.
Leader:	Jesus says: Peace is what I leave you.
ALL:	LET US ACCEPT THE PEACE THAT JESUS OFFERS, AND WORK TO ENABLE IT TO SPREAD.

Emma Wright, aged 18

Song: In many foreign countries
(Tune: Noel Nouvelet (traditional)/Jesus Christ is waiting)

In many foreign countries, justice and peace are gone.
Families live in squalor, poverty and wrong,
Death and disease, from thoughtless western ways;
Help us make a difference, not just take their pay.

Fishermen go hungry, profits borne away.
Unfair trading rules give millionaires their way.
Laws stifle trade, not working as they should;
Help us make a difference, acting for the good.

People lose their culture as a result of war.
Politicians rule, and prices hit the floor.
Crops piled up high, but prices falling low;
Help us make a difference, make our choices show.

Charles Ogilvie, aged 14

Closing responses

Leader:	We live in peace, while many live amidst war and oppression.
	We have hope for our future, while many look forward to uncertainty and fear.
ALL:	HELP US TO SEE THE POINTLESSNESS AND FUTILITY OF CONFLICT.
Leader:	We have plenty to eat and drink.
	We have homes and warmth and security.
ALL:	TEACH US TO SHARE OUR WEALTH UNTIL ALL HAVE THEIR FILL.
Leader:	We can use our time as we wish.
	We can say what we believe without fear of danger.
ALL:	HELP US TO PROMOTE AWARENESS, AND OPEN OUR EYES TO THE INJUSTICE IN THE WORLD.
Leader:	When these things seem too distant, too far away,
	and to take too much time in our busy lives.
ALL:	MAKE US ABLE TO EMPATHISE WITH OTHERS,
	TO REALISE THAT WE ARE ALL INTERCONNECTED.
	HELP US TO USE OUR FREEDOM TO MAKE A DIFFERENCE.

Reflective reading

Read from the centre of the gathering by the same person who read the introductory reflection.

I believe that unarmed truth and unconditional love will have the final word. We have flown the air like birds and swum the sea like fishes, but have yet to learn the simple act of walking the earth as brothers and sisters.

Martin Luther King

Blessing *(said together)*

Living God,
we thank you for this time of worshipping together
and for the thoughts and awarenesses that have been awakened within us.
May the peace of your presence,
the fire of your Spirit,
and the energy of the wind of heaven
fill us, and rekindle the living flame of love in our lives.
Amen

LITURGICAL RESOURCES ON AGEING

The following worship resources were written by Tom Gordon and by Jane Rogers. Tom Gordon is a chaplain with Marie Curie Hospice in Edinburgh. Jane Rogers is retired and works as a volunteer chaplain at a hospital. Both are members of the Iona Community.

THE PHOTO ALBUM OF MY LIFE
Tom Gordon

The photo album of my life

You come to me,
and sit and listen.
I like that.
I like your company,
your interest,
your ready smile.
It breaks my day.
It fills my time,
my room,
my mind
with youth
and newness
and – well –
even things you tell me about
that I'll never understand.

You come to me,
and give me time,
and make me feel I matter again.

But do you know,
can you ever understand
that what you see of me,
and what you know of me,
and what you learn of me,
is not the me I am,
the me I know I am,
but just the part of me
that's here
and now?

Do you know,
can I make you understand
that what you see –
and like, it seems –
is but the final page,
the most recent image
in the album of my life?

Because, you see,
you've started at the last page.
For that's where the album of my life
lay open
when you came along,
open there for you to gaze upon.

I'm glad you like that page.

But do you know,
can I make you understand
that this is not it all?
There's more than this to see
and know
and learn about.

So, take some time
to turn the pages of the album of my life.
Turn back the pages now with me.
Gaze upon the images you didn't know were there,
and look
and learn.

Look there –
that teenager in the mini-skirt
is me,
yes, me!
Would you believe I wore a skirt
as short as that?
These skinny, wrinkled legs you see today
were not always thus!
Look there.
See!
Legs were worth the showing then.

That's part of me!

Ah, and that one too,
that pretty Mum,
a child on either knee –
that's me!
One four,
one two,
both still for just a moment
when the camera clicked,
and never still again!
How proud I look,
how happy then!

That's part of me.

And this,
this band of happy people,
there's me –
and Alf behind –
Oh Alf –
how I miss him so,
those twenty years since he passed on.
But then, a different story,
with friends en masse
on a summer trip to Rothesay.
Oh happy days!

That's part of me.

Look there,
on Christmas Day,
here, in the home,
three years ago, I think,
(or was it four,
or maybe longer since),
with paper hat,
and rosy cheeks –
the Christmas sherry can be blamed for that –
and so much fun,
and not so long ago.

That's part of me.

Enough for now?
Perhaps …

for now …

So go,
and come again another day,
and take your time with me,
to leaf the pages through.
You'll see me there,
with smiles and tears,
so slim, too fat,
alone,
with friends,
with Alf,
you'll see and know and understand
that this
and this
and this …
is me.

Not simply now.
Not just this part.
Not just this final page,
with ancient, wrinkled me.
There's more I need to show
if you can take the time with me.

This album of my life,
just waiting
to be opened up again.

A litany for the service of the years

Leader: Living God, you gave gifts to your people, that they might serve you and
            praise you.
ALL: HELP US TO USE WELL OUR GIFTS IN YOUR SERVICE, SO THAT YOUR
            NAME MIGHT BE PRAISED.

Leader: You saw the faith of Noah's years, and you blessed him and his family with
            your promise of hope and new beginnings.
ALL: GIVE US NOAH'S TRUST IN YOUR WAY, EVEN WHEN ALL AROUND
            SEEMS HOPELESS.

Leader:	You called Abram when he was old, and you gave him a new name and a new beginning.
ALL:	GIVE US ABRAHAM'S FAITH IN YOU, AND CALL US FORWARD TO A JOURNEY OF NEW POSSIBILITIES.

Leader:	You gave Sarah the gift of a child in her old age, so that your Response might live to serve you.
ALL:	GIVE US SARAH'S WONDER AT YOUR WAYS, EVEN WHEN YOUR PURPOSE DOESN'T FIT OUR EXPECTATION, BELIEF OR UNDERSTANDING.

Leader:	You chose Moses and called him to a new career, when royal service and shepherding had already filled the passing years.
ALL:	GIVE US MOSES' RESPONSE TO YOU, AND A BELIEF THAT WHAT'S AHEAD MAY BE EVER BETTER THAN WHAT'S BEEN BEFORE.

Leader:	You gave responsibility to Joshua, to take over when an old man had done his job.
ALL:	GIVE US JOSHUA'S BELIEF THAT WE CAN CHOOSE TO LEARN FROM THE WISDOM OF PAST YEARS AND MAKE A NEW COMMITMENT TO WHAT IS YET TO COME.

Leader:	You called people like us, when they were loyal and faithful and true.
ALL:	GIVE US A TRUST THAT MAKES US MORE LOYAL, A RESPONSE THAT MAKES US MORE FAITHFUL, A BELIEF IN WHAT IS RIGHT AND TRUE.

Leader:	You called people like us, when they were wise and trusting and committed.
ALL:	GIVE US INSIGHT TO KNOW YOUR WISDOM, STRENGTH TO TRUST YOUR GUIDANCE, AND HOPE AND PURPOSE TO MAKE OUR COMMITMENT WITH THEM.

Leader:	You called people like us, when they were unsure, full of questions, overwhelmed with doubt.
ALL:	GIVE US TRUST WHEN WE ARE UNSURE, A RESPONSE EVEN WHEN WE QUESTION, AND A BELIEF THAT TRIUMPHS OVER DOUBT.

Leader:	You called people like us, when they were old and worn out and failing.
ALL:	GIVE US INSIGHT TO RESPOND TO YOU WHEN WE ARE OLD, STRENGTH FROM YOU WHEN WE FEEL WORN OUT, AND HOPE THAT YOU CAN TURN OUR FAILURES INTO YOUR PURPOSE.

Leader:	Living God, you gave gifts to your people, that they might serve you and praise you.
ALL:	HELP US TO USE WELL OUR GIFTS IN YOUR SERVICE, SO THAT YOUR NAME MIGHT BE PRAISED.

A child of God

ALL: I AM A CHILD OF GOD.

Voice l: I am a baby.
Voice 2:   I am a little girl.
Voice 3:   I am a spotty teenager.
Voice 4:   I am a young mother.
Voice 5:   I am a healthy pensioner.
Voice 6:   I am a frail old man
Voice 7:   I am a dying woman.
ALL   I AM A CHILD THAT MATTERS TO GOD.

Voice 1:   I need love and nurture.
Voice 2:   I need safety and security.
Voice 3:   I need understanding and patience.
Voice 4:   I need acknowledgement and support.
Voice 5:   I need affirmation and acceptance.
Voice 6:   I need tolerance and time.
Voice 7:   I need dignity and peace.
ALL   I AM A CHILD WHO HAS A UNIQUENESS IN GOD'S PURPOSE.

Voice 1:   God gives me the gift of life.
Voice 2   God gives me the beauty of innocence.
Voice 3:   God gives me a questioning mind.
Voice 4:   God gives me a capacity to cope.
Voice 5:   God gives me the wisdom of years.
Voice 6:   God gives me memories of a full life.
Voice 7:   God gives me insights into death.
ALL: I AM A CHILD TO WHOM GOD HAS GIVEN GIFTS AND TALENTS TO USE
                TO THE FULL.

Voice 1:   I love my big sister.
Voice 2:   My big brother's really great.
Voice 3:   My mum's just the coolest mum in the street.
Voice 4:   It's great having grandad around.
Voice 5:   My old pal still matters to me.
Voice 6:   Thank God for my family.
Voice 7:   My great-granddaughters bring me such hope and joy.
ALL   I NEED YOU, AND YOU, AND YOU, AND YOU, AND YOU, AND YOU,
                AND YOU ... BECAUSE YOU MATTER TO ME TOO.

Voice 1:   So value my potential, because you've had the chance to value yours.
Voice 2:   Don't destroy my innocence, for with it you will destroy my life.

Voice 3:   Tolerate my rebelliousness, because I *can* change the world for you.

Voice 4:   Please see me as a whole person, 'cause I'm much more than a harassed mother.

Voice 5:   Keep using my experience, and don't discard me yet.

Voice 6:   I'm still here, and I'm more than just this frail body you see.

Voice 7:   Let my dying speak to you of important things, so you can face your mortality with hope.

ALL   I AM A CHILD OF GOD.

          I AM UNIQUE IN ALL THE WORLD.

          I BEND HISTORY.

          I *CAN* STILL MAKE A DIFFERENCE.

          I AM A CREATURE OF A GREAT AND WONDERFUL UNIVERSE.

          LIKE YOU, I AM A SPECIAL CHILD OF GOD.

          THANKS BE TO GOD.

I'm old

I'm old, so they tell me, I'm old.
It's time for my bus-pass, I'm told.
I'm way past my prime,
For my pension, it's time.
'Cause I'm old, no denyin' it, I'm old.

I'm slow on my feet now, I'm slow.
Where my energy's gone, I don't know.
I used to be fit,
Now I'd rather just sit,
'Cause I'm slow, to be honest, I'm slow.

I think I'm beginning to think
That my mind is beginning to shrink!
For my memory's amiss –
Is dementia like this?
'Cause I think that I'm failing to think.

I'm past it! My good days are past.
Oh, I know that you'll look on aghast.
But the person you see
Isn't quite the real me,
'Cause I'm past it, my days are well past.

But …

I'm wise, don't you see it, I'm wise.
And I hope you will now realise
That I've lived a fair bit,
And along with my wit
I'm quite wise, you should know it, I'm wise.

And I'm shrewd, let me tell you, I'm shrewd,
For I've learned from the bad and the good,
The laughter and tears,
Through the unfolding years.
So I'm shrewd, don't forget it, I'm shrewd.

Yes, I'm old, and I know it! I'm old!
But that bell that you've just heard being tolled
Is not for my death.
I've not breathed *my* last breath!
O, I'm old, but not dead yet. Just old!

For there's life in the old dog, some life.
No, I won't cause you trouble and strife.
But there's more I *can* do,
More to offer to *you!*
For there's life in me yet. Yes, my life!

This hand

I sit and look at you,
transfixed by what I see.
Is this the you I've known and loved,
when life was full,
when we were good?
Is this the you
that now I have to know –
so gaunt,
with open mouth
and staring eyes,
so different now
from what I knew of you
so little time ago?

I take your hand in mine,
a slender, bony hand,

too delicate, it seems,
too fragile now for me to hold.
And yet I do.
With gentle touch
I take your precious hand in mine,
and you and I are one
and good again.

This hand,
that touched me with such warmth
when comfort was my need.
This hand,
that held my own with strength
when I your greeting sought.
This hand,
that worked and strove
and never shrank from hardship's toil,
to make a home for such as me.
This hand,
that made such music
as it touched the keys,
that angel hosts might sing.

This hand,
that wrote such tender words
of love and consolation
to many a grief-torn soul.
This hand,
that pointed out with wisdom's depth
the easy paths to go,
and warned of dangers too
for trusting youth to be aware.

This hand ...
so full in all its ancient frailness,
so worthy of its lengthy life.
This hand,
which speaks so much of you.

No, do not try to speak with words.
I do not need your explanation.
For words are not enough

to speak the pain of what is now,
and joy of what has been.

No, just let me hold your hand a while,
your hand in mine.
For in this precious time
it now says all that should be said,
of love and life,
of years and yearning's voice.

This hand is you
and that is all I need.

I take your hand in mine,
a slender, bony hand,
too delicate, it seems,
too fragile now for me to hold.
And yet I do.
With gentle touch
I take your precious hand in mine,
and you and I are one
and good again.

My grandpa

I didn't much like my grandpa. He shook a lot (Parkinson's disease, I discovered later) and that was scary for a wee boy. He drank too much beer – or so my granny always said – and with that and the reek of stale tobacco from his horrible pipe, he didn't smell too good either. He was way too grumpy for my liking. I don't remember him smiling much. He snored like a warthog. (I always shared a room with him and my dad when we stayed on holiday and I detested his snoring!) And my granny and my mum kept telling pretty strange stories about his antics when he was a young farmhand, all about drink and shouting and punching. I'm not sure I ever grasped the details, but it didn't sound like living with him had been a bundle of laughs. So, I didn't much like my grandpa.

But, mostly, we never spoke. He didn't say anything to me. Oh, he'd say plenty about me, like how I was too cheeky for my age, and that I wasn't learning much about good behaviour from the Boys Brigade, and that I should leave things alone that weren't mine, and stuff like that – and I didn't say anything to him; not much I could say, really, apart from calling him a smelly old man and asking him why he was always shaking like that. And I was too scared to be as cheeky as that! So, we never spoke. Just watched and got suspicious and kept our distance.

I wonder now what we would have said if we'd tried to speak. And I wonder if he ever wondered what I'd say to him if we ever conversed. And I wonder what he was really, really like, this grandpa of mine. But my grandpa died before we ever got to know each other, before either of us every really bothered to get to know each other. The gulf was too wide, the differences too vast.

So I remember my grandpa as a man that I didn't really like much. Perhaps it's my granny's oft-used description of him that stays with me most. 'A bad old bugger' she'd call him – and sometimes to his face at that! (Brave lady!)

One thing always intrigued me about my grandpa, though. It's a simple fact that I must have picked up at a very early age. He'd been brought up in an orphanage, Quarriers' Homes in Bridge of Weir. Not a particularly world-shattering piece of information, but an intriguing one just the same. And, years later, it was this single piece of information that changed my mind about my grandpa.

Many years after my own parents had died, I spent some time researching my family tree on the Internet. I keyed in my grandpa's name. And there it was! One census showed him in a family home as a one-year-old with his mother and his brother, the next, ten years later, saw him listed among the boys in an orphanage. I was full of questions … What had happened? What had caused this dramatic change? So I traced his parents. His father had disappeared after he was born, and his mother 'died as the result of a house fire', her death certificate said.

'Died as a result of a house fire.' In an instant a horrible old man became a frightened, lonely child. A shaky, cantankerous grandpa became a disoriented wee boy, devoid of family love. A smelly, argumentative figure, to be reviled, became a tragic victim of hurt and poverty and a terrible trauma.

Whatever had happened in the unfolding of his years, to make this child the father of this man, I shall never know. But what I do now know is that to add to the ending of a life there was now this life's beginning. The old man and the broken child were one and the same.

I didn't much like my grandpa. I still don't. I didn't much care for the old man he'd become. But now I cried for the child he had been, and I wanted to hold him and comfort him and take him in and give him a home. So now my grandpa isn't just my grandpa. He's more than that. I don't know how, but he's more of a person than he was.

I didn't much like my grandpa, but, then, I've begun to realise that he wasn't always a grandpa, was he?

Ben's tears

It was the day the allied troops entered Iraq in 2003. Ben arrived at the Day Hospice as usual for his weekly visit. Settling down in his favourite chair, he picked up one of the morning newspapers from the table in front of him. The headlines were bold. The graphic images were of troops and tanks. The text was about invasion and occupation. As his eyes scanned the pages, big tears started slowly to run down his craggy cheeks. His right fist was clenched, the knuckles white in his bony hand. Slowly and deliberately he began to bang his fist on the arm of the chair. And, half for me and half for himself, he whispered through his tears: 'If only they'd been where I'd been at the end of the War. If only they'd seen the dead soldiers on the beaches. If only they'd been with me as bodies were buried in the sand only to be washed up again the next day with the morning tide. If only they'd learned from what we went through … then they wouldn't be doing this again. No way! They wouldn't be doing this again.' There was nothing to be said in reply. Old Ben was lost in the hopelessness of the moment, his moment of pain, because he felt that 'they' hadn't bothered to learn from what he'd gone through sixty years before.

A dialogue in prayer

The child
God, are you old,
Really old, I mean,
Like grandad,
And Mr Thomson next door,
With whiskers and a funny, old-man smell?
Mummy showed me a picture of you once.
She said it was famous.
She said 'Michael and Jello' had painted it.
Must have been famous painters then.
And, boy, did you look old.
Is that what you're like?
God, are you really old?

The old man
God, I hope you're not old like me.
It's hard enough living next door
To that old so-and-so Thomson,
Him with the funny smell.
I hope you're not like that.
Will heaven be full of old folk,
Me and old Thomson and all the rest?
And will you be like us,
That old God in Michelangelo's paintings?
God, I hope not,
I hope you're not old like me.

The child
God, are you old,
Really old, I mean?
Do you have a stick,
Or one of those metal-walker-things
That Mr Thomson uses when he goes down the shops?
Do you dribble, God,
And slurp your tea?
Do you shout at kids
When their ball goes into your garden?
Do you mutter that
It wasn't like this when you were young?
Were you ever young, God,
Like me, I mean?
God, are you really old?

The old man
God, please don't be old.
Please be what I'd like you to be.
Not too young so I can't keep up.
Not too quick you make me feel uncomfortable.
Not too out-of-control
Like the kids who kick their ball into my garden.
Just right – about my son's age –
Mature,
Yes, that's it.
Don't be old God,
Be good and middle-aged, perhaps.
That'll do.
I could live – eternally – with that.
Just as long as you're not old.

The child
God, are you old,
Really, really old, I mean?
Well, you've got to be, haven't you?
After all, you've been around for ages …
You can't have kids being God,
You can't have teenagers being God either,
Even though my sister thinks she's God already!
Maybe my Dad …
He'd like to be God

And he'd be good at it too – or so he says!
Maybe, just old enough to be a good God would do.
Or do you have to be really old?

The old man
God, don't be old.
I know you're eternal,
But surely that doesn't mean being old.
I know you've been God for every age
And every generation.
So that doesn't mean being old, does it?
I know you're around for me
Just as you've been around for people like me
Ages and ages ago.
So you can't be old,
Really,
Can you?
You are my God
The God I need you to be.
Not old,
Not now.

The child
God, don't be old.
I know you've been around for ever,
But I hope that doesn't mean you're old.
I know you've been God for grandpa
And his grandpa too.
So that can't mean you're old.
You must be different, somehow,
If you're the same for me
And kids like me
For ages and ages.
So you can't be old,
Really,
Can you?
You are my God
The God I need you to be.
Not old,
Not now.

GOD OF ALL TIME

Jane Rogers

Opening responses

Leader:	God of all life, our Creator and Sustainer,
	you support and love each one of us.
	Your love surrounds us from cradle to grave,
	and beyond the grave.
ALL:	YOU REJOICED AT MY FIRST BREATH, MY FIRST STEP,
	MY FIRST WORD.
	YOU REJOICED IN MY CHILDHOOD
	AS I GREW IN STRENGTH, ENERGY AND KNOWLEDGE.
Those aged under 50:	You rejoice in my joys and achievements,
	my relationships, work and responsibilities.
Those aged over 50:	You rejoice in my increasing freedom from family responsibilities
	and in the wisdom that you have given me
	through my experience of life.
ALL:	HOLY SPIRIT OF GOD, YOU ARE WITH AND WITHIN EACH OF US,
	WHETHER WE ARE OLD OR YOUNG, OR SOMEWHERE IN
	BETWEEN.
	TOGETHER MAY WE REJOICE IN YOUR COMPANY
	AND SING YOUR PRAISE. AMEN

Story and prayer

A story, drama or mime showing how older people are often undervalued or derided because of their slower responses or movement, poor hearing or sight. (For example, a mime about someone waiting impatiently at a supermarket checkout for an older person to find change in their purse or to pack their groceries; someone in a hurry to catch a bus with an older person in the way.)

Prayer of confession

Leader:	God, we confess that we have not always properly valued older people as our brothers and sisters in Christ.
	We have often been impatient with their lack of speed in movement and in understanding.
	We have not always had the patience and taken the time to receive from an older person the knowledge and wisdom that they could have given to us.

ALL: FORGIVE US ALL OUR IMPATIENCE AND OUR THOUGHTLESSNESS.

The following, or another declaration of God's forgiveness, is pronounced by someone who is older:

Voice: May God forgive you, Christ renew you, and the Holy Spirit enable you to grow in patience, humility and love.

ALL: AMEN

Scripture readings

Psalm 63:1–8
Psalm 145:1–13
Isaiah 46:3–4
Joel 2:28
Matthew 20:1–16
John 5:2–9
1 Timothy 5:1–3; 9–10
Titus 2:1–4; 6

God of all time

God of all time,
grant me understanding to value the wisdom of experience,
awareness that the voices of the past will not be silenced,
willingness to learn lessons from those who've trod this path before me,
patience to listen to those who've got insights to offer,
time to hear the meaning behind tales of past days,
openness to absorb the teaching of the old and wise,
and enough faith to believe
that the voices of time
can speak of eternal truths,
and bring hope and light to what is now,
and what yet might be.
Amen

A prayer for older people

God, we pray:
Give renewed strength and courage to those who feel weary in their old age after a lifetime of toil.

Give comfort and hope to those who feel lonely and abandoned after the deaths of many that they have loved.
Give patient endurance and peace to those suffering pain and distress from their worn bodies and minds. Amen

A prayer of younger people for greater understanding

Loving, caring God, we pray that next time we meet an older person whom we find it hard to love and understand, that we may show them patience and kindness, and so liberate their gifts to us in accordance with your plan. Amen

A prayer of younger people

It is so easy, Jesus, for us to be wasteful of our time, money and talents while we are young and well and it seems that many years stretch before us.
Let us hear the wisdom of those who are older warning us that life can fly by.
Give us the ability to live our lives to the full, sharing them with you and sharing all your gifts with each other.
So shall we grow together into your presence. Amen

A prayer for carers

God, you care for each one of us.
We pray to you now for all those people who for love's sake alone are the main carer for a spouse, mother, father or friend; and for all those people whose paid work is to care for older people.
May all those who care do so with love, and in their turn be loved and cared for.
May our society come to more fully appreciate the work of all carers, and may the wealth of our community be used to reward fairly their valuable work. Amen

A thanksgiving for 'retired' volunteers

Generous God, we thank you for all those people who no longer need to work full-time to earn their living and who give their time freely in voluntary work to help others.
We remember especially ... *(names of volunteers and/or voluntary organisations relevant to the local situation)*.
May all who give their services without payment to benefit others be blessed by enjoyment and fulfilment in their work, and receive the gratitude and support of the wider community. Amen

A prayer for grandparents and would-be grandparents

Holy God, Father and Mother to us all, we give you thanks and pray for all people who can offer to children the supportive friendship, companionship and love of a good grandparent.

We also remember and commend to your care all those children who have no experience of such a love, and all those older people who have a grandparent's love to give but no children to whom it can be given. Amen

A prayer for those older people with heavy duties of care for others

Caring God, we ask that you will aid with your strength, patience and love all those older people who continue to care for a parent, partner or other family member with a serious physical or mental impairment.

May we all show a willingness to befriend them and aid them in their task, so that they do not become isolated or discouraged. Amen

A prayer for those forced to accept unwanted early retirement or redundancy

Loving God, forgive us that we often value ourselves and one another for the work we do and the money we earn, and for the responsibility, power and status that we get from paid employment.

We pray for those who have no work, especially for those older people who, despite their wishes, feel that they now have little hope of ever working again.

Help us all to know that every one of your children is infinitely precious to you, whether we are strong or weak, young or old, employed or not employed. Amen

A prayer regarding those suffering poverty in later life

Holy God, we pray for all those in our country who are suffering poverty in their later lives, whether by unemployment when they want to work, or through low income in retirement. Grow in our nation a willingness to share, such that every older citizen has sufficient income to have dignity and financial independence. Amen

A prayer concerning allocation of resources

Lord Jesus, on earth you healed the ill and fed the hungry.

You warned the rich and powerful that if they did not give of their plenty to help the poor and powerless they were in danger of hell-fire.

We pray for all our national and local politicians and for ourselves, asking that, through better political decisions which honour all older people, more of our national wealth may go to satisfy the needs of the old, the ill and the hungry, not only in this country but also in those other countries of the world where need is even greater. Amen

A prayer for our community

Spirit of the living God, enable us to surround the older people of our community with comfort and kindness. May we all share in joy and confidence in you, learning that in life or death we have nothing to fear since you love us and care for each one of us. Amen

Prayer of thanksgiving

Voice 1:	God of all ages, we thank you for the many gifts that you give to us all through older people:
Voice 2:	Stores of wisdom and knowledge;
Voice 3:	Concern and interest in the activities of the young;
Voice 4:	Patience and loving forgiveness;
Voice 5:	Courageous endurance in the face of repeated bereavement;
Voice 6:	A strong faith, and faithfulness in prayer for others.
ALL:	THANK YOU GOD. AMEN

Prayer of thanksgiving

God, our Creator and Sustainer,

We easily take for granted all the discoveries of technology and science which have increased the health and well-being of people in this country, so that most of us can now expect to live in good health to 75, 85 or even 90 years of age.

We often forget that for our great-grandmothers and great-grandfathers, and all the generations before them, to live beyond 50 years was exceptional, and painful episodes of disease were a commonplace experience for all.

We thank you for all the opportunities that these many extra years of healthy life provide for us: to discover and enjoy more of your creation, and to live in the service of others.

Make us always thankful for these bonus years of healthy life.

May we respond in gratitude by seeking to share more equitably throughout the world the benefits of science that improve health and lengthen life.

Amen

A prayer of Saint Polycarp

God, the Father of our Lord Jesus Christ, increase in us faith and truth and gentleness, and grant us part and lot among his saints. Amen

(Saint Polycarp was martyred in the year 155, aged at least 86. His feast day is 23rd February.)

Closing responses

Leader:	Almighty God
ALL:	VULNERABLE GOD
Leader:	Help us to build:
ALL:	YOUR KINGDOM OF FREEDOM,
	YOUR KINGDOM OF LOVE.
Leader:	Pour out your Spirit:
ALL:	ON THE OLD,
	ON THE YOUNG,
Leader:	On the poor,
	On the rich,
ALL:	ON ALL OF US ALWAYS. AMEN

Blessing

May the Almighty, all-loving God,
who calls us into life,
be with you and sustain you as you travel onward,
and give you courage to persevere to the end of life and the gate of heaven;
and may the blessing of God,
Creator, Redeemer and Sustainer,
be with you for evermore.
Amen

BLESSED ARE
THE PEACEMAKERS

BLESSED ARE THE PEACEMAKERS

Norman Shanks

In these dark, uncertain times the liturgies in this section assume a striking relevance. Scarcely ever can the Christian vocation of peace-making have appeared more necessary.

In 2001 the World Council of Churches launched its 'Decade to Overcome Violence: Churches Working for Reconciliation and Peace'. This is being promoted not as a set programme of activities but as an attempt to raise awareness and encourage reflection and action at all levels, dependent on local context and circumstances. It recognises 'the urgent need to overcome violence that pervades our lives, our communities, our world and the whole created order'. It is a response 'to the deep yearning (within the churches) to build lasting peace grounded in justice. It is an invitation for all Christian bodies to offer their own gifts for peacemaking according to their own particular calling, to learn from one another and to act together.'[1]

It is undeniable that, both within the pages of scripture and through the history of the church, there is much violence, often represented as consistent with the will and purpose of God. Beyond all these conflicts, however, there echoes a deeper theme, a persistent groundbeat, reflected in the message of the prophets and in the life and teaching of Jesus Christ, making it clear beyond doubt that the vision and values of God's kingdom point towards a world free from fear and violence where weapons of war are transformed into agricultural implements – that goodness is stronger than evil, that light breaks through the darkness, that peacemakers are blessed and called the children of God.

Peace-making is hope in action. The American peace campaigner Daniel Berrigan has described it as 'hard work, almost as hard as war'! Within the Iona Community we express our belief that peace-making is an inescapable part of the life of those who seek to follow in the way of Jesus, through the commitment of members of the Community to action for peace and justice, and through our regular prayers for peace and justice on Iona and elsewhere. Indeed we like repeating the comment of one of our staff that people come to Iona looking for peace and quiet and go away looking for peace and justice!

These liturgies grew out of the conviction that particular peace concerns, for instance about the arms trade, opposition to nuclear weapons, the desire for reconciliation and other issues, must be embodied in our lives through specific actions for peace; that it is not enough to believe that peace is 'a good thing': we must do something about it. And we believe that such actions have to be offered to God: those who take part do so with a deep sense of humility and vulnerability and a recognition of our own weakness and our complicity in the wrongs we seek to put right. So the pattern of the liturgies is highly significant – the themes of confession and repentance, the prayers of concern and the expression of commitment, and the symbolic actions in most of the liturgies.

In worship and in our action for peace and justice we are terribly aware of our weakness and our insignificance in the face of the forces we seek to oppose. I detected a particularly strong sense of powerlessness and vulnerability during those months in 2002/3 when the slide towards war in Iraq seemed so inexorable; and this has continued through all the disconcerting rhetoric about ' a war against terrorism'.

The voices of protest against the war in Iraq were encouragingly loud from the churches. Our 'church leaders' were outspoken and almost unanimous in their call for restraint and further exploration of non-violent means of resolving the situation. Within the churches there was widespread opposition to the war and unprecedented participation in worldwide public demonstrations calling for 'justice not war'. There was much discussion about the possibility of a 'just war' in a context where modern weapons' technology renders the slaughter of innocents inevitable. And, above and undergirding all, people prayed for peace privately and publicly, in regular services, vigils and ad hoc events. And these go on, will go on, as long as they have to.

So we should remember what has been called 'the power of littles' and the encouraging words of Dorothy Day, founder of the Catholic Worker movement, that we can only take one step, lay one brick at a time. And in seeking to 'stand firm' we draw strength from the companionship of those around us (for peace-making need not be a lonely vocation and the mutual support in joint activity is invaluable) and, through it all, from experiencing, however fleetingly, the miracle and mystery of God's grace.

[1]From *Why Violence? Why not Peace*, World Council of Churches, 2002. Used with permission of the World Council of Churches.

ARMING THE WAR MACHINE:

A liturgy of penitence for the arms trade, Iona Abbey 1999

Helen Boothroyd

For this service you will need:
- *A large map of the world placed centrally. A Peters Projection map is recommended.*
- *Cut-out paper or cardboard silhouettes of weapons such as tanks, aircraft and guns; more cut-outs than the anticipated number of the congregation. These are placed on the world map in piles; the size of the pile placed on each country representing the volume of British arms sales to that country.[1]*
- *An information and action sheet to help people take action on the issues after the service.*

Introductory reading from *All Quiet on the Western Front*

I lie huddled in a large shell-hole. I pull out my little dagger. If anyone jumps in here I will go for him. The rattle of machine guns becomes an unbroken chain. Something heavy stumbles, and with a crash a body falls over me into the shell-hole. I strike madly home, and feel only how the body suddenly convulses, then becomes limp, and collapses. When I recover myself, my hand is sticky and wet.

How slowly a man dies! This is the first time I have killed with my hands, whom I can see close at hand, whose death is my doing. I would give much if he would but stay alive. It is hard to lie here and to have to see and hear him.

In the afternoon, about three, he is dead.

I breathe freely again. But only for a short time. Soon the silence is more unbearable than the groans. The silence spreads. I must talk. So I speak to him:

'Comrade, I did not want to kill you. If you jumped in here again I would not do it. But you were only an idea to me before, an abstraction that lived in my mind. It was that abstraction I stabbed. But now, for the first time, I see you are a man like me. I thought of your hand-grenades, of your bayonet, of your rifle; now I see your wife and your face and our fellowship. Forgive me comrade. We always see it too late. Why do they never tell us that you are poor devils like us, that your mothers are just as anxious as ours, and that we have the same fear of death, and the same dying and the same agony – Forgive me comrade; how could you be my enemy? If we threw away these rifles and this uniform, you could be my brother, just like Kat and Albert. Take twenty years of my life, comrade, and stand up – take more, for I do not know what I can even attempt to do with it now.'

Litany of war *(Read slowly)*

Voice 1:   A German soldier in the novel *All Quiet on the Western Front*, describing the experience of killing in the trenches. World War One. The war to end all wars.

Voice 2:   Only twenty years later. World War Two. Unspeakable atrocities. Millions of civilians slaughtered. The war to destroy evil.

Voice 3:   The Cold War. Peace through deterrence. The threat of nuclear annihilation hangs over the world. But no armed conflict between the rich countries.

Voice 4:   No peace in the rest of the world though. More than 150 major wars with over 23 million people killed in them.[2] Mostly in the poorer countries. Mostly civilians.[3]

Voice 5:   The vast majority of arms in these wars have been and are being supplied by the richer countries – like Britain, one of the biggest arms exporters in the world.[4] Britain sells arms to over 150 countries; since 1997 the UK government has licensed arms to 20 countries engaged in serious conflict.[5] About £760 million of UK public spending each year is used to support these arms sales.[6] That means that each taxpayer here pays over £25 a year to subsidise the trade in arms, the trade in death.[7]

Song: O Lord the clouds are gathering (CG)

Scripture reading: Micah 4:1–4

Litany of British arms sales

Reader:[8]   'This is the first time I have killed with my hands, whom I can see close at hand, whose death is my doing ... I did not want to kill you ... But you were only an idea to me before, an abstraction that lived in my mind. But now, for the first time, I see you are a man like me ... Now I see your wife and your face and our fellowship. Why do they never tell us that your mothers are just as anxious as ours, and that we have the same fear of death, and the same dying and the same agony.'

Voice 4:   When British companies sell arms to fuel war and repression they do not see the killing close at hand. They do not see the dead husbands, wives and children, the faces of those 'whose death is their doing'. They do not experience the fear and agony of death; they do not know the anguish of the bereaved. They see only the customer, the new market, the balance sheet.

They think in abstractions – of 'end users' and 'collateral damage'. They think of business relationships, not of the business of the dictatorships they support.

Voice 5:   In the presence of God and of each other, let us listen in sorrow to the sinful story of British arms sales:

Voice 4:   September 11th 1973. General Pinochet, armed with planes bought from Britain, overthrows the democratically elected government in Chile and instigates a dictatorship of terror, murder and disappearances, supported by further British arms sales.[9]

Voice 5:   1986. Al Yamamah. Britain's biggest ever arms deal. With Saudi Arabia: a dictatorship with an appalling human rights record; a dictatorship that practises torture, execution, imprisonment without trial; a dictatorship which does not allow Christians to practise their faith freely.[10]

Voice 4:   1979–1990. Britain supplies manufacturing tools and parts for military equipment to Saddam Hussein's regime in Iraq, equipment used both in the war against Iran and also for attacking the Kurdish inhabitants of Northern Iraq.[11]

Voice 5:   1975–1999. British planes and other weaponry help the Indonesian military to terrorise the people of East Timor. 200,000 East Timorese die in twenty-five years of brutal oppression.[12]

Voice 4:   Today. 2005. Britain still has major arms contracts with regimes carrying out internal repression. *(Insert examples current at the time of the service, e.g. Saudi Arabia, Indonesia, Sudan ...)*[13]

Voice 5:   Today. 2005. Britain still sells arms used in areas of tension and conflict, fuelling existing and future war. *(Insert examples current at the time of the service, e.g. southern Africa, the Indian sub-continent, the Middle East ...)*[14]

Prayer of confession

Leader: God of peace, for choosing to put our trust in weapons of war:
ALL: WE COME BEFORE YOU IN SORROW AND CONFESSION.
Leader: God of life, for our silent complicity with the industry of death:
ALL: WE COME BEFORE YOU IN SORROW AND CONFESSION.
Leader: God of generosity, for supporting the arms trade through our work or our taxes, or for profiting from it through our shares and investments.
ALL: WE COME BEFORE YOU IN SORROW AND CONFESSION.
Leader: God of hope, for our doubt and despair in the face of evil.
ALL: WE COME BEFORE YOU IN SORROW AND CONFESSION.
Leader: God of courage, for our fear to speak out or to take bold action.
ALL: WE COME BEFORE YOU IN SORROW AND CONFESSION.
    AMEN

Introduction to congregational action

Some words of Cardinal Basil Hume: 'The world community can continue to pursue the arms race ... Or it can move deliberately and ungrudgingly toward the provision of basic needs for our global family. It cannot do both. Either we invest in death or we invest in life.'

Let us choose to invest in life. Let us make our voices heard in the corridors of power. Our political representatives are heavily influenced by their mail bags. Our government does care about public opinion. And our power as consumers is greater than we think.

We are all invited to join in a symbolic action now, and in doing so to commit ourselves to take real action against the arms trade. This action could take a variety of forms:

- You might decide to join one of the campaigning organisations.
- You might decide to investigate ethical investment and banking, and to boycott goods from companies that also produce arms, so that you no longer support the arms trade through what you buy or what you decide to do with your money.
- You might decide to write to your MP about Britain's arms sales. Specific current issues to raise with them include ...

It is appropriate here to highlight issues such as:
– Sales to oppressive regimes or war zones.
– Government subsidy of arms sales.
– Government promotion of arms sales.
– Government support for international arms fairs.
– Loopholes in arms control, such as production under licence from UK manufacturers
  by overseas companies, and UK companies continuing to broker deals abroad.
– Lack of transparency of arms sales.

(These issues are highlighted in the information and action sheet for people to take away.)

You will see that paper cut-outs of weapons such as tanks, aircraft and guns are piled on various parts of the map of the world. These symbolise British arms sales to the countries or regions on which they are placed. You are all invited to come to the map now, to remove one of these weapons and take it away with you, together with an action sheet.

Congregational action *with quiet background music or a group singing* Come now, O Prince of Peace (CG)

Prayer of intercession

Leader: God of the poor and marginalised,
           God of the victims of oppression and of war,
           we cry to you for peace in our world.
ALL: JESUS CHRIST, PRINCE OF PEACE, HELP US TO ACT FOR PEACE.

(The chant Come now, O Prince of Peace *might be sung between intercessions.)*

Leader: We pray for all victims of the arms trade worldwide.
           People in ... *(insert here current examples of conflict zones and of poor coun-*
           tries which give priority to arms spending) ...
           and many other places where conflict has been prolonged and exacer-
           bated by the flow of arms, or where money spent on arms is depriving
           people of their basic needs.
           We hold before God all those who have lost loved ones, lost limbs, lost
           sanity, lost homes, lost livelihoods, lost hope as a result of the trade in
           arms.
ALL: JESUS CHRIST, PRINCE OF PEACE, HELP US TO ACT FOR PEACE.
Leader: We pray for leaders and decision-makers,
           that policies may be redirected towards peace and human rights, rather
           than the continuation of war and oppression.
ALL: JESUS CHRIST, PRINCE OF PEACE, HELP US TO ACT FOR PEACE.
Leader: We pray for all who are involved in the arms trade,
           that they may realise the real consequences of their actions.
           We pray for the conversion of hearts and minds;
           and for the conversion of the arms industry towards productive purposes.
ALL: JESUS CHRIST, PRINCE OF PEACE, HELP US TO ACT FOR PEACE.
Leader: We pray for ourselves.
           Give us the courage to speak out against the export of death.
           Give us the strength to work for an end to the arms trade.
           Give us the resolve to withdraw our financial support,
           even at a cost to ourselves.
           We offer these prayers in the name of our Saviour, Jesus Christ, Prince of
           Peace.
ALL: JESUS CHRIST, PRINCE OF PEACE, HELP US TO ACT FOR PEACE.

Song: Abundant life (CG)

Blessing

Be strong in the Lord and in the strength of his power. Put on the whole armour of God so that you may be able to withstand on that evil day. Having done everything, stand firm. Fasten the belt of truth around your waist and put on the breastplate of righteousness. As shoes for your feet put on whatever will make you ready to proclaim the gospel of peace. Take the shield of faith with which you will be able to quench all the flaming arrows of the evil one. Take the helmet of salvation, and the sword of the Spirit, which is the word of God. (*Ephesians 6:10–17*)

May God be with us.
May the Prince of Peace accompany us.
May the Holy Spirit guide our actions.
AMEN

Alternative songs

Christ, be our light (CG)
Here I am Lord (CG)
Make me a channel of your peace (Prayer of St Francis) (SOGP)
Sent by the Lord am I (CG)
Singing, we gladly worship the Lord together (CG)
What shall we pray? (CG)

Notes

[1] The latest *United Kingdom Strategic Export Controls Annual Report* can be found on the Foreign and Commonwealth Office website: www.fco.gov.uk and contains a country by country breakdown of British arms exports.

[2] Information from *State of the World's Children*, UNICEF, 1996, cited by Campaign Against the Arms Trade in *Paying the Price* briefing, 2002. On an average yearly basis the number of war deaths in this period was more than double that of the nineteenth century and seven times greater than the eighteenth century.

[3] By the end of the 1990s nearly 90% of war victims were non-combatants and at least half of these were children – According to Campaign Against the Arms Trade website: www.caat.org.uk

[4] Britain is currently the world's second largest arms exporter. In 2002 the UK's total arms exports were worth £2513 million – Statistics from Richard F Grimmett, United States Congressional Research Service, September 2003, quoted on Campaign Against the Arms Trade website: www.caat.org.uk

[5] From *Fanning the Flames*, Campaign Against the Arms Trade, 2003.

[6] Information from *The Subsidy Trap*, Oxford Research Group and Saferworld, 2001.

[7] There were 29.4 million taxpayers in the UK in 2002/3 according to the website of the Inland

Revenue: www.inlandrevenue.gov.uk

[8] These extracts to be reread slowly, with a pause between each sentence, by the same voice that read the passage from *All Quiet on the Western Front* the first time.

[9] Information from *The Independent* 1.7.99. and *Hansard* 6.2.01.

[10] Information from *The Missing Link in Labour's Foreign Policy* by David Mepham and Paul Eavis, Institute for Public Policy Research and Saferworld, 2002 and *Shattered Lives*, Amnesty International and Oxfam, 2003.

[11] Information from *The Subsidy Trap*, Oxford Research Group and Saferworld, 2001 and *The Missing Link in Labour's Foreign Policy*, op. cit.

[12] Information from *A Matter of Life and Death* by Chris Cole, Pax Christi, 2000 and *The Missing Link in Labour's Foreign Policy*, op. cit.

[13] Information from *The Missing Link in Labour's Foreign Policy*, op. cit.; ' *Shattered Lives*, op. cit. and CAAT News, October-November 2004.

[14] Information from *The Missing Link in Labour's Foreign Policy*, op.cit.; ' *Shattered Lives*, op. cit. and CAAT News, October–November 2004.

PRAYER VIGIL OUTSIDE BAE SYSTEMS ARMS FACTORY, WARTON, LANCASHIRE

For many years, a small group has gathered for a prayer vigil outside the BAE Systems factory at Warton in Lancashire. On the first Monday of every month they have come together to protest the arms trade, in which BAE Systems is Britain's major player. This liturgy comprises material used at these vigils. It could be adapted for use at any place of arms manufacture and sale. Or it could be used to inspire a similar act of worship.

Leader: Britain is currently the world's second largest arms exporter. In 2002 (the latest figures available) the UK's total arms exports were worth £2513 million.[1] The UK exported arms to over 150 countries in that year. Since 1997, the UK government has licensed arms to 20 countries engaged in serious conflict.[2]

(Silence)

Gathering song: Come now, O Prince of Peace (CG)

Introduction

We are here today to reflect on the arms trade and to pray for its victims – for sisters and brothers suffering the violence of conflict and war, human rights abuses, homelessness, hunger …

Some of us here will have heard first-hand the stories of those fleeing from situations of war, persecution and grinding poverty. The rest of us will have seen these terrible images on our television screens.

(First-hand story or a story from a newspaper.)

Today, as we gather in the shadow of one of the most powerful arms manufacturers in the world, we reflect on our need of repentance and conversion, and on our call by God to be peacemakers in the face of this lethal business. As I speak, there are about thirty wars going on around the world, mostly in poor countries. Meanwhile, one billion people in these poorer countries cannot satisfy their most basic needs. Seventy per cent of all arms sales are to poor countries. Britain bears a heavy responsibility for this.

Crosses – stained red to symbolise the shedding of blood in war and conflict and bearing the names of countries, communities and individuals who have suffered as a result of the trade in arms – are brought forward and placed in front of the group.[3] Reports and documents showing BAE's annual profits are placed on the ground near the crosses.

Scripture reading: Deuteronomy 30:15–20

See, I have set before you today life and prosperity, death and adversity. If you obey the commandments of the Lord your God that I am commanding you today, by loving the Lord your God, walking in his ways, and observing his commandments, decrees, and ordinances, then you shall live and become numerous, and the Lord your God will bless you in the land that you are entering to possess. But if your heart turns away and you do not hear, but are led astray to bow down to other gods and serve them, I declare to you today that you shall perish; you shall not live long in the land that you are crossing the Jordan to possess. I call heaven and earth to witness against you today that I have set before you life and death, blessing and curses. Choose life so that you and your descendants may live, loving the Lord your God, obeying him, and holding fast to him; for that means life to you and length of days, so that you may live in the land that the Lord swore to give to your ancestors, to Abraham, to Isaac, and to Jacob.

(NRSV version)

Prayer of confession *(said together)*

God, you have entrusted us with the care of each other.
Forgive us that we profit from the oppression and injury of our brothers and sisters.
Forgive us that we develop so readily the means of destruction
at the expense of the things that create community.
Forgive us that when we are asked for bread we sell bombs,
and that we have made the livelihood of so many dependent upon trading in death.
Enable the victims of the arms trade to forgive us.
Enable us to give ourselves in commitment to the eradication of this evil.
Enable us to help those with power to work for justice and peace.
Lord, you have given us all we need;
so now make us ready to forfeit all the hurtful things that are not needed.
God, who is against the arms trade and for the people, give us your love.

Copies of BAE Systems reports and documents are burnt (as a sign that those present reject the arms trade and repent of the exploitation of the world's poorest).

(Silence)

Chant: Come now, O Prince of Peace

Prayer of intercession

Leader: We pray for all who suffer because of the sale of arms: those caught up in war and conflict, those who go hungry, those who are persecuted, remembering especially …

ALL: O LORD, OUR GOD, HAVE MERCY ON US.
                MAKE US INSTRUMENTS OF YOUR PEACE.

Leader: We pray for the management, workers and shareholders at BAE Systems. We pray for all who are involved in the arms industry, that they may find other ways to use their skills – ways that celebrate life rather than threaten its destruction.

ALL: O LORD, OUR GOD, HAVE MERCY ON US.
                MAKE US INSTRUMENTS OF YOUR PEACE.

Leader: We pray for a conversion of hearts and minds from ways of war to ways of peace, especially remembering all decision-makers, and all those who carry out the decisions that are made.

ALL: O LORD, OUR GOD, HAVE MERCY ON US.
                MAKE US INSTRUMENTS OF YOUR PEACE.

Leader: We pray that the cry for peace will be heard above the clamour for war. And we pray for ourselves, that we will never tire of speaking up for peace. We pray for those who aren't free to speak out and to protest.

ALL: O LORD, OUR GOD, HAVE MERCY ON US.
                MAKE US INSTRUMENTS OF YOUR PEACE.

Song: Do not be afraid (*based on Isaiah 43:1–4*) (SOGP)

Naming the victims

The names on the crosses (of countries, communities and individuals who have suffered as a result of the trade in arms) are read aloud. As each name is read, a candle is lit.

Closing prayer *(said together)*

God, we repent of this evil in which we are complicit.
God, we pray for a conversion of our hearts,
our churches, our governments and nations,
that together we may seek justice for all peoples and build a new security
built not on weapons of war,
but on the hope of God's love.
We carry these lights to the factory gates.
We bring light to darkness.

The candles are taken and left at the gates of the arms factory.

Song: Make me a channel of your peace (*prayer of St Francis*) (SOGP)

Notes

[1] In 2002 the UK's total arms exports were worth £2513 million – Statistics from Richard F Grimmett, United States Congressional Research Service, September 2003, quoted on Campaign Against the Arms Trade website: www.caat.org.uk

[2] From *Fanning the Flames*, Campaign Against the Arms Trade, 2003.

[3] For example, prior to the independence of East Timor (now Timor-Leste) in 2000, the individuals and communities suffering oppression or killed by the Indonesian military, supplied with weapons by BAE, were remembered in this way at each vigil. Pertinent current examples include the Democratic Republic of the Congo, the Kurdish community in Turkey, the people of Tanzania (whose government has given priority to an expensive arms purchase from BAE) and the people of Kashmir (suffering continued tension as the arms race between India and Pakistan continues, fuelled by BAE exports).

WE WILL REMEMBER:
A prayer vigil for peace

This liturgy comes from Wellspring, a worship group in the United Kingdom. The liturgy was originally prepared for Remembrance Sunday, and was subsequently adapted for use as a vigil for peace.

Opening responses

Reader: Bruised, black clouds shed heavy tears on the fields of Flanders,
    fields become graveyards
    in which were buried the flowers of a generation.
ALL: AND GOD WEPT, FOR THESE WERE HIS CHILDREN.
Reader: Bruised and black clouds shed heavy tears on the cities of Europe
    and of Japan,
    cities shrouded in the dust of desolation,
    camps wreathed in the smoke of human cremations,
    people in confusion whispering – 'Please God, never again.'
ALL: AND GOD WEPT, FOR THESE WERE HIS CHILDREN.
Reader: Bruised and black clouds shroud cities,
    shopping streets,
    business centres,
    refugee camps,
    and people gaze on devastation
    wrought by evil on innocence.
ALL: AND GOD WEEPS, FOR THESE ARE HIS CHILDREN.
Reader: Bruised and black clouds shed tears over a whole world,
    bowed, bloodied by battle,
    cowed and weary of war,
    her roads clogged by refugees –
    with nowhere but earth to call home.
ALL: AND GOD WEEPS, FOR THESE ARE HIS CHILDREN.
Reader God of life,
    drawing life and death together in yourself,
    uniting the lost and the loving,
    be among us as we gather;
ALL: GUIDE OUR PRAYING AND LOVING,
    CHERISH OUR REMEMBERING,
    GOD, OUR GOD,
    WHO FORGETS NO ONE.

Suggested scriptures

Psalm 4
Isaiah 2:4
Isaiah 9:2–7
Wisdom 3:1–9
Wisdom 4:7–15
John 5:24–29
1 Thessalonians 4:13–18
James 3:13–18

A sung response

Ritual action

Emotions of anxiety, sadness, anger and frustration are likely to be present among those gathered. There is a place for all of these feelings and it is important to try to find space for them within the liturgy. Using a ritual action can give voice to emotions too deep to put into words. Select one of the following actions or devise your own:

1. *Place a large map of the world at the foot of a cross, or in the middle of the gathering if the group is sitting in a circle. Invite people to come forward and place a night light on either:*

   - *A troubled country or region in the world.*
   - *Places where decisions are being made, for example powerful countries, the seat of the United Nations.*
   - *A country where many people live in hunger and poverty yet vast sums are being redirected from humanitarian aid to weaponry.*
     (The night lights represent a prayer to God to be a light to the people of those places.)

   A litany may be used during this action, naming aloud places and their people in the categories suggested above. Suitable words might be:

   > We light a light for the people of …We remember them.
   > *or*
   > We pray for the people of …
   > *or*
   > Be gracious to the people of … and bless them.
   > *or*
   > Do not abandon the people of … for these are your children.

2. Provide a selection of images of war and conflict. Invite members of the congregation to pick up an image from a central area and to lay it at the foot of a cross. Quiet music is a suitable accompaniment to this action.

3. Provide a variety of symbols connected with the theme of the liturgy, for example a photo of a soldier, a train ticket (representing refugees fleeing conflict), a soft toy (representing children caught up in conflict), a handkerchief (representing those who weep), etc. Pass these symbols among the congregation and invite congregation members to write a short intercession or reflection, and then to come forward and place these at the foot of a cross or by a lighted candle. This suggestion will require pens and paper to be provided for all members of the congregation.

4. Invite people to write the names of nations and peoples in conflict on a Roll of Remembrance. Once all the congregation have had a chance to write on the Roll of Remembrance, place this at the foot of a cross, or in the midst of the gathering with a lighted candle and posy of flowers next to it.

5. Before the service prepare a stack of cards, sufficient for one each for the anticipated congregation, each with the name of a country or a picture of a person representative of a country or circumstance – for example, a child in Iraq, a soldier preparing for war, a Palestinian in a refugee camp, a bereaved Israeli, a homeless Afghani. Photographs from newspapers could also be used. Invite people to take one card or picture and to spend some time in quiet, focusing their prayer on that situation. Suggest that they continue to pray for the situation by taking the card home and placing it on a desk, bedside table or notice board, so that simply glancing at it becomes a prayer. This suggestion is based on the understanding that the pain of the world is too great for one person to pray for, and that it is therefore helpful to focus on a specific situation, knowing that other specific situations are being held in the prayers of other people.

Closing responses

Reader:	From the rising of the sun until its setting
ALL:	GOD OF PEACE
	GOD OF JUSTICE
	GOD OF INFINITE MERCY –
	REMEMBER YOUR PEOPLE.
Reader:	From the bleakness of war to the lavish warmth of peace

ALL: GOD OF PEACE
              GOD OF JUSTICE
              GOD OF INFINITE MERCY –
              REMEMBER YOUR PEOPLE.
Reader: From the pain of the present moment to the peace of eternity
ALL: GOD OF PEACE
              GOD OF JUSTICE
              GOD OF INFINITE MERCY –
              REMEMBER YOUR PEOPLE.
Reader: We turn to you, God,
              asking that you enfold our planet in your justice, peace and truth.
              Enlighten the minds of those making decisions,
              melt the hearts of those inflicting cruelty upon your children,
              and strengthen the resolve of all who pray for peace.
              And may God bless us – and the peoples who share our planet.
ALL: IN THE NAME OF THE FATHER, THE SON AND THE HOLY SPIRIT.
Reader: May God hold our world and all its people in the palm of his hand.
ALL: AMEN

FASLANE BLOCKADE:
February 2001
Kathy Galloway

Faslane is the UK Trident nuclear submarine base at Helensburgh in Scotland.

Many of the most significant acts of worship for members of the Iona Community on the mainland have not been in churches. They have been outdoors, on demonstrations and marches and picket-lines, outside military bases and the Ministry of Defence, in city squares and at embassies. Equally important, though perhaps less dramatically, they have been in homes and community centres, in schools and factories and hospitals, all the places where people struggle on the knife-edge and we among them. At the very least, we can take our bodies, and our prayers, and say with them, 'I beg to differ'; we can witness to our conviction that 'it is better to light a candle than to curse the darkness'.

Kathy Galloway, *The Pattern of Our Days*

Call to worship

Come to us, Lord Jesus Christ.
As you stood among your disciples in your resurrection body,
so be present with us now.

Chant: Come Holy Spirit ... Come Holy Spirit (x2) Maranatha ... Maranatha, Come Lord come ... Come Lord come

Prayer

Blessed be God the Creator,
Blessed be Jesus Christ our Lord,
Blessed be the Holy Spirit who dwells within us,
Blessed be God, Trinity unending.

Song: St Patrick's breastplate (COSH)
(Words by St Patrick; Cecil Frances Alexander, 1818–95)

I bind unto myself today
The strong name of the Trinity,
By invocation of the same,
The Three in One, and One in Three.

I bind unto myself today
The virtues of the star-lit heaven,
The glorious sun's life-giving ray,
The whiteness of the moon at even,
The flashing of the lightning free,
The whirling wind's tempestuous shocks,
The stable earth, the deep salt sea
Around the old eternal rocks.

Christ be with me, Christ within me, Christ behind me, Christ before me,
Christ beside me, Christ to win me, Christ to comfort and restore me,
Christ beneath me, Christ above me, Christ in quiet, Christ in danger,
Christ in hearts of all that love me, Christ in mouth of friend and stranger.

Words of greeting

Sisters and brothers who are here today, we greet you with the greeting of peace. We have come because we want to commit ourselves to uphold and respect the lives of persons and peoples, the life of all creation. We remember all whose lives have been sacrificed to the powers of death, to acknowledge that our own communities and nations have been party to those powers, to express our common longing for a new world, and to commit ourselves to building it together: men, women and children of goodwill from different countries, different faiths, sharing the same hope of peace based on justice and the integrity of creation.

Gospel

Prayer

Lord Jesus,
here are your disciples
and those we represent
who need to meet you in our doubt.

Help us to hold graciously
those questions to which there are no easy answers,
enable us to discern the inability to believe
which comes from our unwillingness to obey,
and in the pain and scarring of the world,
help us to identify your hands,
wounded among us.
Amen

Statements from church leaders

Leader: Jesus said: Blessed are the peacemakers, they shall be called children of God.

After each statement, an Alleluia is sung.

Prayers

Leader: Loving God, we remember and pray in solidarity with those who work for peace in the face of the threat of war and fear of nuclear destruction.

ALL: LORD HEAR US … LORD GRACIOUSLY HEAR US.

Leader: We pray for all who have been victims of nuclear testing, dumping or bombing. Help us to remember the sufferings of those who are still deeply wounded in body and spirit.

ALL: LORD HEAR US … LORD GRACIOUSLY HEAR US.

Leader: We pray for lands and seas which have been contaminated and for the life which depended on them.

ALL: LORD HEAR US … LORD GRACIOUSLY HEAR US.

Leader: We pray for the men and women who work in this and other bases.

ALL: LORD HEAR US … LORD GRACIOUSLY HEAR US.

Leader: We pray for politicians and policy-makers, that they may be guided in the ways of peace.

ALL: LORD HEAR US … LORD GRACIOUSLY HEAR US.

Holy Spirit, Spirit of the living God,
You breathe in us, on all that is inadequate and fragile.
You make living water spring even from our hurts themselves.
And, through you, the valley of fears becomes a place of wellsprings.
So, in an inner life with neither beginning nor end,
Your continual presence makes new freshness break through.
We pray in your name and in your Spirit of peace. Amen

A prayer from Sri Lanka

Song: St Patrick's breastplate (COSH)

I bind unto myself today
The power of God to hold and lead,
God's eye to watch, God's might to stay,
God's ear to hearken to our need,
The wisdom of our God to teach,
God's hand to guide, God's shield to ward,

The word of God to give us speech,
God's heavenly host to be our guard.

I bind unto myself today
The strong name of the Trinity,
By invocation of the same,
The Three in One, and One in Three,
Of whom all nature hath creation,
Eternal Father, Spirit, Word.
Praise to the Lord of our salvation,
Salvation is of Christ the Lord.

Closing responses

Leader:	Mothering God, you gave us birth in the bright morning of this world.
ALL:	CREATOR, SOURCE OF EVERY BREATH, YOU ARE OUR RAIN, OUR WIND, OUR SUN.
Leader:	Mothering Christ, you took our form, offering us your food of light.
ALL:	GRAIN OF LIFE AND GRAPE OF LOVE, YOUR VERY BODY FOR OUR PEACE.
Leader:	Mothering Spirit, nurturing one, in arms of patience hold us close,
ALL:	SO THAT IN FAITH WE ROOT AND GROW, UNTIL WE FLOWER, UNTIL WE KNOW.
Leader:	Glory be to God who made us, and to Christ who loved us and to the Holy Spirit who keeps us in peace.
ALL:	AS IT WAS IN THE BEGINNING, IS NOW AND SHALL BE FOR EVER, AMEN.

NUCLEAR WEAPONS:
An Ash Wednesday service of repentance, Faslane, 2002
The Adomnán of Iona Affinity Group
(written by Maire-Colette Wilkie with Jean Oliver)

The Adomnán of Iona Affinity Group is composed of members and associates of the Iona Community who are committed to non-violent direct action for nuclear disarmament. The group are named in memory of Adomnán mac Ronain, the ninth abbot of Iona. In AD 697 Adomnán devised and promulgated the 'Law of the Innocents'. This law was an early attempt to limit the effects of war by protecting from attack all those who were non-combatants. The Adomnán of Iona Affinity Group stand in the tradition of Adomnán by arguing and acting for full nuclear disarmament by all nations to prevent the indiscriminate and mass killing of non-combatants that the use of nuclear weapons would inevitably entail.

A similar service to this was held on Ash Wednesday, 2003 in Parliament Square in Edinburgh, shortly before the United States and Britain went to war on Iraq, purportedly over the issue of weapons of mass destruction. The service was an opportunity to repent all weapons of mass destruction, and of the warmongering of the British nation.

Before worship, ashes are prepared; and a number of small cardboard effigies of the Trident nuclear submarine are made, which will also be reduced to ash by burning during the service.

Gathering song: The peace of the Earth be with you (CG) *or another simple chant with a peace theme. This song is repeated for several minutes to enable people to find a place to stand and quietly prepare for worship.*

(Short silence)

Litany of repentance

Leader: We have come this day to worship God with a sign of our repentance.
            Today many Christians are celebrating Ash Wednesday, which heralds the
            start of the season of Lent.
            During Lent we recall and enter into the great journey and drama of the life
            and death of Jesus; his ultimate self-sacrifice to overcome sin and death.

Voice 1:   Christ has overcome the power of darkness.
            Yet still we tread in the valley of the shadow of death.
            We do not always live as followers of Christ in the world.
            We do not walk his way of justice, truth and peace.
            So we repent.

ALL:	FATHER, FORGIVE US, WE DO KNOW WHAT WE DO.
Voice 2:	We come to this place to repent our collective guilt
	in the squandering of the Earth's resources
	by the deployment of Trident and all weapons of mass destruction.
ALL:	FATHER, FORGIVE US, WE DO KNOW WHAT WE DO.
Voice 3:	We come to this place to repent our very imagining
	that weapons of this type could ever be used
	on our brothers and sisters.
ALL:	FATHER, FORGIVE US, WE DO KNOW WHAT WE DO.
Voice 4:	We come to this place to repent that
	we have not yet enabled leaders of state
	to relinquish such folly and absurdity.
ALL:	FATHER, FORGIVE US, WE DO KNOW WHAT WE DO.
Voice 5:	We come to this place to repent our hypocrisy
	in possessing and threatening the use of weapons of mass destruction
	while we condemn the same thing in others.
ALL:	FATHER, FORGIVE US, WE DO KNOW WHAT WE DO.
Voice 6:	We come to this place to repent of
	all those lives that we put at risk by our folly.
ALL:	FATHER, FORGIVE US, WE DO KNOW WHAT WE DO.
Voice 7:	We come to this place to repent that
	we put our very land to such insane use.
ALL:	FATHER, FORGIVE US, WE DO KNOW WHAT WE DO.
Voice 8:	We come to this place to repent the squandering
	of the people's wealth
	and of the resources that would lead to their welfare.
ALL:	FATHER, FORGIVE US, WE DO KNOW WHAT WE DO.
Voice 9:	We come to this place
	as a sign of our willingness to change our ways,
	to name that which is our sin,
	and to receive the mark of ashes
	as a witness to our will to change, to stand firm,
	and to resist that which is evil and its embodiment in Trident.
ALL:	FATHER, FORGIVE US, WE DO KNOW WHAT WE DO.
Leader:	We invite any of good will to join with us in this act of repentance.

The peace of the Earth be with you *is sung again, during which any people who are watching on the fringe of the group may respond to the invitation and draw closer.*

Leader: Lord, you are merciful to all and hate nothing you have created. You forgive the sins of humankind and bring us to repentance. Protect us in our struggle against evil. As we begin the discipline of Lent, make this day a holy celebration of your goodness to us and bless our efforts to do your will. Amen

Reader 1:   Let us hear the words of the Prophet Isaiah. Words Jesus would have known well, and words that are still so applicable to us in our time, both as individuals and as a nation.

Scripture reading: Isaiah 58

Reader 1:   The mouth of the Lord has spoken.
ALL: AMEN

Song: If the war goes on

1. If the war goes on
    and the children die of hunger,
    and the old men weep
    for the young men are no more,
    and the women learn
    how to dance without a partner
    who will keep the score?

2. If the war goes on
    and the truth is taken hostage,
    and new horrors lead
    to the need to euphemise,
    when the calls for peace
    are declared unpatriotic,
    who'll expose the lies?

3. If the war goes on
    and the daily bread is terror,
    and the voiceless poor
    take the road as refugees;
    when a nation's pride
    destines millions to be homeless,
    who will heed their pleas?

4. If the war goes on
    and the rich increase their fortunes
    and the arms sales soar
    as new weapons are displayed,
    when a fertile field
    turns to no-man's-land tomorrow,
    who'll approve such trade?

5. If the war goes on
    will we close the doors to heaven,
    if the war goes on,
    will we breach the gates of hell;
    if the war goes on,
    will we ever be forgiven,
    If the war goes on … and on … and on …?

John L Bell

Prayer or reflection (concerning our pursuit of security and might based on weapons of mass destruction)[1]

(Short silence)

Reader 2:   As we remember that we are children of God our task becomes clear. St Paul exemplifies our urgent duty and calling to bring our nation to repentance. It will not be easy, but it is a glorious call.

Scripture reading: 2 Corinthians 5:20 – 6:10

Reader 2:   The mouth of the Lord has spoken.
ALL: AMEN

The peace of the Earth be with you *is sung again.*

Litany of the witnesses

Leader: We are not the first witnesses to Christ's reconciling power,
             nor shall we be the last.
             So take courage!
             We surround ourselves with a great cloud of witnesses.
             Let us call to mind and to be present with us
             those who have lived, worked, spoken
             and witnessed for peace
             in this and other ages:

Names are called out and, after each name, a chorus is sung of the African song Stand firm
*(SBTL). The Adomnán group starts, by each individual naming one of the following people
who preached non-violence: St Francis of Assisi, St Columba, St Margaret of Scotland,
Martin Luther King, Mohandas Gandhi, Dorothy Day, George Fox, George MacLeod, Roger
Gray, Reg Comley. They end by all naming together Adomnán of Iona.*

Others are then invited to name witnesses in the same manner.

Distribution of ashes

Leader: For centuries Christians have used ashes on Ash Wednesday as a vivid
reminder of the biblical idea of public penance. It is a very appropriate
sign to use ashes in this place. Should Trident be used, millions of human
beings would be reduced to ashes. Vast swathes of the earth would be
turned to radioactive dust for centuries. Part of the ashes with which we
will be marked will come from burning these effigies of the four Trident
submarines, symbolising our hope that soon the actual submarines will be
rendered harmless before they can be used for real. I invite those of you
who are holding models of the submarines to place them in this small fire.

*The effigies of Trident are burnt in a metal container in silence. These ashes are added to
the ashes that were prepared before the service.*

Leader: Soon we will ask God to bless this ash, which we use as a sign of our
repentance, and as a memorial of those who have gone before us in
nuclear and other conflict. Let us remember them now.

            (Silence)

Leader: Lord, bless the sinner who asks for forgiveness. Keep us faithful to your
word and strong in your service. Amen

The ash is blessed.

Leader: I now invite those who wish to receive these ashes as a mark of their
repentance to come forward.

Distribution of ashes

*This can be done in various ways. E.g. each person could mark their neighbour with ashes
and bless them with words such as 'Love one another'. After receiving ash each person may
turn to face the direction of the object of the protest and join hands with their neighbours.*

During the distribution of ashes the song Goodness is stronger than evil *(LAA) is sung
repeatedly.*

Commissioning

Leader: What we have heard and what we have seen cannot remain mere gestures, empty words. A symbol contains the seed of reality. Jesus did not merely preach, he went about doing good. In that tradition, Adomnán of Iona called upon his contemporaries and his heirs to follow the law of God by ensuring the protection of the innocents. He asked for his spiritual heirs to ensure that his Law of Protection be observed throughout Britain, and that they be supported by the prayers and good will of the citizenry. Today, I call on those heirs of Adomnán free to act: will you put your words into action?

Adomnán Group: We will.

Leader: We bless you and bind God's love and protection about you.

Adomnán arrestees and sponsors come forward and are commissioned.

Song: Will you come and follow me? (CG)

At the beginning of verse 4 of the song, Adomnán arrestees move to blockade the gate to the submarine base.

At the end of verse 4:
Leader: Friends of Adomnán's heirs, are you free to put your words into action?

Others risking arrest then move to blockade the gate also.

(Silence)

Once arrests start, Stand firm *is sung again for each arrestee, using the person's name.*

When arrests are over:
Leader: We thank you, Lord, for the gift of each other. Be with those now in custody for your Name's sake. Guide them and those who hold them. Be with us in our ongoing celebration of your creation. Be with us in our witness to all that is good, in our resistance to the evil of Trident.

All present are invited to wish each other 'Peace' as they leave, and The peace of the Earth be with you *is sung again repeatedly during departures.*

Notes

[1]The UN Earth Prayer was used in the original service.

A TIME FOR LISTENING, A TIME FOR HOPE:
An interfaith service for peace

This service was held in the Cathedral Church of St Peter in Lancaster on 26th January 2003 as the prospect of Britain going to war on Iraq without the authorisation of the United Nations loomed closer.

The initiative was co-ordinated by Bishop Patrick O'Donoghue, Roman Catholic Bishop of Lancaster. Bishop Patrick worked with Muslim, Jewish, Hindu, Anglican and Methodist leaders from the local faith communities to plan and lead the service. The Cathedral was packed to the doors with over 1500 people in attendance, many standing at the back and others sitting on every available floor and seating area of the vast church.

The address was given by Dr Hugh Miall, a lecturer in peace studies at Lancaster University.

A TIME FOR GATHERING

The service opens with calls to prayer from Jewish, Islamic, Hindu and Christian traditions:
The blowing of the Shofar, the Jewish call to atonement.
The Islamic refrain 'Hayya alas Salaah', translated as 'Come to prayer'.
Hindu mantras.
The ringing of the cathedral bells, the Christian call to worship.

Song: For the healing of the nations

Young people carry the following words, written on pieces of card, to the front of the cathedral and leave them on the altar: hope, love, dialogue, community, faith, prayer, mercy, justice, tolerance, patience, understanding, peace.

Greeting

Sisters and brothers, the conflict of nations can sadly escalate into war, however unwanted. When that happens, a mixture of thoughts and feelings fill us all: fear for those standing in harm's way, worry about the possible length of the conflict, concern for our own safety and that of our loved ones, sorrow that war can seem necessary for the sake of peace. As people of faith and citizens of a nation that values freedom and justice, peace is indeed our deepest desire: peace for our hearts, peace for our lands, and peace for all the world. Therefore let us call upon God, the One who alone can bring peace that endures.

A TIME FOR LISTENING

A reading from the Psalms

Pray for the peace of Jerusalem:
May they prosper who love you.
Peace be within your walls,
And security within your towers.
For the sake of my relatives and friends
I will say, 'Peace be within you.'
For the sake of the House of the Lord, our God,
I will seek your good.

Psalm 122

Sung responsorial psalm: Psalm 84

All sing the refrain: The Lord speaks of peace.

A reading from the Qur'an

And who could be better of speech
Than he who calls others unto God
And does what is just and right
And says: I am of those who have surrendered
Themselves to God.
Good and evil are not equal;
Repair the evil that is done to you with something better.
And lo! The enemy who did evil to you may turn into a close and true friend.
Yet to achieve this is not given to any but those who are
Wont to be patient in adversity.
It is not given to any but those endowed with the greatest fortune.
If it should happen that a pointing from Satan stirs you to blind anger,
Seek refuge with God.
Behold, He alone is all hearing, all knowing.

Sura 41

Music: *(In the original service a flute solo was played.) The idea is to intersperse the different readings with appropriate music from different cultures and traditions. For example, Middle Eastern music, a sitar solo …*

A reading from the Atharva Veda

Peace be to the earth and to airy spaces.
Peace be to heaven, peace to the waters.
Peace to the plants and peace to the trees.
May all the gods grant me peace.
By this invocation of peace may peace be diffused.
By this invocation of peace may peace bring peace.
With this peace the dreadful I appease.
With this peace the cruel I appease.
So that peace may prevail, happiness prevail.
May everything for us be peaceful.

Music

A reading from the New Testament

Who is wise and understanding among you? Show by your good life that your works
are done with gentleness born of wisdom. But if you have bitter envy and selfish ambition in your hearts, do not be boastful and false to the truth. Such wisdom does not
come down from above, but is earthly, unspiritual, devilish. For where there is envy
and selfish ambition, there will also be disorder and wickedness of every kind. But the
wisdom from above is first pure, then peaceable, gentle, willing to yield, full of mercy
and good fruits, without a trace of partiality or hypocrisy. And a harvest of righteousness is sown in peace for those who make peace.

James 3

A song for peace: Make me a channel of your peace (words by St Francis) (SOGP)

A TIME FOR DISCERNING

Address: At the threshold of war

We are at the threshold of war. To cross the threshold and unleash violence is to accept
the certainty of causing suffering. It is time to stop, to pause, to reflect.

We should reflect, first of all, on the innocent Iraqi civilians, who are caught
between the Iraqi dictatorship and the approaching machines of war. A friend, Scilla
Elworthy, was in Baghdad this month. She visited the Al Amarya Shelter, which was

bombed in the last war. Lest we forget what we are unleashing, may I quote what she saw: 'This shelter, which looks like a rectangular concrete box, was bombed at 4.30 a.m. on 13th February 1991, by two laser-guided bombs each weighing two tons. The first penetrated two metres of concrete ceiling like a drill; we saw the hole with reinforcements hanging down. 422 women and children were sleeping below on bunks. 408 of them died, mostly burned to death in 400 degrees centigrade temperatures, because the second bomb went into the ventilation system and created an oven of the entire building. The whole thing took four minutes.'

We should reflect on violence, aware of its consequences: aware that every child, woman and man is precious and irreplaceable.

We should reflect on the unpredictable consequences of violence, and its tendency to escalate. We know that our government, and the United States' government, and the Israeli government, have adopted policies of using nuclear weapons in response to weapons of mass destruction. If the Iraqi regime does indeed possess chemical and biological weapons, it may use them in this war. We should reflect on what the world would be like, and what our own place in the world would be like, if a war were to reach such a pass as this.

We should reflect on the unpredictable consequences for the region. We know how deeply people have reacted against colonialism and against American troops in Saudi Arabia. Have the consequences of placing American and British troops for a long time in Iraq been sufficiently considered? Has it really been understood how people in the region will see the imposition of another Western-backed regime in the heart of the Arab lands? Will this action pacify or inflame the other conflicts in the region?

We should reflect on the consequences for terrorism. This is supposed to be a war on terrorism. But nothing seems more calculated to provoke a terrorist response than the present course of action.

We should reflect on the consequences for the peace of the world if the United States starts a pre-emptive war without the authority of the United Nations. It is difficult to construe such action as being compatible with international law.

We should reflect, too, on our hopes for a different kind of response to violence: a response inspired by the spiritual traditions represented here. A response that is non-violent. A response that waters the seeds of compassion and healing, rather than the seeds of anger. A response that sees violence and suffering as a cycle of actions, but a cycle that can be broken. A response that reaches out to redress the root causes of humiliation, rage and fear.

There are other paths forward than war. The French and German governments, and many in Britain, argue for giving the United Nations inspectors more time. The Saudi government has proposed a way out for Saddam. Rosemary Hollis, Director of the Middle East programme at Chatham House, has proposed linking a new approach to Palestine with enlisting the co-operation of the Arab states and seeking political reform in Iraq. Britain could better pursue an alternative approach with the Europeans than follow the United States into a dangerous and unnecessary war.

We need to tackle weapons of mass destruction not by countries bombing other countries that won't comply, but within the framework of multilateral United Nations' agreements. We need to strengthen the Nuclear Non-Proliferation Regime, not undermine it by threatening to use nuclear weapons first against non-nuclear states.

If we resist the path of violence, we do not have to cross this threshold. We can seek a different path forward in hope and trust. If we look for it together, with open minds and hearts, it will be there.

Silence during which young people bring candles to the front of the cathedral.

A TIME FOR PRAYER

Litany of peace

Reader:	Lord of the nations, God of peace and love,
	in your hands are all the people of this world:
	one flesh, one blood, created by you.
	You alone, O God, can curb the passions
	that take us from you and turn us upon each other.
	You alone can save us from ourselves.
ALL:	BE WITH US NOW, O LORD, AND HEAR OUR PRAYER FOR PEACE.
Reader:	Forgive us for participating in that which turns people against each other;
	for fuelling anger and harbouring vengeance,
	and not heeding your call to love one another.
ALL:	FORGIVE US LORD.
Reader:	Forgive us for not always sharing with the world
	the blessings of prosperity that we have received as a nation.
	In our comfort, we have not always seen the uncomfortable.
	In the caring for our own, we have not always cared for the least of your kingdom.
ALL:	FORGIVE US LORD.
Reader:	Renew us in faith, Lord, and grant us peace.
ALL:	RENEW US IN FAITH, LORD, AND GRANT US PEACE.
Reader:	Open our eyes and help us to see the world around us as you see it.
ALL:	RENEW US IN FAITH, LORD, AND GRANT US PEACE.
Reader:	Open our eyes and help us to see where your love is needed most.
ALL:	RENEW US IN FAITH, LORD, AND GRANT US PEACE.
Reader:	Open our eyes and hearts to your truth.
ALL:	RENEW US IN FAITH, LORD, AND GRANT US PEACE.

Reader: As we seek justice, make us just.
             As we seek forgiveness, make us forgive.
ALL: RENEW US IN FAITH, LORD, AND GRANT US PEACE.
Reader: Guard and protect those who stand in harm's way.
             Inspire the leaders of nations to pursue equity and peace.
ALL: RENEW US IN FAITH, LORD, AND GRANT US PEACE.
Reader: Grant wisdom to our leaders, and to the United Nations.
ALL: RENEW US IN FAITH, LORD, AND GRANT US PEACE.
Reader: Grant peace in our land, in our homes, and in our places of work.
ALL: RENEW US IN FAITH, LORD, AND GRANT US PEACE.
Reader: God of our ancestors, God of all who are in need,
             heed our call and answer our prayer.
             Send peace in our time,
             peace for our hearts, peace for our land, peace for all the world,
             peace that abides as we abide in you.
ALL: AMEN

A TIME FOR HOPE

A sign of peace is shared among all those present.

Concluding prayer *(The universal prayer for peace)*

Almighty God, you lead us from death to life, from falsehood to truth, from despair to hope, from fear to trust, from hate to love, from war to peace. Let peace fill our hearts, our world, our universe. Amen

Closing song: Tell out my soul

CHALLENGING PREJUDICE

CHALLENGING PREJUDICE

Zam Walker

I write this on Holocaust Memorial Day, the 60th anniversary of the liberation of Auschwitz-Birkenau death camps. When anyone is marginalised or actively discriminated against because of who they are this is the logical end result. It is still the case that in any school playground boys will use the term 'woman' as a way to insult each other. Or use terms denoting race, sexuality or differing abilities – always depicting the other not just as different, but as inferior, as someone, something, to be feared and despised.

In scripture we are urged not to conform to the ways of the world. Some Christian groups have adopted a quietist approach and withdrawn from daily life, refusing to engage with the political process or even to have contact with those who are 'impure' or not part of their select group. I think God intends otherwise. St Paul is clear in naming the 'ways of the world' as those attitudes and behaviours which are judgemental, exclusive, discriminatory; which refuse to recognise God in each person and which limit the availability of God's grace. 'Don't be like the people of this world, but let God change the way you think.' (*Romans 12:2 CEV*) Repentance, after all, means turning around, being transformed.

The six liturgies in this chapter address prejudice, name issues, and challenge each of us to overcome our fear and face reality, to be transformed in the power of the Spirit. Each liturgy centres on personal stories or names individual people who have experienced pain, who have taken action to overcome discrimination, to be the people who God created them to be. Each liturgy involves naming, listening, confession, affirmation, a commitment to action for change and a celebration of our glorious diversity. It involves the whole person – body, mind and soul. We each have a part to play. All are included. Even Jesus was challenged and was prepared to change his mind to be more inclusive (see 'A simple liturgy challenging racism').

As Yvonne Morland says in her liturgy 'We are all broken, we are all gifted': '… to be truly inclusive of any marginalised group, we need to recognise that we are all the people of God and that all of our journeys contain chaff and grain, wounds and gifts.'

I was blessed indeed to be a participant at the two services held in Iona Abbey which appear here. The atmosphere on each occasion was incredible. During both services members of the congregation were enabled to participate who had previously felt marginalised or even excluded from churches. The joy on their faces was truly marvellous to behold. As someone said to me, 'This is the Kingdom!'

The liturgies contained within this section reveal a God who challenges us to include all – even ourselves; to see beyond the label, to look through other people's eyes and into our own hearts, to celebrate our wonderful diversity and to see each other as reflections of the all-embracing rainbow God in whose image we are *each* made.

> To all the colours of the rainbow:
> WE STAND WITH YOU WHEN WE ARE PERSECUTED.
> To all the colours of the rainbow:
> WE CELEBRATE OUR DIVERSITY.
> To all the colours of the rainbow:
> WE ARE WELCOME AT CHRIST'S TABLE.

Blessing from *The soul loves the body*

A SIMPLE LITURGY CHALLENGING RACISM

Yousouf Gooljary

Introduction

Leader: Racism is a sin against God and against our fellow human beings. It is contrary to the justice and the love of God. It destroys the human dignity of both the racist and the victim. Let us condemn racism in all its forms.

'Whoever says I am in the light while hating a brother or sister is still in the darkness.' (1 John 2:9).

Song

Many of the worship songs associated with the liberation struggle in South Africa could be used here, for example Mayenziwe ('Your will on earth be done, O Lord'), Senzenina (A cry of the oppressed: 'What have we done?') *or* Thuma mina ('Send me Lord').

Scripture reading: Mark 7:24–30

Scriptural reflection

Read slowly with the chant Kindle a flame *sung by a lone voice or small group between each section.*

Voice 1:   *Rereads Mark 7:24*
Voice 2:   Jesus moves from his country to a foreign land, from his comfort zone to a place outside his ethnic security.
Sung response: Kindle a flame to lighten the dark and take all fear away.

Voice 1:   *Rereads Mark 7:25–26*
Voice 2:   Jesus does not want to get involved. He tries to keep a low profile but is confronted by a stranger pleading for his help: someone of a different nationality, a different ethnic origin, a different religion. A woman.
Sung response: Kindle a flame to lighten the dark and take all fear away.

Voice 1:   *Rereads Mark 7:27*
Voice 2:   Jesus answers her harshly.
Voice 3:   I am from a different ethnicity, a different cultural background. I have to look after my own.
Voice 2:   Why does Jesus respond like this? Is he leading the woman? What does he expect her to say?
Sung response: Kindle a flame to lighten the dark and take all fear away.

Voice 1:	*Rereads Mark 7:28*
Voice 2:	The woman responds courageously.
Voice 4:	I may be a different religion, a different ethnicity, a different colour, a different gender, a different culture, but I have rights too. I am entitled to something. At least give me the crumbs.
Sung response:	Kindle a flame to lighten the dark and take all fear away.

Voice 1:	*Rereads Mark 7:29–30*
Voice 2:	She has risen to Jesus's challenge. Now he treats her as an equal and gives her more than she had dared to hope.
Voice 3:	Your daughter is healed: fully, completely, now. I do not give you the crumbs. I give you the whole banquet. For you too are a child of God.
Sung response:	Kindle a flame to lighten the dark and take all fear away.

Or:

One of my favourite stories is the one about the Syrophoenician woman (Matthew 15:21–28; Mark 7:24–30), a foreigner, who came to ask Jesus to heal her sick daughter when he was visiting her territory to get away for a little while from the danger that was now pursuing him and, presumably, to get a little peace and quiet. Some Christians go into paroxysms of re-interpreting and pietising in order to avoid the unavoidable fact that, in this story, Jesus does not show up in a good light. A visitor to her country, he is insulting to her people in a way that nowadays would be deemed quite explicitly racist. But I like the story precisely because, in it, he acts like a man of his time and place, with the cultural baggage of any human being. When the woman challenges him, he has the openness to look at his behaviour, to see the assumptions in it, and to go beyond it. He recognises the necessity to venture beyond the lines. He has the courage and humility to learn and to change. I do not find much hope for change or salvation in impossibly inhuman perfection. But I do find it in Jesus in this story.

Kathy Galloway

Song: If you believe and I believe (CG)

A story from today

The sharing of an appropriate story illustrating the experience of racism, or of how racism has been overcome and attitudes changed. This may be done, for example, by a reading, testimony, drama or dialogue.

Prayer for God's help and healing

Leader: Redeeming God,
            in a world of violence
            we acknowledge our own selfishness and prejudice,
            which are contrary to your all-embracing love.
            Help us to act justly, to love mercy
            and to walk humbly with Christ, in respect for all your children.
ALL: WE PRAY FOR FORGIVENESS AND REDEMPTION;
            WE PRAY FOR HELP AND HEALING.
Leader: Gracious God,
            mindful of our own need for your forgiveness and grace,
            enable us to be challenging yet compassionate
            towards those who show bigotry and commit racist violence.
            May their hatred and prejudice be overcome
            through the strength and liberation of your redeeming love.
ALL: WE PRAY FOR FORGIVENESS AND REDEMPTION;
            WE PRAY FOR HELP AND HEALING.
Leader: Caring God,
            your Son Jesus showed solidarity with the weak and vulnerable.
            Touch with your love
            all those who have been the victims of racist violence.
            Heal their wounds of body, mind and spirit
            and lead them on the journey to justice and reparation.
ALL: WE PRAY FOR FORGIVENESS AND REDEMPTION;
            WE PRAY FOR HELP AND HEALING.
Leader: Liberating God,
            you offer freedom to all people.
            Send your Holy Spirit to strengthen the victims
            of racist bullying, threats, persecution and abuse.
            Break the bonds of fear and isolation,
            and empower us in our struggle.
ALL: WE PRAY FOR FORGIVENESS AND REDEMPTION;
            WE PRAY FOR HELP AND HEALING.
Leader: Reconciling God,
            help us to overcome all our ethnic divisions.
            Increase our understanding
            of how to develop a truly inclusive culture.
            Most of all, this day and every day,
            challenge us to challenge racism.
ALL: AMEN

Closing responses

Leader: God of justice,
          give us voice,
          take away our fear;
          shake up our prejudices and move us to a different place,
          so that we may stand on common ground
          with those who struggle for justice.

ALL: TEACH US LOVE. TEACH US COMPASSION.
          ABOVE ALL, OUT OF LOVE AND COMPASSION,
          TEACH US TO ACT.
          AMEN

Sung blessing: The peace of the Earth be with you (CG) or Thuma mina (CG)

THE SOUL LOVES THE BODY:
Affirming sexuality and celebrating diversity

Bev Chidgey, Georgia Duncan, Mel Duncan, Sophia Griffiths, Jennine Lennox, Kristie Meehan Miles, Dafydd Owen, Neil Paynter, Jenni Sophia Fuchs, Veni Vounatsou

This service was held in Iona Abbey on the evening of Monday, 5th August 1998. Members of the Iona Community were gathered on Iona for their annual Community Week. They came together in this act of worship, led by Iona Community staff, to affirm and celebrate that all people, of whatever sexuality, are made by God and in the image of God, and are full members of Christ's family.

In contrast, on the same day, Anglican primates, gathered from around the world at the Lambeth Conference, passed a resolution on the issue of sexuality. This resolution rejected homosexual practice as 'incompatible with scripture' and advised against Church blessing of same sex unions or the ordaining of those involved in same gender unions. A gathering of Anglican primates in October 2003 reaffirmed this resolution. A statement from the Vatican in June 2003 was worded even more strongly, stating that 'homosexual acts go against the natural moral law … Under no circumstances can they be approved.'[1]

Coloured tissue paper streamers are handed to all members of the congregation as they enter the church.

The soul loves the body
As the congregation is gathering, musicians and dancers sing and move to this chant.

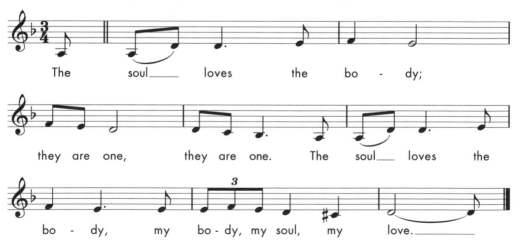

Music © Trisha Watts. Text © Monica O'Brien.

Introduction and welcome

In the original service, some words were spoken about the vote that day at the Lambeth Conference, followed by:

At each Communion Service here in Iona Abbey we say that *all* are welcome at Christ's table. Yet not everyone has felt welcomed, including people who are gay, lesbian, bisexual and transgender.

Tonight we throw open the arms of the Iona Community, arms that are strong and loving, arms that proclaim *all truly are welcome*: at Christ's table, in our families, our communities, our churches, our work places, our neighbourhoods and our hearts.

Opening responses

Leader: Creator Spirit, wellspring of our lives,
            As a stream flows steadily on, defying all the odds of stone and water,
ALL: FLOW OVER EVERY BOUNDARY AND BORDER THAT
            SEPARATES US FROM EACH OTHER.
Leader: As the waters of Iona welcome each of us,
ALL: RENEW US NOW IN NEWNESS OF LIFE AND UNITY OF LOVE.
Leader: As we were once held in the waters of our mother's womb,
ALL: HOLD US IN THE POWER AND ACCEPTANCE OF YOUR UNCONDITIONAL LOVE.

Song: A touching place (verses 1–3) (CG)

Scripture readings: 1 Samuel 18:1–5; 2 Samuel 1:25–26 (David's lament for Jonathan)

(Silence)

David's story

David grew up in rural Minnesota. Gentle David has been a close family friend for decades. He used to babysit our oldest son Brad. In the late 1970s he moved to New York to become an opera star. Shortly after moving there he was followed by three men on his way home one night. As he quickened his pace they sped up as well.

When he reached the front door of his building he fumbled for his keys. They pushed him into the foyer and started to hit him. When David fell to the ground the men began to kick him. With each kick to the ribs and each kick to the head they shouted obscene names at him.

This was the first of the three times that David has been beaten for nothing more than being who God created him to be.[2]

(Silence)

Persecution in Zimbabwe

The mob howled at the tiny group of men and women staffing the small stand at the Zimbabwe book fair. 'We don't want any hosos here,' they shouted. 'We'll smash them. We'll kill them.'

Soon the crowd's insults turned to violence. They burned books belonging to the Gays and Lesbians of Zimbabwe organisation (GALZ), turning on the handful of homosexual campaigners.

Homosexuality is illegal and publicly unacceptable in Zimbabwe. President Mugabe has publicly denounced homosexuals, branding them 'sexual perverts – pigs and dogs who deserve no rights'.

The Zimbabwe government banned GALZ from having a stall at the fair, but the decision was overturned by the High Court. As the mob gathered around the stall, Herbert Ushewokunze, a public prosecutor, told the crowd: 'We don't want gays here. We don't care what the High Court says. This is the court of the people, not a court of poofs.'

(Silence)

Song/poem: Maybe the poet (is gay) by Bruce Cockburn, or Glad to be gay by Tom Robinson *(sung solo)*

Prayer of intercession

Leader: For the quarter of a million homosexuals
            murdered in Nazi concentration camps,
            and those who remained imprisoned despite the Allied victory,
            and now live in history's closet:
ALL: WE PRAY, O GOD, FOR THOSE WHO DIED IN CLOSETS.
Leader: For millions of lesbians and gay men in countries
            in which there are no support systems or groups,
            in which revelation leads to imprisonment, castration or death:
ALL: WE PRAY, O GOD, FOR THOSE WHO FEAR IN CLOSETS.
Leader: For priests, nuns, ministers and lay church leaders
            who, to serve the Church, cannot come out,
            while bringing liberation to others who are oppressed:
ALL: WE PRAY, O GOD, FOR THOSE WHO LIBERATE FROM CLOSETS.

Song: If you believe and I believe (CG)

Dialogue

Peter:	Eh, Jesus?
Jesus:	Yes, Peter?
Peter:	I was just wondering ...
Jesus:	Yes, Peter?
Peter:	Um, what would you do if someone came along, you know, who wanted to join us, who loved men?
Jesus:	I love men, Peter.
Peter:	I know that Jesus but ...
Jesus:	Yes, Peter?
Peter:	Who loved men, *you know*. Or a woman who loved women.
Jesus:	Who was gay Peter? Who was queer?
Peter:	Yes Jesus ...What would you do?
Jesus:	What do you mean, Peter?
Peter:	I mean, would you stand and cast the demon out of them and tell them to repent?
Jesus:	Because they *loved*, Peter? No.
Peter:	Would you pray for them then?
Jesus:	Perhaps not as much as I'd pray for you, Peter.
Peter:	What Jesus? ... I mean, there hasn't been anyone up until now, but ...
Jesus:	There hasn't?
Peter:	Who loves men, Jesus? Who's gay? ... Has there, Jesus? Has there?
Jesus:	Oh, Peter.
Peter:	Who Jesus? Who is it? Is it Simon, Jesus? Is it Philip? It's Bartholomew. It's Bartholomew, isn't it?
Jesus:	Peter, don't you have more important things to think about?
Peter:	Yes Jesus.
	(Pause)
Jesus:	Eh, Peter?
Peter:	Yes, Jesus.
Jesus:	Love one another.
Peter:	Pardon? Oh, yes Jesus.

(Silence)

Reflection

Society needs gay people because they are human – they belong. It benefits from gay people precisely because they are different – whether as social critics, as explorers of gender, as models of different approaches to gentleness and strength, as the inheritors of the ancient cultural traditions of same sex affection and friendship, as people skilled in creating social networks based on grace and acceptance, as exemplars of a less predatory way of males relating to women, as those able or willing to exercise social functions that other members of society find difficult. The quest for a new relationship between gay people and society finds part of its key in an understanding of the role of diversity within … human culture.

Michael Vasey

(Silence)

Introduction to the litany of celebration

We come now to our litany of celebration. In this litany we will call names aloud and, in so doing, will remember many people whose lives have graced our world. *Some are gays and lesbians, others are those who had the courage and freedom of body, mind and spirit to defy the gender and sexual conventions of their day.* We will call the names in groups of six and at the end of each group all are invited to join in the response: 'We celebrate you!' and to wave the coloured streamers as the response is said. At the conclusion of the formal litany there will be time for anyone here to name aloud people whose lives you would like to celebrate. Please feel free to allow the names to tumble as they will. Following the litany all are invited to join in decorating the leader's chair, the font and the communion table with rainbows of colour using the streamers. Please move to whichever area is nearest you to share in the decoration.

Litany of celebration

Voice 1:   Chris Smith, MP
Voice 2:   Martina Navratilova, tennis player
Voice 3:   David Bowie, musician
Voice 4:   Brigid of Ireland, saint
Voice 5:   Walt Whitman, writer
Voice 6:   Ellen DeGeneres, actress
ALL: WE CELEBRATE YOU!
Voice 1:   Tchaikovsky, composer
Voice 2:   Sir Ian McKellan, actor

Voice 3:	Karen Clark, political leader
Voice 4:	Stephen Twigg, MP
Voice 5:	Greg Louganis, Olympic diver
Voice 6:	Adrienne Rich, poet
ALL	WE CELEBRATE YOU!
Voice 1:	Virginia Woolf, novelist
Voice 2:	David Zimmerman, friend
Voice 3:	Bayard Rustin, civil rights activist
Voice 4:	Freddie Mercury, pop star
Voice 5:	Perpetua and Felicity, saints
Voice 6:	Stephen Fry, comedian
ALL:	WE CELEBRATE YOU!
Voice 1:	Billy Jean King, tennis player
Voice 2:	Lionel Blue, rabbi
Voice 3:	K.D. Laing, musician
Voice 4:	Uncumber, saint
Voice 5:	Oscar Wilde, writer
Voice 6:	Boy George, pop star
ALL:	WE CELEBRATE YOU!
Voice 1:	Anselm of Canterbury, saint
Voice 2:	Gertrude Stein, writer
Voice 3:	E.M. Forster, novelist
Voice 4:	Colette, writer
Voice 5:	Rhona Cameron, comedian
Voice 6:	W.H. Auden, writer
ALL:	WE CELEBRATE YOU!
Voice 1:	George Michael, pop star
Voice 2:	Sappho, Greek poet
Voice 3:	John Henry Newman, cardinal
Voice 4:	Sir John Gielgud, actor
Voice 5:	Noel Coward, entertainer
Voice 6:	Vita Sackville-West, writer
ALL	WE CELEBRATE YOU!
Voice 1:	Malcolm Boyd, theologian
Voice 2:	Julian Clary, comedian
Voice 3:	Emily Dickinson, poet
Voice 4:	Eleanor Roosevelt, first lady
Voice 5:	Teresa of Avila, saint
Voice 6:	Elton John, musician
ALL:	WE CELEBRATE YOU!

Voice 1:   Rock Hudson, actor
Voice 2:   Leonard Bernstein, composer
Voice 3:   Melissa Etheridge, musician
Voice 4:   Plato, philosopher
Voice 5:   Ben Bradshaw, MP
Voice 6:   Marlene Dietrich, actress
ALL: WE CELEBRATE YOU!
Voice 1:   Liberace, pianist
Voice 2:   Herman Melville, author
Voice 3:   Allen Ginsberg, poet
Voice 4:   Queen Anne
Voice 5:   Sergius and Bacchus, saints
Voice 6:   May Sarton, poet
ALL: WE CELEBRATE YOU!
Voice 1:   Peter Allen, entertainer
Voice 2:   Rudolph Nureyev, dancer
Voice 3:   Joan of Arc, saint
Voice 4:   Sandi Toksvig, comedian
Voice 5:   Garcia Lorca, poet
Voice 6:   Graham Norton, comedian
ALL: WE CELEBRATE YOU!

Congregation call out names of people they know and want to celebrate, concluding with:

ALL: WE CELEBRATE YOU! WE CELEBRATE YOU! WE CELEBRATE YOU!

At the conclusion of the litany the song I am what I am, *recorded by soul-singer Gloria Gaynor, is played on tape while rainbows of colour are created with the streamers by all the congregation over the leader's desk, font and communion table.*

Poem: It happens all the time in heaven

It happens all the time in heaven,
And some day

It will begin to happen
Again on earth –

That men and women who are married,
And men and men who are
Lovers,

And women and women
Who give each other
Light,

Often will get down on their knees

And while so tenderly
Holding their lover's hand,

With tears in their eyes,
Will sincerely speak, saying

'My dear,
how can I be more loving to you;

How can I be more
Kind?'

Hafiz

Closing responses

Leader: To all the colours of the rainbow:
ALL: WE STAND WITH YOU WHEN WE ARE PERSECUTED.
Leader: To all the colours of the rainbow:
ALL: WE CELEBRATE OUR DIVERSITY.
Leader: To all the colours of the rainbow:
ALL: WE ARE WELCOME AT CHRIST'S TABLE.

Your Song *by Elton John is sung solo as the congregation leave the church.*

Notes

[1]Vatican statement June 2003 – from *Considerations regarding proposals to give legal recognition to unions between homosexual persons*, web site of the Offices of the Congregation for the Doctrine of the Faith, Rome.
[2]Two surveys by the Gay London Policing Group in the early 1990s found that 40% of gay men and 25% of lesbians had been beaten up by queerbashers at least once in their lives.

GOD MAKES FRIENDS:
A liturgy about gender
David Coleman and Zam Walker

Zam Walker and David Coleman are members of the Iona Community. They are passionate about the need for the world to answer God's call to build inclusive community through costly commitment and action, and believe that subversiveness is a mark of orthodox Christianity. Each has been involved in a variety of justice issues.

Before the service, the worship space is decorated with colours, candles and nice smells, with anything that helps people to use their senses and to celebrate their bodies. The use of slides or multimedia projection would also be effective.

Opening responses

Leader: Living God, our source, we are made in your image.
ALL: SHOW US THAT IMAGE IN EVERYONE WE MEET.
Leader: Jesus, our brother, you call us your friends.
ALL: HELP US BEFRIEND EACH OTHER AND OUR SELVES.
Leader: Holy Spirit, our flame of love, inspire us with your joy.
ALL: FIRE US WITH THE CHALLENGE OF YOUR CALL AND WELCOME.

Song: Dance and sing (IAMB)

Litany of friendship

Leader: How does God make us?
ALL: GOD MAKES US FRIENDS.

Leader: For friendship is life that is shared;
            shared without insisting upon rights,
            though not denying them.
            Shared with respect
            and love for self
            to set the standard
            and starting point
            for that greater love
            that risks the self that God has given.

Leader: Who does God make us?
ALL: GOD MAKES US FRIENDS

Leader: With work to be done,
   a world to be cherished.

   God first made a person.
   Good like God.
   But only one.
   And the person worked well.
   But come the day's end, the person wept.

Leader: How does God comfort us?
ALL: GOD MAKES US FRIENDS.

Leader: For everything was good
   except being alone.
   That was the problem.

   And so God made friends.
   And everyone saw that it was good.
   Friendship made good
   the will of God for people.

Leader: Why is there gender?
ALL: GOD MAKES US FRIENDS.

Leader: Friendship in male.
   Friendship in female.
   To fill a world with friendship
   through bodies that God makes holy.
   Lovers and parents.
   Living in many and various ways
   the highest calling God can offer.

Leader: What, then, is the best that God can make us?
ALL: GOD MAKES US FRIENDS.

Song: Loving Spirit (CG) or Enemy of apathy (CG)

Prayer of confession

God, since your image is not to be grasped
Except in the diversity of male and female:
So to Her we turn
To Him we cry
To God gendered within us
We bring brokenness and faithlessness,
Our abuse of the gift that would bring us into community.

Silence, followed by prayers with eyes open.

Either the following phrases are read slowly and with pauses, or the phrases are brought into the view of the congregation in silence on cards, banners or Powerpoint slides, preferably with appropriate illustrations:

violence: against women, children, men, partners;
homophobia; heterosexism; sexual abuse;
intimidation, humiliation;
refusal to love self;
twisting of religion;
collusion with the way things are.

Silence we need
To hear the charges.
Time we need
To let them sink in.
Yet if Christ's disciples keep silence,
Stones, for sure, will shout aloud.
So let those who have hands or voices
Claim what we need
To grow in love.

Confessional action

The congregation are invited to share in the burning of the sins named in the prayer by writing one or more of the sins on a small piece of paper and coming forward to burn the paper in a central fireproof container. The action may be done either in silence or while a chant is sung: Behold the Lamb of God (SOGP) or a Kyrie eleison (e.g. SOGP)

Proclamation of forgiveness and wholeness

Leader:	Healing: ours
ALL:	THROUGH JESUS, THE BROKEN.
Leader:	Forgiveness: ours
ALL:	THROUGH CHRIST WHO WAS WRONGED.
Leader:	Community: ours
ALL:	THROUGH GOD WHO MADE FRIENDS.

Positive action

The congregation are invited to share in a positive action, e.g. anointing each other or building a cairn, during which a chant or song is sung: Take, O take me as I am (CAYP) or Take this moment (CG)

Sharing of the peace

Scripture reading: John 11:1–7; 11–15; 17–19; 32–44 & 12:1–3

Song: Dignity and grace (CG) or What a friend we have in Jesus

Celebration and intercession

God gendered within us,
not shut out from any aspect of human life and love,
we lift up to you:
those in whom your image struggles to emerge
because of restrictions placed in their way:

Open intercession for people and situations suffering from gender stereotyping. These may be individuals, groups or places.

God, before us, beside us, within us,
involved in our past, present and future,
we lift up to you:
our hearts made complete by sisters and brothers of our time and all time:

Open thanksgiving for those who have challenged restrictions imposed because of their gender and so liberated themselves and others from these restrictions. The following names might be used, along with others as the Spirit leads:

Julian of Norwich, who wrote of the Motherhood of Christ.
Aelred of Rievaulx, who developed a theology of friendship.
George Fox, who proclaimed the vision of the Spirit in all.

Guru Nanak, who promoted the equality of women and men.

Florence Nightingale, who was called to ordination but denied her vocation; instead she channelled her energy into nursing and sanitation reform.

Constance Coltman, the first British woman to be ordained, in 1917.

Mary Seacole, a nurse and campaigner for social reform.

Sophia Jex Blake, a medical pioneer.

James Barrie, a female surgeon who disguised her true identity in order to practise medicine.

The Tolpuddle Martyrs, who strove for better working conditions.

Sojourner Truth, a prophet and campaigner for justice.

Josephine Butler, who was engaged in law reform.

David Livingstone and Mary Slessor, who campaigned against slavery and promoted partnership in trade.

Emmeline Pankhurst and other suffragists and suffragettes.

Conscientious objectors and peacemakers.

The women's movement and all who strive for equality.

The men's movement and those who strive for an end to machismo.

The gay, lesbian, bisexual and transgendered movement, striving for justice and celebrating our wonderful variety.

Song: I call you my friends *(based on John 15:9–17)*
Tune: The Cruel War, English traditional

As I have been treasured,
As I have been adored,
So have I been strengthened
To call you my friends.

In love I give guidance
For those who dare remain.
As I have been guided
I call you my friends.

I ask of you nothing
That my flesh has not known;
Nor lonely your journey
I call you my friends.

And joy in completeness
Will come your serving way;
Your laughter is holy
When you are my friends.

Though death may extinguish
The peace for which I cried;
I lived life for justice
To call you my friends.

In friendship you know me,
My life's still laid down when
You call earthly sisters
And brothers my friends.

Blessing *(said together)*

As we are fully women, fully men
in all our rainbow glory,
so walk with us, and embrace us.
With your blessing,
kiss the lips that praise you;
now and always
make it so.
Amen

Alternative songs

As man and woman we were made (SOGP)
Come my Way, my Truth, my Life (CG)
Come now, O Prince of Peace (CG)
Jesu, Jesu (SOGP)
Women and men as God intended (OITB)

A SILENT DESPERATION OF THE SOUL:
Liturgical material about mental health

Iain Whyte and the Edinburgh Community Mental Health Chaplaincy Group

This liturgy comprises material that was written by members of the Edinburgh Community Mental Health Chaplaincy group. The group meets each week at a drop-in in Edinburgh and, in 2003, travelled to Iona for four days in community, where some of this liturgy was composed. The liturgy has been assembled by Iain Whyte, a Church of Scotland minister serving as a community mental health chaplain in Lothian, and a member of the Iona Community. Two members of the Edinburgh Community Mental Health Chaplaincy group are chaplains and two are nurses. Most are, or have been, users of mental health services.

Introduction

At the preparation meeting for the visit to Iona one of the members of the chaplaincy group asked: 'How will our group be described?'

This question expresses one of the common anxieties that surround mental health. It is the experience of many people that once they are diagnosed 'schizophrenic' or 'manic depressive' these become labels.

In 2002, an anti-stigma campaign on mental health in Scotland was launched called *'See me: I'm a person, not a label'*. In the chaplaincy, we seek this as a first step for churches and faith communities. We believe that Jesus always saw people rather than labels.

The second step is to recognise that within faith communities there are so many people with so much hidden and locked-up potential. Those who have struggled with mental health problems invariably have a sensitivity and compassion that can contribute creatively to any caring organisation and to society. A member of our group plays the guitar in a day centre for children with Down's Syndrome and has unlocked some of the shackles of their world. We believe that Jesus brought out potential in people that others never even recognised was there.

Thirdly, we need to recognise our common need for healing. Although the statistics say that one in three of us have mental health problems, all of us have known depression or anxiety or felt despair to some degree and are somewhere on the mental health spectrum. If we take that to heart, then there is no more 'us' and 'them'. We believe that Jesus challenged us to recognise our mutual dependence.

Iain Whyte

Song: Dignity and grace (CG) [1]

Opening prayer

Leader: We confess that we have crossed the road, moved to another seat, neglected visiting others, because mental ill-health confuses and challenges us.

ALL: GOD, WHO CALLS US TO A CHANGE OF MIND, FORGIVE US.

Leader: We confess that we have too easily accepted labels given to others or participated in the language of derision and stigma because it has felt awkward to challenge it.

ALL: CHRIST, WHO ALWAYS RECOGNISED PEOPLE RATHER THAN STEREO-TYPES, FORGIVE US.

Leader: We confess that we have excluded or limited people, and often have been unwilling to see God's gifts in everyone.

ALL: HOLY SPIRIT, WHOSE FREEDOM CALLS ALL TO FULLNESS OF LIFE, FORGIVE US.

Leader: Forgiving God, help us to build a community where all are included, accepted and loved.

ALL: AMEN

Poem: Loneliness – A silent desperation of the soul

When you laugh the world laughs with you.
When you cry you cry alone.
No one hears the silent screams.

In the abyss of my mind there is darkness, there is a void.
There is a black place that no one can reach.
Only myself. It is the very essence of me.
It is the very life force in which I glow.
In the prison of my mind I long to be free from this mortal body that weighs me down and is a burden to me.

I wish I was an eagle soaring above the clouds.
No one can touch me there. I am free.
My mind, body, spirit and soul are floating high above the heavens.
In my adventure I see a clear blue sky and the dawning of a new horizon, and flying east, the rays of the sun engulf me.

I embrace the warmth of the sun and dance around its glowing waves with wings;
with grace and elegance I swiftly glide down near the ocean.
I can see the reflection of the sun like droplets of rubies and sapphires,
glimmering and glistening on the ocean surface.

With the wind beckoning me and the faith in my heart,
I fly towards the snow-filled mountains – to that place of joy and hope
where dreams come true and love greets you with open arms.

Where eternity meets infinity.
In the midst of her is the wellspring of life, and the hope of the eternal.

Tony Chan (Edinburgh Community Mental Health Chaplaincy group)

Scripture reading: Mark 5:1–17[2]

Reflection, testimony, personal story: from someone who has experienced mental health challenges, or from someone who works in the mental health field.

Prayer of thanksgiving

Leader: For the lifting of curtains from mental health, for legislation promoting equal rights, for new resources and creative paths towards better mental health,
ALL: THANKS BE TO GOD.
Leader: For the courage of those who struggle to keep going, for the faith of those who discover meaning in their lives, for the cheerfulness of those who dispel fear with laughter,
ALL: THANKS BE TO GOD.
Leader: For medical care; scientific advance; for art, music, writing and community in which potential can be realised; and for the enduring love of friends and carers,
ALL: THANKS BE TO GOD.

Song: We cannot measure how you heal (CG)[3]

Prayer of intercession

Leader: We pray for those who are fearful of their feelings and fearful to seek help, who feel trapped in darkness and devoid of hope.
ALL: GOD OF INFINITE COMPASSION, LET THEM FEEL YOUR LOVE SURROUNDING THEM, AND YOUR HAND LEADING THEM THROUGH.

Leader:	We pray for those who are gripped by guilt and weighed down by low self-esteem, believing that their life is a failure.
ALL:	CHRIST, ENCOURAGER AND UPLIFTER OF THE BURDENED, BRING THE ASSURANCE THAT WE ARE ALL CALLED TO A DIVINE DESTINY.
Leader:	We pray for those who stand alongside others as carers, companions and loved ones, often feeling helpless and exhausted.
ALL:	HOLY SPIRIT, COME TO THEM, WITH THE WIND THAT REFRESHES, RENEWS AND EMPOWERS, THAT THEY MAY KNOW THAT THEY ARE NOT ALONE.

Poem: The dark was clear

This poem could be read just before or after the closing hymn, or during the hymn, over the music.

An eagle held me yesterday.
I rose with his wings.
He led me through the night
With his penetrating eye.

The dark was clear to him.
We travelled high
To places I had never seen.
The stars were nearer.

Nearer to God
We seemed to fly;
My prayers he carried
Beyond the sky
Where love will never die.

Helen Campbell (Edinburgh Community Mental Health Chaplaincy group)

Closing song: Those who wait on the Lord (American traditional) (SOGP)

1. Those who wait on the Lord shall renew their strength,
   they shall rise up on wings as eagles
   they shall run and not be weary, they shall walk and not faint:
   help us Lord, help us Lord in your way.

2. Those who serve the suffering world shall renew their strength,

3. Those who live the risen life shall renew their strength,

4. Those who love the Mystery shall renew their strength,

5. Those who die on the march shall renew their strength,

6. Those who wait on the Lord shall renew their strength,

Blessing

May you come safely to shore
across the dark ocean

and know
that even in the darkest depths

there is hope to be found
and peace

or (said together)

Where can I go from your spirit?
Or where can I flee from your presence?
If I ascend to heaven, you are there;
If I make my bed in Sheol, you are there.
If I take the wings of the morning
and settle at the farthest limits of the sea,
even there your hand shall lead me,
and your right hand shall hold me fast.
If I say, 'Surely the darkness shall cover me,
and the light around me become night',
even the darkness is not dark to you;
the night is as bright as the day,
for darkness is as light to you.
Psalm 139:7–12

Notes

[1] Poor self-esteem is very common in mental ill-health. This hymn addresses that issue in a simple but profound way.

[2] This reading is for many the most dramatic and helpful Gospel incident that touches on mental health. Jesus seeks to meet the man's needs even before he reaches him, goes boldly into a situation that others have abandoned through fear, treats the man as an individual with a name, and sits with him in calmness and restoration.

[3] So many people who have struggled for years with their mental health are sceptical of anything that smacks of a quick cure. They hold in tension 'the pain that will not go away' and 'the private agonies inside' but also the 'love which tends', often enough in 'the touch of friends'.

HEARTS AND HANDS AND VOICES:
A commitment liturgy for Deaf and hearing people

Paul Whittaker

During September 2003, one of the guest programmes at the Iona Community's MacLeod Centre on Iona was entitled 'Hearts and Hands and Voices'. Guests, both Deaf[1]and hearing, shared together in an exploration of God's word and worship using sign language. The programme was led by Paul Whittaker, an associate member of the Iona Community and Artistic Director of the charity 'Music and the Deaf', and Cathy Nightingale, a minister in the Church of England, both of whom are Deaf.

Paul and Cathy prepared and led a service of commitment in Iona Abbey during the week, together with guests from the 'Hearts and Hands and Voices' programme, who jointly wrote the affirmation used in the service. The whole service was led in British Sign Language (BSL), with a voice-over for hearing members of the congregation who did not know BSL. The final affirmation was spoken by the congregation, at the same time as it was signed by a Deaf congregation member whose first language is BSL. Paul explains the thinking behind the service:

'I wanted the congregation to think about worshipping through non-verbal communication; and actually seeing the words – rather than just saying or hearing them – does make a congregation think more deeply about what is happening. Getting them all to sign the song *Lord of life, we come to you* as part of the act of commitment was a chance for them to experience it personally: to watch their hands – their direction – and to come physically closer to God. The spoken and signed affirmation at the end of the service was a drawing together of both Deaf and hearing people, of verbal and non-verbal communication, realising the validity and beauty of both. The service was written in English and translated into BSL. Trying to sign the English words in the service will not work as the two languages are separate ones.'

Some of the resources introduced during the 'Hearts and Hands and Voices' programme are included at the end of this liturgy, and could be incorporated into the service. They were supplied by Hannah Lewis, an associate member of the Iona Community, who is Deaf and is bilingual in BSL and English. Hannah has recently completed a PhD in Deaf liberation theology.

Hannah Lewis and Cathy Nightingale are two of eleven ordained Deaf people who use sign language as a first language in the Church of England.

It should be noted that in all the material that follows, where BSL versions are given, the words in BSL are only an approximation of the meaning, to try to indicate the signs used. BSL is a visual language and, as such, it is not really possible to write it down.

Opening responses

Voice 1:	Among the proud,
Voice 2:	among the poor,
Voice 1:	among the persecuted,
Voice 2:	among the privileged,
Voice 1:	Christ is coming,
ALL:	HE IS COMING TO MAKE ALL THINGS NEW.
Voice 1:	In the private house,
Voice 2:	in the market place,
Voice 1:	in the wedding feast,
Voice 2:	in the judgement hall,
Voice 1:	Christ is coming,
ALL:	HE IS COMING TO MAKE ALL THINGS NEW.
Voice 1:	With a gentle touch,
Voice 2:	with an angry word,
Voice 1:	with a clear conscience,
Voice 2:	with burning love,
Voice 1:	Christ is coming,
ALL:	HE IS COMING TO MAKE ALL THINGS NEW.
Voice 1:	That the kingdom might come,
Voice 2:	that the world might believe,
Voice 1:	that the powerful might stumble,
Voice 2:	that the humble might be raised,
Voice 1:	Christ is coming,
ALL:	HE IS COMING TO MAKE ALL THINGS NEW.
Voice 1:	Within us,
Voice 2:	without us
Voice 1:	among us,
Voice 2:	before us
Voice 1:	in this place,
Voice 2:	in every place
Voice 1:	for this time,
Voice 2:	for all time,
Voice 1:	Christ is coming,
ALL:	HE IS COMING TO MAKE ALL THINGS NEW.

Song: Oh the love of my Lord is the essence (SOGP)

Scripture verses

These Gospel verses all give short descriptive pictures of Jesus. It is effective if each is read by a different voice.

Mark 6:31
John 11:33
Matthew 21:12

Reflection: Images of Jesus

We all have our own ideas of what Jesus looks like. Perhaps this comes from childhood or from a particular experience in our lives. The reality is that none of us actually know what Jesus did look like, yet each culture has its own specific image of him. We invite you this evening to consider how your image of Jesus affects your faith. Does it make you passive? Active? Meditative? Angry? Compassionate?

In a moment we will project four different images for you to look at. They may provoke a strong reaction or no reaction at all. They may be wildly different from how you imagine Jesus to look. Please look at them in silence for a moment and then, if you wish, share with someone nearby which image challenges you the most and why.

After the song 'Lord of life, we come to you' is sung once as a solo, please sit quietly again and re-consider the images and how they challenge or stimulate your faith.

The images are projected and the reflection time follows.[2]

Act of commitment and affirmation

The congregation are invited to join in signing the song 'Lord of life, we come to you' as an act of commitment. It is helpful if the signing of this song is taught to the congregation prior to the beginning of the service rather than at this point in the liturgy. The song is sung solo again while the congregation sign it. This part of the commitment is concluded with a prayer.

Leader: As you hear the words of 'Lord of life, we come to you', and as you sign it yourself, watch your own hands and be aware of drawing close to God.

Signed song: Lord of life, we come to you (CG)

Prayer

O Christ, may our minds never become closed by belief
but always be open to the surprise of you,
the newness of you,
to the whoosh of wonder that comes with the
discovery of you in unexpected places. Amen

Leader: We say together the affirmation of commitment. Please speak it slowly so that we can think about the meaning of the words.

The affirmation is also signed.

Affirmation *(said together)*

We believe in God, our loving parent, who created us as equals, and who rested on the seventh day to value the beauty of what he made.

We believe in Jesus, our loving brother, who came as helper, teacher, healer and to be a friend to outsiders. He suffered and died as an outcast and through his resurrection to new life defeated all that holds us back from living as equals in the family of God.

We believe in the Holy Spirit, our loving sister, who comforts, pushes, encourages and challenges us, both to rest in God and to work in the world, and who helps us in our communication with God and with each other.

We believe in God, Jesus and the Holy Spirit. We are called to be God's family living in a loving and just community. Amen

A transcript of the BSL version:

We believe God, loving parent, God created equal. Rest seventh day worth beauty God's creation.

We believe Jesus loving brother came down helper teacher healer friend to outsiders Jesus suffered died same outcast. Rise to new life. Destroys all hold us back same equals – all family of God.

We believe Holy Spirit, loving sister, comfort, push, encourage, challenge us. Help rest in God and work in world both. Spirit help us communicate to God and each other.

We believe God, Jesus, Holy Spirit. We called same God's family, living loving just community. Amen

Song: Make me a channel of your peace (words by St Francis) (SOGP)

Closing responses

Leader: On our hearts and on our houses,
ALL: THE BLESSING OF GOD.
Leader: In our coming and our going,
ALL: THE PEACE OF GOD.

Leader: In our life and our believing,
ALL: THE LOVE OF GOD.
Leader: At our end and new beginning,
ALL: THE ARMS OF GOD TO WELCOME US AND BRING US HOME.
           AMEN

ADDITIONAL RESOURCES

A new Psalm: Psalm 152

This psalm was created by a group of Deaf lay ministry students during a workshop in October 1999. Many of these students continue to be involved in an ongoing group which has an annual theology/worship summer school for Deaf lay people. The psalm was originally created in British Sign Language. The signs were written down and then translated by an interpreter into English.

Original version *(a transcript of the BSL version)*

'tap'[3]
look at me Lord
Want sign at you so much. See you? I can't

Hearing world understand us? Not!
You understand us?
You understand us!

Hearing those
Music have, bells have, singing have
You show attention

Our prayers signed silent
You know us?

But we praise you – will!
Waving hands, clapping hands,
Stamp together. Our praise you feel.
Hold hands. Smile!
Candles alight. Fireworks!

Why? Clouds move away
You look at me
At last! At last!

English translation

Lord – look at me
I want to tell you something, but I can't see you.

The hearing world does not understand us.
Do you understand us?
You do understand us!

Those hearing ones
Have music, bells and singing.
They get your attention through sound.

Our prayers are signed silently.
We are here. Do you know that?

We will praise you.
We will wave our hands and clap.
We will stamp together so you feel our praise.
We will hold hands together as we smile our praise.
We will light candles – and set off fireworks!

Then the clouds will roll away
And you will notice us at last!
At last!

A Deaf person's creed

I believe in God
Who made everything in heaven and on earth
Including me.
Full Deaf and made
In the image of God.

I believe in the only Son of God,
Jesus Christ.
Who was born, lived and died for the sake of us all.
Who knew what it meant to be despised and rejected, mocked and ignored
     for who he was.
I believe Jesus was killed, then rose again,
And by his resurrection we have been saved from the bondage of sin and death;
From the bondage of oppression and a world that wants me to pretend to be hearing.

I believe in the Holy Spirit of God,
Who breathes life into each one of us.
Who calls us forward when we would hang back;
Who empowers us to believe in who we are
And what we can do
And who in the beauty of Sign Language speaks to the very depths of my soul.

And I believe in a church
Where I can be myself,
Where all are equal
And where this Good News of Jesus Christ is challenged, expanded and made real
In its worship and in its work.
For now and for ever.
Amen

A Deaf person's creed *(a transcript of the BSL version)*

I believe God
Created everything heaven earth both
Including me.
Full Deaf
Created face like God.

I believe God only Son,
Jesus Christ.
Jesus born, lived, died, why?
Because[4]-us.
Jesus knew meaning looked-down-on rejected mocked ignored why? Because–himself.
I believe Jesus crucified, buried. Then rose again
Through his resurrection we saved from prison sin death;
from prison oppression world wants me pretend hearing.

I believe God Holy Spirit
that's-it breathes life each-one
When we hang back pulls forward
strengthens us believe person are
and can achieve.
Holy Spirit signs beautiful sign language
enters-into depths-inside all-of-body

I believe church
There be myself.
There all people equal
There Good News Jesus Christ
challenged, expanded, created real
Through worship and through work
Now for ever.
Amen

Notes

[1] Generally 'Deaf' (capitalisation) signifies someone born deaf whose first language is British Sign Language (BSL), while 'deaf' (no capitalisation) is used to describe other people with a hearing impairment.

[2] The four images used in the original service were a black Christ and disciples in traditional African dress, an angry Christ with finger pointed as if in accusation, a laughing Christ, and a weeping Christ.

[3] A gesture – as if you were tapping God on the shoulder.

[4] The sign for 'because' is repeating the 'why' sign with a different facial expression.

WE ARE ALL BROKEN, WE ARE ALL GIFTED:
A liturgy of inclusiveness

Yvonne Morland

I have become concerned about inadvertently creating new 'ghettos' by how we focus our attention and action in attempts to be inclusive. The theme of this liturgy has evolved in recognition of the fact that to be truly inclusive of any marginalised group we need to recognise that we are all the people of God and that all of our journeys contain chaff and grain, wounds and gifts.

It is true that, by the nature of the world we have created so far, many people are systematically excluded from fullness of life and opportunity. This happens not just as a result of direct acts of oppression or suppression but because of ignorance and lack of understanding. These elements can be observed in the behaviour even of people who can otherwise be seen to be good, compassionate, justice-seeking and committed in their hearts to inclusiveness.

A prayer used regularly by members of the Iona Community when they meet asks God 'that hidden things may be revealed to us, and new ways found to touch the hearts of all'. I believe some of these hidden things can be discovered in sharing more richly the diverse gifts of all. This requires practical action informed by listening to the people whom we do not easily include.

And let us not forget that woundedness is a gift too. The death and resurrection of Jesus as the supreme sign of God's undying love for his son and for all humanity removes any doubt on that score. Nonetheless, as we inhabit and embody the lives God has given us, we must acknowledge, accept and live through our woundedness in order to find the gifts that are contained therein. And we need the loving support and understanding of each other to bear this journey and to discover the hidden gifts.

Gathering words

Leader: We come to this place:
ALL: TO BE TOGETHER AND TO CLAIM THAT WE ARE GOD'S PEOPLE.
Leader: We look to ourselves and to each other:
ALL: TO EXPRESS THE LOVE OF GOD AS A SIGN OF HOPE FOR THE WORLD.
Leader: We abandon ourselves:
ALL: TO THE WORKING OF THE HOLY SPIRIT, TRUSTING IN GOD'S MERCY.

Song: All are welcome (CG) or Great God, your love (CG) or The love of God comes close (LAA)

Recognising woundedness and acknowledging costs

Either:

A number of stories are read out about people who have experienced exclusion or alienation, for example as a result of illness or 'disability', together with statements of concern about how the failure to recognise the wounding and cost of this exclusion and alienation demeans our world community.

Or, if the gathering is one where a significant degree of trust and caring is already present: *People are invited to voice briefly their own stories of exclusion and alienation, pain and struggle into a time of collective quiet and reflection, perhaps with each story separated by a chant.*

Suggested chants between statements or stories: God to enfold you (CG) or Listen, Lord (CAYP) or Stand firm (MAG) or a Taizé chant

The section ends with the response:

Leader:	In the silence and in words:
ALL:	WE HEAR AND ACKNOWLEDGE THE EXPRESSION OF BROKENNESS;
	WE COMMEND TO GOD THOSE PEOPLE AND SITUATIONS, NAMED AND UNNAMED;
	WE WILL REMEMBER AND ACT ON WHAT WE HAVE HEARD.
	AMEN

Reflection

This reflection is offered as an option. Other options for this part of the service can include, for example, scripture readings, participative prayer, dance, drama, or a combination of these.

There are several stories in scripture of Christ recognising the woundedness of people ostracised by mainstream society, going forward to meet them and, in one way or another, challenging the crowd by restoring the wounded person to an honoured place. Many of these stories are referred to as 'the healing miracles' and, on one level, they are about curing sickness.

Unfortunately, our interpretations of these stories have often avoided examining what Christ and God mean by healing in its deeper sense. We have found it too easy to ascribe sinfulness to people who are not well, to associate, particularly, mental ill-health with demon possession, and to assume that people who do not 'get better' do not have a strong enough faith. We have also been guilty of claiming that homosexuality can be 'cured', that families experiencing strife are a testament to the breakdown of family values, and that 'disabled people' need to be looked after in a way that disempowers them. In doing so, we distance ourselves from the reality of many people's lives and from our own responsibility to work to build relationships based on love, not fear. We refuse to take up Christ's challenge to recognise the woundedness of our world society and we therefore deprive ourselves of a true appreciation of its actual and potential giftedness.

Let us listen to these words of Jean Vanier, founder of L'Arche Community, where people termed 'able-bodied' and those termed 'disabled' live together; where good is not 'done to people' but where community is based on friendship and mutual service:

If you enter into relationship
with a lonely or suffering person
you will discover something else;
that it is you who are being healed.
The broken person will reveal to you your own hurt
and the hardness of your heart,
but *also* how much *you* are loved.
Thus the one you came to heal
becomes your healer.

If you let yourself be moulded thus
by the cry of the poor
and accept their healing friendship,
then they may guide your footsteps into community
and lead you into a new vision of humanity,
a new world order,
not governed by power and fear
but where the poor and weak are at the centre.
They will lead you into the kingdom Jesus speaks of.

(Silence)

May we recognise our own frailty as a potential source of healing for others; may we learn not to fear it but to let it make us more compassionate.

Prayer

Leader: In the knowledge that our human frailty is a gift from you, O God:
ALL: OPEN UP OUR MINDS TO GREATER UNDERSTANDING OF EACH OTHER AND OF YOU.
Leader: Open up our hearts to greater wisdom in our prayers and in our actions.
ALL: REMOVE FROM US THE FEAR THAT KEEPS US CLOSED TO NEW ENCOUNTER.
Leader: Release us from the pain of all that we have done and failed to do.
ALL: FOR WE ARE YOUR PEOPLE, GOD, AND WE SEEK TO DO YOUR WILL. AMEN

Song: As a fire is meant for burning (CG) or As many stones (CG) or Come now, O Prince of Peace (CG) or Dignity and grace (CG)

Celebrating gifts: Participative action

This section can be structured in a variety of ways, for example:

- *Art materials could be made available for people to create images and colour as a celebration. Some direction will be needed in this case.*
- *There might be sharing in small groups of a gift of personality or ability from each person.*
- *People might be asked to bring to the occasion of the liturgy something they want to celebrate, for example a picture, a piece of fabric or clothing, food. Alternatively, a variety of objects could be provided for people to choose and to lay down in a central area; objects that somehow express or symbolise a certain aspect of their personality, or an important experience.*

Whichever action is chosen, there should be a gathering of the whole group and/or the images and symbols towards the end of the time together. This gathering could include:

- *Some silence to allow reflection on the experience, which can be followed by concluding words from the worship leader.*
- *Some free time of spoken reflection for voicing celebrations. The following words could be used by the whole gathering as a response to each statement:*

> ALL: WE CELEBRATE WITH YOU AND AFFIRM THE GIFTEDNESS OF OUR GOD-GIVEN LIVES.

Recessional song: You shall go out with joy (CG) or Mayenziwe (CG) or Sent by the Lord am I (CG) or Goodness is stronger than evil (TIOAU, LAA)

WITH ALL CREATION

WITH ALL CREATION

John Harrison

'We will not offer to God offerings that cost us nothing.' [1]

Words from the closing responses of the daily morning service in Iona Abbey. Easy to say; but not so easy to obey once we leave the confines of the church. Whether it is climate change, biodiversity, pollution, recycling, squandering of resources, animal welfare, or genetic modification, it is so easy to acknowledge that there is a problem, that we should be doing something about it, and then to do nothing or very little – certainly nothing that imposes a cost to our lifestyles, our time or our pockets. How many of us have reduced our fossil fuel energy usage over the past twelve months? How many of us have not switched to a 'green tariff' electricity supply because we believe it will cost more? How many of us have stopped buying goods that have been flown in, at great 'carbon cost', in favour of local produce? How many of us buy exclusively fairly traded goods, even if they are more 'costly' than other brands? How many of us are prepared to reject highly polluting and costly air travel for our holidays? To do any of these things would be at least a token acceptance of our responsibility to God's creation. It would be an offering to God that did not cost us nothing.

John Mead, in a recent article in *Green Christian*, the magazine of Christian Ecology Link, writes of 'Christian denial', with specific reference to climate change. But he also says that 'denial about climate change is just one manifestation of a much wider state of denial about our affluent culture as a whole'. He quotes the economist Herman Daly who refers to 'the enormous forces of denial' embodied in the cultural assumptions of rich societies. John Mead says that these are 'assumptions that have to be overcome before we can begin to live sustainably; that is, in ways which do not wreck the planet'.[2]

The liturgies here help to draw our attention to just a few of the challenging and often costly issues which we must face if we are to accept our responsibilities for the care of God's creation and turn aside from Christian denial. Let us not deny that there is a growing threat to planet Earth from our indiscriminate and greedy use of the precious resources God has provided. Let us in planning our worship try to find ways to inform others of the threat and what we and they can do to overcome it. And let us acknowledge our Christian responsibilities without the need for a reminder from a crowing cockerel. (Matthew 14:66–72)

Notes

[1] *Iona Abbey Worship Book*, Wild Goose Publications, 2001
[2] 'Climate Change: Unmasking Christian Denial', *Green Christian*, Issue 55, Summer 2004. www.christian-ecology.org.uk

CRUCIFIED EARTH:
A service of prayers for the environment, Iona Abbey 2000
Neil Paynter

'You see, there is no such thing as dead matter now. And Christ is the light of the whole world, spiritual and material. His crown of thorns is twined with every thorn. His cross is every tree.'
George MacLeod, Sermon in Stone

In the prophetic words of the campaigning group Earth First!: 'The earth is dying, it is being murdered and the people murdering it have names and addresses.'

I hear the dying cries of Jesus in the cement city, in the denuded countryside, when I turn on the TV news and see ragged, hungry children crawling over mountain ranges of garbage.

I heard the cries of Jesus one night and in response wrote this liturgy. I was watching the TV news and there was an apocalyptic image of a Brazilian rainforest burning. You could see it burning from outer space, they said. In only fifty years there wouldn't be any rainforest left. Rainforests are the 'lungs of the earth', a scientist said.

I thought of fatty hamburgers and herds of cattle giving off methane; I thought of wage slaves and the cheap little plastic toys they give out at fast-food restaurants; I thought of the legacy of Western culture; I thought of whole tribes being cut down, and thousands of precious, unknown species lost ... I thought of God watching his rainforest burn the same way he watched his only son being beaten and crucified. Suddenly the TV picture cut to the great statue of Jesus Christ that towers over Rio de Janeiro.

'Father, forgive them, they know not what they do,' I heard Jesus speak.

'And truly I say to you,' pronounced the TV anchorman, recapping the evening's news, 'as you did it to the least of these, so you did it to me.'

I remembered Earth Day, 1990, in Ottawa, Canada, where I lived at the time: children dancing in the summer sunshine on the front lawn of the Parliament buildings; the heady feeling in the air that we were finally going to get it together, that the environment was no longer going to take a back seat in the political agenda, that we would no longer sacrifice the earth for a 'healthy' economy. I remembered the speech by author, activist and prophet Farley Mowat. He stepped up to the microphone – then howled like a timber wolf. It was the most eloquent speech I'd ever heard. It said it all.

I remembered a couple thousand of us standing silently 'being trees'. For a minute it felt silly. Then the exercise became a profound meditation – people from all different beliefs and backgrounds were connected to a common cause; it felt like the environmental movement was really taking root. In the distance we could hear the city sound of automobiles, big business, power politics. It felt like we'd stepped out of the machine. It felt like we still had some time.

Later someone spoke about thousand-year-old redwood trees and heroic young people blocking logging roads; about the ancient, deep wisdom of First Nation peoples. Someone else said that involved in every action is a moral choice – that we needed to be more aware of our choices, that people had the power. It was up to us.

Recently, I read this:

'Jonathan Porritt, searching for the reasons why people do not take ecological issues seriously, said:

' "Simply, not enough people are dying yet in our Western countries: of skin cancer, of UV rays, or from pollution toxification illnesses. Nor are enough coastal communities drowning yet from rising sea-levels due to global warming. The visible, tangible, avoidable consequences of ecodisaster are not yet powerful enough to persuade sufficient people to change today's priorities."

'But they're dying in other places. They're dying in Nigeria and Brazil, they're dying in the Solomon Islands and Bangladesh. What kind of human beings are we?

'Is this what we are headed for in the West? Is our denial of reality so great, our denial of our finitude and the planet's finitude so strong that, having rolled back our boundaries so firmly over other people and species, having externalised our costs to such a degree, we have lost the ability to self-limit, and must wait for the limitations laid upon us by catastrophe and tragedy?' (Kathy Galloway)

Someone told me that this liturgy is 'theologically flawed', and that it is more pagan than Christian. Fine. Maybe the person is right.

I am so angry about what we are doing to the planet. So, call me a pagan or a pantheist. I don't care. I know what I feel in my heart and gut. Maybe you feel it too? We are crucifying this beautiful, precious, miracle of a planet.

The Earth is dying. Our sisters and brothers are dying. We need to turn our priorities upside down. We need to help to effect a revolution in consciousness. We need to start somewhere. There are so many good people everywhere who want to live differently, who want to live more gently and simply and more in harmony with God's creation. We are living in dark days. We have to get off our fat, complacent backsides. American technology won't save us all in the final reel. We won't colonise the planet Mars.

Through Jesus Christ, a new heaven and earth will be created (Isaiah 65:17; 66:22; 2 Peter 3:13; Revelation 21:1–5).

We are Christ's hands and feet in the world. Let's get working.

Before the service, sufficient candles for each member of the congregation are placed on the communion table or other central table, together with environmental campaign information and addresses for letter writing.

Introductory prayer

Invisible we see you, Christ beneath us.
With earthly eyes we see beneath us stones and dust
and dross, fit subjects for the analyst's table.
But with the eye of faith, we know you uphold.
In you all things consist and hang together:
> The very atom is light energy,
> The grass is vibrant,
> The rocks pulsate.
All is in flux; turn but a stone and an angel moves.

George MacLeod

Opening responses

Leader:	O God, who called all life into being,
ALL:	THE EARTH, SEA AND SKY ARE YOURS.
Leader:	Your presence is all around us,
ALL:	EVERY ATOM IS FULL OF YOUR ENERGY.
Leader:	Your Spirit enlivens all who walk the earth,
ALL:	WITH HER WE YEARN FOR JUSTICE TO BE DONE,
Leader:	For creation to be freed from bondage,
ALL:	FOR THE HUNGRY TO BE FED,
Leader:	For captives to be released,
ALL:	FOR YOUR KINGDOM OF PEACE TO COME ON EARTH.

Song: How great Thou art (CG)
(It will work well if the songs in this service are sung unaccompanied. This will help to give the worship a simple, stark, earthy feel.)

Scripture reading: The Crucifixion

John 19:1–16 and Matthew 27:32–50 and John 19:31–37 and Matthew 27:51–54, read slowly as a single narrative.

During the reading of the crucifixion – at about the point where Simon carries the cross – a member of the congregation carries a large wooden cross[1] from the nave of the church up the central aisle to the communion table, or otherwise to a central point in the worship space; the cross is hung with plastic carrier bags.

Litany of environmental abuse and degradation

Instances of environmental abuse and degradation current at the time of the service are read out. Newspapers, books and websites can be used to find timely examples. A Kyrie is sung after each voice.

For example:

Voice 1:   In January 2004 *The British Journal of Nature* reported that one million animal and plant species will disappear in the next fifty years if global temperature continues to rise at the present rate.

Kyrie eleison

Voice 2:   Around the world, natural forests are being cut down at the rate of 50 hectares a minute.[2]

Kyrie eleison ...

Prayer of confession

Christ, 'in you all things consist and hang together'.
You are alive and vibrant in the natural world.
You are in every tree, every flower,
in every living stone, in every person.
Forgive us for the ways in which we daily crucify you:
For the ways we strip and beat and flog you.
For the ways we bind you with fences and
pay you mock homage.
For the ways we spit on the ground of your being.
For the ways we offer you poisoned streams to drink.
For the ways we pierce your side with spears and
watch the blood and water run out.

For the way, when asked whom we serve,
we respond that we have no God,
and serve only the powers of the fallen world, crying:
'Crucify, crucify!'

Christ, your blood is on our hands.
Forgive us for the ways in which we daily betray you.
Forgive us, light and life of the world,
we know not what we do.

Time of silence

People are invited to consider ways by which they might live more in harmony with creation; more in communion with the earth. Ways are suggested: e.g. choosing less-packaged food, recycling more faithfully, using cars less often, saving water, becoming a supporter or a member of an environmental rights organisation ...

Action

People are invited to the communion table, or other central table, to light a candle (as a symbol of their commitment to be more aware of creation), and to take away the campaign information and addresses for letter writing.

Before the action the leader might read out the quote from the campaigning group Earth First!:

'The earth is dying, it is being murdered and the people murdering it have names and addresses.'

Affirmation: Psalm 8

ALL:	WONDERFUL GOD, CREATOR,
	THE WHOLE EARTH DECLARES YOUR GREATNESS.
A:	Your glory glows in the heavens.
	It is babbled by babies and sung by children.
B:	You are safe from all your enemies:
	those who oppose you are silenced.
A:	When I look at the sky which you have made,
	the moon and the stars that you set in place:
B:	Where do human beings fit in the pattern?
	What are we, that you care for us?
A:	You have made us only a little lower than yourself;
	and crowned us with glory and honour.
B:	You share with us responsibility
	to care for sheep and cattle, wild things, birds and fish,
	everything that lives in the sea:
	to work with you, within creation.
ALL:	WONDERFUL GOD, CREATOR,
	THE WHOLE EARTH DECLARES YOUR GREATNESS.

Prayers of intercession

A period of free and open prayer in which people are given space to pray for particular environmental concerns, e.g. global warming, peoples and countries suffering from environmental degradation, conflict over the Earth's resources, environmental disasters, species threatened with extinction. The response to each intercession might be: Christ in your mercy/ HEAR OUR PRAYER.

Prayers of thanksgiving and hope

(These prayers flow from the intercessions. This prayer could be shortened and the issues limited to connect with the issues raised in the litany of environmental abuse.)

Leader: God, we give thanks for those organisations and people who are working to heal and save the Earth.

Names are read out; some examples follow:

God bless Earth First!
God bless Friends of the Earth.
God bless Greenpeace.

God bless all who know the true value of the land
and who have the courage and faith to put themselves on the line:

God bless the brave women of the Chipko movement in India,
who halt commercial logging by hugging trees.

God bless the indigenous people of 'Sour Lake', who are taking the corporation Chevron Texaco to court for the millions of gallons of spilled oil Texaco is charged with leaving in Ecuador after they stopped drilling there in the 1990s. May the indigenous peoples of the world be listened to and win justice.

God bless the Greenbelt movement in Kenya, and Wangari Maathai, winner of the Nobel Peace Prize in 2004. God bless the people of the 'South World', who are teaching the people of the North World what is truly valuable.

God bless the World Wildlife Fund, and all organisations working to save endangered and vulnerable species and to protect biodiversity.

God bless the Nigerian activist Odigha Odigha, who, in the face of much resistance and intimidation, has worked to protect Nigeria's rainforest, the home of 1.5 million people, primates, plants, rare butterflies.

God bless development organisations like Oxfam, Christian Aid, CAFOD ... working to aid victims of conflict over scarce resources and environmental degradation.

God bless all those groups campaigning for safe, clean drinking water.

God bless individuals like Von Hernandez of the Philippines, whose campaigning efforts achieved the world's first nationwide ban on waste incinerators.

God bless aboriginal elders Eileen Kampakuta Brown and Eileen Wani Wingfield, who are campaigning to block the construction of a nuclear waste dump in their homeland.

God bless all artists – writers, photographers, film-makers, painters, musicians – who use their talents and vision to move people to wonder and to action.

God bless prophetic publications like *Resurgence* magazine and *The New Internationalist* ...

God bless everyone who is working to recycle more and to consume less – all who are 'thinking globally and acting locally'.

God bless local environmental initiatives ... *(Name some of these.)*

God bless those who are working to set up environmentally sustainable businesses.

God bless the anti-capitalist and anti-globalisation movement and the prophets of our time *(Read out some names, e.g. Vandana Shiva, Satish Kumar ...)*

God bless all who are rejecting consumerism
and a life based on the incessant consumption of the Earth's finite resources –
a life based on throwing things and people away.

God bless all who are trying to 'live more simply so that others may simply live'.
God bless all who are working for change,
and who, as Jesus did, face ridicule, threats, violence, crucifixion.

Scripture reading: Luke 24:1–11 or Romans 8:18–25

Leader: God, we often find it difficult to recognise signs of your kingdom, to believe that things are in any way getting better.
God, open our eyes; give us hope for this planet and ourselves ...

God, we give thanks now for good news and signs of hope:

Good news items from newspapers, magazines and websites are read out; some examples follow:

Voice 1:   For news of the passing of improved air quality laws and targets in Mexico City, and in the Guangdong province in China.
Voice 2:   For the Bolivian government's 'gift to the earth' of three wetlands, home of hundreds of species of animals and plants.
Voice 3:   For recent measures to help protect Australia's Great Barrier Reef.

Voice 4:	For the hopeful news that the Great Lakes, the world's largest fresh water system, are beginning to purify themselves.
Voice 5:	For news that humpback whales in the South Pacific and sea lions in Alaska are making a comeback.
Voice 6:	For increased research and use of safer, more environmentally friendly energy sources.

Space for prayers of thanks for good news from the congregation.

Song: Oh the life of the world (CG)

Closing prayer *(said together)*

O CHRIST, THERE IS NO PLANT IN THE GROUND
BUT IS FULL OF YOUR VIRTUE.
THERE IS NO FORM IN THE STRAND
BUT IT IS FULL OF YOUR BLESSING.
THERE IS NO LIFE IN THE SEA,
THERE IS NO CREATURE IN THE OCEAN,
THERE IS NOTHING IN THE HEAVENS
BUT PROCLAIMS YOUR GOODNESS.
THERE IS NO BIRD ON THE WING,
THERE IS NO STAR IN THE SKY,
THERE IS NOTHING BENEATH THE SUN
BUT PROCLAIMS YOUR GOODNESS.
AMEN

Blessing

Deep peace of the running wave to you,
deep peace of the flowing air to you,
deep peace of the quiet earth to you,
deep peace of the shining stars to you,
deep peace of the Son of Peace to you.

Notes

[1] On Iona the cross was made from driftwood.
[2] Information from World Wildlife Fund.

FOOTPRINTS IN THE COSMOS

John Harrison

This liturgy uses the symbol of footprints to represent the impact of human action upon the Earth, its climate and its resources. The service draws upon the concept of the 'ecological footprint' found in the worldwide campaigning movement for environmental awareness and action.[1]

For this service you will need cardboard cut-outs of human footprints of three different sizes to reflect the footprint (impact) of:

- *The United States: cut from a cardboard rectangle 1740 x 680 millimetres.*
- *The United Kingdom: cut from a cardboard rectangle 910 x 360 millimetres.*
- *A sustainable use of resources: cut from a cardboard rectangle 270 x 110 millimetres.*

These footprints are laid out in a trail around the worship space with symbols of creation and of the beauty of the earth placed at points along the trail – shells, piles of stones, branches, leaves, pine cones …

One footprint of each size is kept by the leader for use during the reflection.

Opening responses *(based on Sirach/Ecclesiasticus 51:13–20)*

Leader:	Before I set out on my journey, I sought Wisdom in my prayer;
ALL:	AND I WILL SEARCH FOR HER UNTIL THE END.
Leader:	From the first blossom to the ripening grape:
ALL:	MY HEART HAS DELIGHTED IN WISDOM.
Leader:	From my youth I have followed Wisdom's gentle footprint;
ALL:	AND SO MY FEET WALK UPON THE STRAIGHT PATH.
Leader:	In the footsteps of Wisdom I learn understanding,
ALL:	AND CALL ON GOD, WHO WILL NEVER ABANDON ME.

Song: Sing praise to God (LFB)

Scripture reading: Deuteronomy 8:6–10

Reflection

Voice 1:	God created the Earth beautiful and whole and entrusted it to our care, giving its gifts for our delight.

Voice 2:   But the footprints of humanity have damaged the Earth:
resources destroyed,
forests cut down,
oceans polluted,
the ozone layer torn and the atmosphere warming.
We are changing the climate and ransoming the future.

(Pause)

Voice 1:   Not all humanity treads with a heavy footfall.
Some of us wear hobnailed boots,
while others walk barefoot.
If we were all to use resources sustainably and equitably,
our ecological footprint would not damage the Earth.

The smallest of the three cut-out footprints is held up for all to see and then laid in the centre of the worship space.

Voice 3:   It is the wealthy countries whose footprints are damaging the Earth.
If all the world were to live as the United Kingdom,
we would need the resources of three planets like Earth to sustain our lifestyle.

The middle-sized of the three cut-out footprints is held up for all to see and then laid in the centre of the worship space.

Voice 1:   Heavy footfall.

(Pause)

Voice 3:   If all the world were to live like the United States,
we would need the resources of six planets like Earth to sustain our lifestyle.

The largest of the three cut-out footprints is held up for all to see and then laid in the centre of the worship space.

Voice 1:   Hobnailed boots ... Now, let's hear about the state of Kerala in India:[2]

Voice 4:   Kerala, by our standards and values, is one of the poorest states in India. Yet the infant mortality rate is lower than in much of Europe; life expectancy is 72 years; 95 percent of those over 7 years old can read and write; and a higher proportion of its population has postgraduate degrees than in the USA. And Kerala's ecological footprint – that is, the productive

Voice 1: land and sea necessary to support its lifestyle – is at a sustainable level well below the world's average.

Voice 1: How did Kerala achieve all this? ... They made a choice. A choice as a society: to put people before profit, fairness before riches, and care for the Earth before resource exploitation.

Voice 4: The people of Kerala make a tiny footprint.

If all the world were to live like Kerala,

there would be more than enough resources for all;

our planet would be safeguarded, its environment restored.

Voice 1: The lightest of treads.

Scripture reading: Isaiah 24:4–6a

Prayer of confession

Leader: O God, your fertile earth is slowly being stripped of its riches,

ALL: OPEN OUR EYES TO SEE.

Leader: O God, your living waters are slowly being choked with chemicals,

ALL: OPEN OUR EYES TO SEE.

Leader: O God, your clear air is slowly being filled with pollutants,

ALL: OPEN OUR EYES TO SEE.

Leader: O God, your creatures are slowly dying and your people are suffering,

ALL: OPEN OUR EYES TO SEE.

Leader: God our maker, so move us by the wonder of your creation,

ALL: THAT WE REPENT AND CARE MORE DEEPLY.

Leader: So move us to grieve the loss of life,

ALL: THAT WE LEARN TO WALK WITH GENTLE FOOTFALL UPON YOUR WORLD.

Song: Touch the earth lightly (CG)

Meditative action

The congregation are invited to walk slowly and prayerfully around the footprint trail, as a sign of their commitment to live more sustainably and to reduce their ecological footprint in the world. Quiet music might be played during this time. (If possible, it would be powerful to follow the footprint trail outside, and to continue the service there, under trees or stars or on God's good earth.)

Prayer of intercession

Voice 1:   Creator God, take our feet off the path of destruction. Help us to treasure and conserve the resources of the Earth. Help us to share your bounty fairly.

Teach us in the rich nations to live more simply. Take away our greed. May we use only what we need and not continue, in our arrogance and power, to take whatever we want.

May we learn from the people of Kerala that happiness and well-being are not to be found in more things and in unending economic growth, but in treading the path of justice and fairness.

Creating God, you have given us a vision of a new heaven and a new earth …

Voice 2:   resources conserved
Voice 3:   earth tended
Voice 2:   atmosphere cleansed
Voice 3:   trees planted
Voice 2:   injustice ended
Voice 3:   oceans teeming
Voice 4:   nations at peace.

Voice 1:   Creator, Redeemer, Sustainer
Voice 2:   alert nations, enthuse churches,
Voice 3:   receive our commitment and so entwine our lives with your purpose
Voice 4:   earth and heaven will then sing of your glory

Song: Sara shriste (You are author and Lord of creation) (MAG)

Closing responses

Leader: The Earth does not belong to us.
ALL: WE BELONG TO THE EARTH.
Leader: All things are connected and interdependent.
ALL: LIKE THE BLOOD THAT UNITES A FAMILY.
Leader: We did not weave the web of life.
ALL: WE ARE MERELY A STRAND IN IT.
Leader: Whatever we do to the web,
ALL: WE DO TO OURSELVES AND TO OUR DESCENDANTS.
Leader: Let us give thanks for God's gift of creation.
ALL: WE GIVE THANKS THAT ALL THINGS ARE HELD TOGETHER IN CHRIST.

Blessing *(said together)*

Bless to us, O God,
the earth beneath our feet.
Bless to us, O God,
the path whereon we go.
Bless to us, O God,
the people whom we meet.
Amen

Alternative songs

Other songs from the Wild Goose Resource Group that would be suitable for this service include: While Earth remains (OITB) and We will not take what is not ours (LAA).

Notes

[1] The concept of the ecological footprint is found in 'Ecological Footprints – the rich wear big boots' in *The Little Earth Book*, James Bruges, Alastair Sawday Publishing, 2000, ISBN 1 901970 23 X. It is also found in many other publications.

[2] Information about Kerala is found in 'Ecological Footprints – the rich wear big boots' op. cit. Also *New Internationalist* magazine, Issue 241, March 1993. Alternatively, another appropriate country, state or community could be used as an example at this point in the liturgy, using the knowledge and experience of those preparing for worship.

WHAT A WASTE!
A liturgy of commitment

John Harrison

Before the service, a big pile of household refuse is tipped into the centre of the worship space. (Cans, plastic, etc, should be clean, and only raw food that can be easily and safely picked up, such as cauliflower leaves or banana skins, should be included.) A number of large containers (see-through if possible) are placed around the edges of the pile. The containers are labelled 'Plastic', 'Glass', 'Cans', 'Compost', 'Paper', 'Electrical goods' and 'Other'.

Scripture reading: Genesis 1:1–13

Opening responses

Leader:	Creator God,
	in whose image we are made and
	in whose sight everyone and everything are precious,
ALL:	WE ARE HERE TO PRAISE AND SERVE YOU.
Leader:	Redeeming God,
	by whose grace we are renewed,
ALL:	WE ARE HERE TO PRAISE AND SERVE YOU.
Leader:	Sustaining Spirit,
	by whose love all creation is embraced,
ALL:	WE ARE HERE TO PRAISE AND SERVE YOU.
Leader:	Creative, redeeming, sustaining God,
	your world is miraculous and wonderful;
	your love for us is amazing.
ALL:	LET US SING ALOUD IN PRAISE OF OUR CREATOR.

Song: Come and let us worship God (OITB)

Scripture reading: Matthew 14:15–20 (The feeding of the five thousand)

Reflection

Voice 1:   God's precious creation. Used well. Shared. Treasured. Savoured. The left-overs carefully collected up. When we listen to this story, we focus on the miraculous feeding of so many people from such a small offering, and marvel at the number of baskets filled with recovered scraps. But what else was Jesus showing us? What example was he setting? What was he

	saying about the way we should care for God's precious creation?
Voice 2:	Every hour of every day in Britain enough waste is generated to fill the Albert Hall.[1]
Voice 3:	The municipal waste collection vehicle clatters along the road. Workers scuttle from house to house dragging wheely bins, feeding the contents into the chasm of the vehicle's stomach. Later today another landfill will be stuffed full.
Voice 4:	Can nothing be recycled?
Voice 1:	Household waste, consumer goods …
Voice 2:	New styles, fashions, fads –
Voice 3:	Bought one minute then discarded the next.
Voice 4:	Within 6 weeks of sale, 90% of the material used in producing or contained within consumer goods becomes waste. [2] Why don't we recycle?
Voice 1:	Throw-away society.
Voice 3:	Supermarket workers bustle from shelf to shelf, from cool cabinet to cool cabinet, removing all the date-expired goods. Can't send them to charities any more. Fear of litigation. Throw it away, for safety's sake. And all the packaging too.
Voice 4:	Can nothing be recycled?
Voice 2:	Landfill sites. Scrapheaps.
Voice 3:	Crumpled cars piled on crumpled cars. Rusting metal, dripping oil, leaking brake fluid, oozing grease. Cars, cars, cars. MOT failures, write-offs, discards for a newer model. Soon to be crushed beyond any recognition and use.
ALL:	HOW MUCH WILL BE RECYCLED?

Prayer of confession

Leader:	God, forgive us. 81% of our rubbish goes into landfill sites.[3] Landfill sites that give off greenhouse gases (which contribute to global warming) and create toxic fluids that seep into the groundwater. For our carelessness with your creation:
ALL:	NURTURING GOD, HAVE MERCY, FORGIVE AND CHANGE US.
Leader:	God, forgive us. We rely more and more on incineration to solve our waste disposal problems[4], yet our increased use of incineration creates toxic ash[5] and fills our air with poisons. For our carelessness with your creation:
ALL:	NURTURING GOD, HAVE MERCY, FORGIVE AND CHANGE US.
Leader:	God, forgive us.

We could recycle 80% of our rubbish,
but currently we only recycle 11%.[6]
For our carelessness with your creation:

ALL: NURTURING GOD, HAVE MERCY, FORGIVE AND CHANGE US.

Song: God of new beginnings (OITB)

Action

The congregation are invited to join together in a symbolic action as a sign of their commitment to recycle more.

They are invited to pick up a few items from the pile of household rubbish in the centre of the worship space, and to place them in the appropriate labelled containers for recycling.

After the action is completed the leader points out that all the bins contain items – except the empty container labelled 'Other'.

Prayer

Voice 1:   Creator God, open our hearts to the wonder and preciousness of your world. Help us to see its true value and to be good stewards of creation.

Voice 2:   Redeeming Christ, change our attitudes and priorities; be with us as we strive to follow your example.

Voice 3:   Sustaining Spirit, support and strengthen us as we campaign for grass-roots issues such as recycling, issues that are the basis of a gentler, more sustainable lifestyle.

ALL: TRANSFORM US, TRIUNE GOD, AND LEAD US INTO ACTION.

Song: Don't tell me of a faith that fears (LAA)

Closing responses

Leader: This is the day that God has made;
ALL: WE WILL REJOICE AND BE GLAD IN IT.
Leader: We will not offer to God;
ALL: OFFERINGS THAT COST US NOTHING.
Leader: Go in peace to love and to serve;
ALL: WE WILL SEEK PEACE AND PURSUE IT.
Leader: In the name of the Trinity of love;
ALL: GOD IN COMMUNITY, HOLY AND ONE.
         AMEN

Sung blessing: Now go in peace (CG)

Notes

[1] Information from *Earthmatters* magazine, issue 50, autumn 2001.

[2] Information from 'Go M.A.D.', *Ecologist* magazine, 2nd edition, 2003. (The title is an abbreviation for 'go make a difference'.)

[3] Information from the Centre for Alternative Technology.

[4] Information from the Centre for Alternative Technology.

[5] Information from *Green Homes Handbook*, FOE Scotland, 1996 and *Earthmatters* magazine, issue 49, summer 2001. Incineration leaves 15–35% of total volume as highly toxic ash that has to be disposed of elsewhere.

[6] Information from 'Go M.A.D.', *Ecologist* magazine, 2nd edition, 2003 and *Sustainable Development Indicators in Your Pocket 2004*, DEFRA publications, 2004.

ENGAGED COMMUNITY

ENGAGED COMMUNITY

Brian Woodcock

You might think spirituality is the opposite of worldliness. In a sense it is, for it is neither materialistic nor earthbound. Its language is imaginative and poetic. It comes from the heart and speaks to the soul. Its kingdom is not of this world. So people tend to pursue it in places far removed from their everyday lives.

Yet it was on Iona, the most remote place in which I have ever lived, that I came across the expression 'engaged spirituality'. And engaged spirituality is certainly not about getting away from it at all. Or if it is, it is about getting away just long enough to be propelled back into the thick of it.

Engaged spirituality goes to the very heart of Christianity. To the Incarnation. To God revealed amid the ordinariness and suffering of our world. In Jesus. In all human life. In everything God has made and called good. If it takes a remote island to bring this home to us, that's fine – provided we *do* take it home.

Whatever it is that drives so many pilgrims to this ancient Hebridean island, Iona Abbey offers no escape route from the conflicts of the world. Its worship continually focuses on the issues of our lives and times. It also focuses on God of course, but that is not necessarily so different. The line between heaven and earth can be very thin there. Because the island is a heavenly place, some say. But also because the Iona Community has a particularly earthy view of the Faith. Its members are dispersed around the country and in other parts of the world, connecting work and worship, prayer and politics, as they try to rebuild community.

The worship resources from the Abbey in this section are a typical example. They were a response to a specific situation: the invasion of Iraq. The suggested readings came not from some sacred vacuum but from real situations of their own time.

With Corrymeela it is more visible. Northern Ireland is compact. The issues are clearer, and well known. Corrymeela is a community of reconciliation, courageously challenging the forces of division, violence and prejudice. Though the centre is in a beautiful setting, it is accessible to all who want to use it, and has been dangerously close to the violence. Litanies about accepting one another's gifts, and affirming differences, have an edge about them.

For the L'Arche Community worship is a natural part of the life of the houses where people with special needs and their helpers form community together. The liturgy offered here uses a simple physical act as the basis of a meaningful service for all levels of understanding. It is an expression of mutual caring within trusting relationships that is common to all L'Arche groupings. But there is also something subversive about this service. It confronts the Church's failure to achieve inter-communion. The doctrinal subtleties that prevent Christians sharing Communion together make little sense to people with the needs and gifts of this community. So they replace the bread and wine with bowl and towel in an act that remains undeniably a sacrament, with similar format and wording.

If Iona, Corrymeela and L'Arche bring worship and issues ever closer together, Camas removes the divide altogether. The two become one. Set worship disappears completely; life takes over. To many Camas guests, the words, symbols and formality of the church are alien. Shared reflection must arise from the guests themselves, when they are ready, with their words and their symbols. They literally share themselves – their struggles and their dreams.

Camas cannot provide us with worship resources to use elsewhere. Strictly speaking, nor can the other centres if it is *engaged* spirituality we are talking about. Much of what is offered here would at least have to be adapted. Engaged spirituality is very specific. It engages with *our* lives and concerns. If we want our worship to connect with our own lives, localities and times, we really have to write it ourselves. Or with one another. What we find in these pages are ideas to help us do just that.

In the end I am not sure that engaged spirituality is about services of worship at all. Engaged spirituality is actually the spirituality of the events *themselves*. It is what happens when we come out of our services, churches and spiritual centres, and see the real world in a new way. Engaged spirituality is the spirituality of work, of politics, of bereavement, of sharing a meal. It is discovering God in the common life. As George MacLeod saw Iona Abbey gradually returning to its former glory, he put it this way in one of his prayers:

> *Take us outside, O Lord, outside holiness,*
> *out to where soldiers curse and nations clash*
> *at the crossroads of the world.*
> *So may this building be justified.*

AN ACT OF COMMITMENT TO A COMMON WORK OF RECONCILIATION

The Corrymeela Community

The Corrymeela Community is a dispersed community of people of all ages and Christian traditions who, individually and together, are committed to the healing of social, religious and political divisions in Northern Ireland and throughout the world.

This liturgy is sometimes used on Monday mornings at the Corrymeela centres and at the beginning of a new work week during the summer programme. It is also suitable for any time of rededication, and whenever supporters of the work of Corrymeela are gathered.

This liturgy might be adapted for use by any engaged Christian community.

Before the worship begins cards bearing the names of all those working at the Centre, or all those involved in the group that is meeting, are placed on a central table. As people enter the worship space they are invited to take one or more of the cards.

Opening responses

Leader: 'There are different gifts, but it is the same Lord who is served through them all.'
Welcome to this worship at the beginning of a new week.
As we meet together, we listen to God's message.
We seek God's guidance and help in the days ahead.

ALL: WE RECOMMIT OURSELVES TO BECOMING INSTRUMENTS OF GOD'S PEACE.

Scripture reading

The following suggested readings are drawn from a list of Bible passages designed to help see the work of Corrymeela in the context of God's purposes and the way of love revealed by Jesus and found in the common life of his followers:

Isaiah 42:1–9
Matthew 5:13–16
Luke 6:27–31; 32–36
Acts 2:43–47
1 Corinthians 13
Ephesians 4:1–6

Colossians 3:12–15 or 17
1 John 4:7–12

Reflection

A short reading, poem or meditation that brings out some of the thoughts in the scripture reading; or invite people to reflect silently on a few words from the reading and to hear its meaning for them at that moment.

Prayers for others and ourselves

To begin the time of prayer all are asked to pray silently for those whose names are on the cards that they received when they came into the room.

Leader: We pray for all those at the centre during the past week.
            Pause
            God, welcomer of all
ALL: HEAR OUR PRAYER.
Leader: We pray for all those expected to come in the week ahead
            and for all those who for whatever reason may arrive unexpectedly with
            us.
            Pause
            God, welcomer of all
ALL: HEAR OUR PRAYER.
Leader: We pray for each other.
            Pause
            God, welcomer of all
ALL: HEAR OUR PRAYER.
Leader: We pray for any other special needs or concerns.
            Pause
            God, we trust to your love all those for whom we have prayed through
            Jesus Christ our Lord.
ALL: AMEN

Litany of dedication

Leader: As we begin another week's work, let us remember our need for each
            other and the importance of all the roles we fulfil.
ALL: THERE ARE DIFFERENT GIFTS, BUT IT IS THE SAME SPIRIT
            WHO GIVES THEM.
            THERE ARE DIFFERENT WAYS OF SERVING GOD, BUT IT IS THE SAME
            LORD WHO IS SERVED.

GOD WORKS THROUGH DIFFERENT PEOPLE IN DIFFERENT WAYS,
BUT GOD'S PURPOSE IS ACHIEVED THROUGH THEM ALL.
FOR EACH ONE IS GIVEN A GIFT BY THE SPIRIT TO USE FOR THE
COMMON GOOD,
AND IT IS ONLY TOGETHER THAT WE CAN BE THE BODY OF CHRIST.

Leader: Though we have different gifts, together we are a community of reconciliation led by Christ. In his name let us dedicate all of our work to the service of God.

ALL: JESUS THE SERVANT, USE US IN YOUR SERVICE,
GIVING US WISDOM AND COURAGE TO FOLLOW WHERE YOU LEAD,
SO THAT IN ALL THAT WE SAY AND DO WE MAY SPREAD YOUR PEACE IN
THE WORLD.
AMEN

The Prayer of Saint Francis of Assisi *(said together)*

Lord, make us instruments of your peace:
where there is hatred, let us sow love,
where there is injury, pardon,
where there is doubt, faith,
where there is despair, hope,
where there is darkness, light,
where there is sadness, joy.
O divine Master, grant that we may not so much seek
to be consoled as to console,
to be understood as to understand,
to be loved as to love;
for it is in giving that we receive,
in pardoning that we are pardoned,
and in dying that we are born to eternal life.
Amen

Song: Now go in peace (CG 91) or Sent by the Lord (CG 105) or Singing, we gladly worship (CG 114)

Closing responses

Leader: Let us go in peace
ALL: AND MAY THE PEACE OF CHRIST PASS FROM US TO ALL THOSE WE MEET.
AMEN

WORSHIP IN A TIME OF WAR:
Worship resources from Iona
Resident group of the Iona Community

In the days immediately before the United States and the United Kingdom went to war on Iraq in March 2003, the resident staff group working for the Iona Community at the centres of hospitality on Iona felt compelled to prepare some relevant liturgical material as a response to the situation. The following material was used in Iona Abbey and was distributed to guests and day visitors to Iona.

The Iona Community Justice and Peace Commitment states the Community's belief:

- That the Gospel commands us to seek peace founded on justice and that costly reconciliation is at the heart of the Gospel.
- That work for justice, peace and an equitable society is a matter of extreme urgency.
- That everyone should have the quality and dignity of a full life that requires adequate physical, social and political opportunity, without the oppression of poverty, injustice and fear.
- That the use or threatened use of nuclear and other weapons of mass destruction is theologically and morally indefensible and that opposition to their existence is an imperative of the Christian faith.

Suggested scripture readings

Jeremiah 6:13–15a
Micah 4:3–4
Luke 10:25–37
Romans 12:14–21
Philippians 4·4–7
Colossians 3:9–15

Prayer of confession

Leader: God, who made the atom and the ocean,
you see the way that small things,
small movements and small intentions,
come together in the crashing waves of the sea
and the crashing waves of men and machines at war.
Forgive us that we have set our feet
on the road which leads to war.

ALL:	FORGIVE US AND TURN US BACK.
Leader:	Each time we harboured fear and hatred of the people of Iraq, even those who were seeking our protection, we took a step along the road.
ALL:	FORGIVE US AND TURN US BACK.
Leader:	Each time that we consumed and wasted the natural resources of your earth, we stepped closer to the oilfields of the East.
ALL:	FORGIVE US AND TURN US BACK.
Leader:	Each time that we failed to caution our leaders; in our own voices, to ask the questions in our hearts, we advanced further towards destruction.
ALL:	FORGIVE US AND TURN US BACK.
Leader:	Each time that we believe that we are superior, that what is other is evil, we bring within our sights the men, women and children like us, who will feel our anger.
ALL:	FORGIVE US AND TURN US BACK.
Leader:	Forgive us that we have come so far down the road and help us, even at this late hour, to turn back.
ALL:	AMEN

Prayers of concern

We hold before God in prayer the following groups of people caught up in the present situation:

(Pause)

We pray for all leaders and decision-makers at a national and international level. Speak to them, God, with your wisdom, compassion and restraint.

(Silence)

We pray for the thousands of ordinary people affected by fear or filled with a sense of outrage, that their voices may be heard. At this time we pray especially for the people in Iraq and the surrounding region.

(Silence)

We pray for those whose livelihoods depend on the design, manufacture and deployment of weapons. May alternative uses be found for their skills; may they be kept in work that does not lead to war.

(Silence)

We pray for the intelligence-gatherers – those you have trusted with knowledge, who have access to the 'truth' when we are often confused by conflicting information. Give them insight and discernment.

(Silence)

We pray for those working in the media, that their influence may be positive, rather than feeding fear and prejudice.

(Silence)

We pray for Jew and Arab, Christian and Muslim, rich and poor, empowered and powerless; for an end to bitterness and vengeance, for reconciliation and understanding.

A call to commitment and action

Dear God,
as we think of Jesus
we think not just of prayer and quiet retreat
but of a life of action,
of tables overturned,
of lives touched and healed,
endless walks through arid deserts to the next place of hurt and need.

And as we consider our troubled, torn planet,
even now on the brink of yet more
death and destruction,
stir us, we pray, to work, and to work
for the transforming of this beautiful world.

And for justice for those oppressed by tyrants.
And for justice for those whose lives, even now,
are blighted by endless forgotten wars.

Give us wisdom, guide our actions.
Make us fearless and passionate
for the earth
and all its suffering people.
Amen

A SERVICE OF THE WASHING OF FEET

L'Arche Community

This service was contributed by the Liverpool community of L'Arche, who use it regularly in their community, and who shared it in Iona Abbey during their visit in 1998.

The original celebration liturgy of the washing of the feet was written by an ecumenical group commissioned by the International Council of L'Arche. It was used for an interdenominational retreat in Belfast in 1996 and it served as an inspiration for a service of the World Council of Churches in Geneva in 1997 and the Lambeth Conference of bishops of the Anglican Communion in 1998.

'L'Arche is an international federation of communities for people with learning disabilities and assistants. Whatever their gifts or limitations, people are all bound together in a common humanity. Everyone is of unique and sacred value and everyone has the same dignity and the same rights. The fundamental rights of each person include the rights to life, to care, to a home, to education and to work. Since the deepest need of a human being is to love and to be loved, each person has a right to friendship, to communion and to a spiritual life.' *(From L'Arche website)*

Carrying the Bible

The service begins with the carrying of the Bible into the worship space by two people, accompanied by the celebrant.

Scripture reading: John 13:12–14

Chant: Veni Sancte Spiritus (Taizé)

Opening responses

Celebrant: But now in Christ Jesus you who were far off have been brought near by the blood of Christ. (*Ephesians 2:13*)
ALL: CHRIST IS OUR PEACE.
Celebrant: Christ makes us one and has broken down the dividing wall of hostility. (*Ephesians 2:14*)
ALL: CHRIST IS OUR PEACE.
Celebrant: He emptied himself, taking the form of a servant. *(Philippians 2:7)*
ALL: CHRIST IS OUR PEACE.
Celebrant: In a world that empties human life of meaning,
    we are called to a vision of humanity restored to fullness

through welcome and covenant.

ALL: CHRIST IS OUR PEACE.

Celebrant: In a world devoured by despair,
we are called to live and proclaim the Good News.

ALL: CHRIST IS OUR PEACE.

Celebrant: In a world where many forces deter us from obeying the voice of Christ,
we are called to be faithful to our call.

ALL: CHRIST IS OUR PEACE.

Celebrant: In a world of division and discord, we are called to oneness.

ALL: CHRIST IS OUR PEACE.

(Silence)

Prayer of confession

Celebrant: Almighty God, we have sinned against you, our neighbours, all humanity
and the whole created order.

We have let pride, negligence, ignorance and wilful disobedience get in
the way of your love.

We have closed our hearts to those around us, especially to the weak
and poor.

We have allowed our differences to mar our relationship with you and
with each other.

We have hurt one another in thought, word and deed.

We have denied our need for transformation and change.

For all the suffering and pain that indifference, resentment and prejudice
have caused,

ALL: KYRIE ELEISON.

Celebrant: For the pride that has prevented forgiveness, understanding and openness to each other,

ALL: KYRIE ELEISON.

Celebrant: For the times we failed to see the beauty in the other,
For the times we failed to listen to the other,
For the times we failed to talk with the other,

ALL: KYRIE ELEISON.

Celebrant: For the violence we do to each other, which spills into our world,

ALL: KYRIE ELEISON.

Celebrant: For our greed and selfishness that causes many to fear this and every
night alone: hopeless, homeless, insecure, hungry, fearful, confused or
locked up in institutions,

ALL: KYRIE ELEISON.

Assurance of forgiveness

So if anyone is in Christ, there is a new creation: everything old has passed away; see, everything has become new! All this is from God, who reconciled us to himself through Christ, and has given us the ministry of reconciliation; that is, in Christ God was reconciling the world to himself, not counting their trespasses against them, and entrusting the message of reconciliation to us. *(2 Corinthians 5:17–19)*

Scripture readings

Isaiah 58:6–12
Philippians 2:5–11
John 13:1–17

A sung Alleluia may be used before and after the Gospel reading.

Homily

Creed *(based on the Nicene Creed)*

Celebrant: Do you believe and trust in God, the Father, who made the world?
ALL: I BELIEVE IN GOD, THE FATHER ALMIGHTY, CREATOR OF HEAVEN AND EARTH.
Celebrant: Do you believe and trust in his Son Jesus Christ, who redeemed humankind?
ALL: I BELIEVE IN JESUS CHRIST, HIS ONLY SON OUR LORD.
             HE WAS CONCEIVED BY THE POWER OF THE HOLY SPIRIT AND BORN OF THE VIRGIN MARY.
             HE SUFFERED UNDER PONTIUS PILATE, WAS CRUCIFIED, DIED AND WAS BURIED.
             HE DESCENDED TO THE DEAD.
             ON THE THIRD DAY HE ROSE AGAIN.
             HE ASCENDED INTO HEAVEN, AND IS SEATED AT THE RIGHT HAND OF THE FATHER.
             HE WILL COME AGAIN TO JUDGE THE LIVING AND THE DEAD.
Celebrant: Do you believe and trust in his Holy Spirit, who gives life to the people of God?
ALL: I BELIEVE IN THE HOLY SPIRIT, THE HOLY UNIVERSAL CHURCH, THE COMMUNION OF SAINTS, THE FORGIVENESS OF SINS, THE RESURREC-TION OF THE BODY, AND LIFE EVERLASTING.
             AMEN
Celebrant: This is the faith of the Church.

ALL: THIS IS OUR FAITH.

               WE BELIEVE AND TRUST IN ONE GOD, FATHER, SON AND HOLY SPIRIT.

Prayer of intercession

Reader 1:   Today Christians from different churches cannot eat around the same table of the broken bread, transformed into the body of Christ.

               But we can eat together around the table that welcomes the broken, the poor and the weak.

               Today Christians from different churches cannot drink from the same chalice of the blood of Christ.

               But we and all our brothers and sisters in Christ can drink together from the same chalice of suffering, of division, of anguish in our Church, our country and our world.

               Together we can pour out the sweet oil of compassion upon the wounds of humanity.

               We pray that unity will come.

ALL: AMEN, COME LORD JESUS!

Reader 2:   Come through the treasure of your holy word,

               sharper than a two-edged sword

               that pierces into us, cleansing us from all shame and deceit.

ALL: AMEN, COME LORD JESUS!

Reader 3:   Come through the treasure of your body broken, risen, strengthening, nurturing that we know in the Eucharist.

ALL: AMEN, COME LORD JESUS!

Reader 4:   Come through the treasure of our own weakness, vulnerability and pain.

               Come through all our brothers and sisters in L'Arche.

               Come through our differences and in those we see as an enemy.

ALL: AMEN, COME LORD JESUS!

Reader 5:   Come then, as you came among your disciples to wash their feet.

               Send your Holy Spirit upon us

               that we who seek your grace may live by your power.

ALL: AMEN, COME LORD JESUS!

Song

Prayer before the washing of the feet

The first part of this prayer is based on Philippians 2:3–11 and the central section on John 13.

Celebrant: All powerful and ever-living God,

               we do well always and everywhere to give you thanks,

through Jesus Christ our Lord.
You sent your Son to live among us,
so that we might learn from him humility and obedience.
His nature was divine, yet he did not cling to equality with God,
but emptied himself to assume the condition of a slave.
He became as we are and was humbler yet,
accepting death, even death on a cross.
But you, Father, raised him high, and gave him a name
that is above all names,
so that we can acclaim 'Jesus is Lord' to your honour and glory,
and join with the whole company of heaven and earth saying:
Holy, holy, holy Lord,
God of power and might.
Heaven and earth are full of your glory.
Hosanna in the highest.
Blessed is he who comes in the name of the Lord.
Hosanna in the highest.
Ever-loving God, we thank you for the great gift of Jesus your Son,
for the example he gave us of love and service,
for his promise to be with those who love and follow him.
Having loved his own, he loved them to the end.
On the night before he gave his life for us,
knowing that you had put everything into his hands,
he met with his disciples and gave them his new commandment:

ALL: LOVE ONE ANOTHER AS I HAVE LOVED YOU.

Celebrant: Getting up from table, he took a towel and water, washed his disciples'
              feet, and said:

ALL: I HAVE GIVEN YOU AN EXAMPLE.
              YOU ARE TO DO FOR ONE ANOTHER WHAT I HAVE DONE FOR YOU.

Celebrant: As we remember Jesus, his life, his love even unto death,
              his desire for our unity in his love, his resurrection,
              we rejoice that he has given us his Spirit
              to be his hands and body now in the world.
              May the Holy Spirit create in us the mind that was in Christ Jesus
              to enable us to love and live as he did, without counting the cost,
              to desire a unity in love as he did, without losing heart.

ALL: HEAL THE BROKEN BODY OF HUMANITY,
              THE BROKEN BODY OF YOUR CHURCH.

Celebrant: Father, we know ourselves to be weak and vulnerable,
              we too are poor,

but it is in our poverty and brokenness that you come to us,
and reveal the depths of your love.
For all this we give you thanks through Jesus Christ your Son
who lives and reigns with you and the Holy Spirit
one God for ever and ever.
Amen

The washing of the feet

Each group leader begins by washing the feet of a neighbour. The one whose feet has been washed then places a hand on the head of the person who has done the washing. They pray silently together. Then the one who had their feet washed washes the feet of the next person. And so on, until the last person washes the feet of the group leader.

Song

Lord's Prayer

Each person says the Lord's Prayer in their own first language.

Blessing and sharing of the peace

Celebrant: May the Lord bless you and keep you.
ALL: AMEN
Celebrant: May the Lord let his face shine on you and be gracious to you.
ALL: AMEN
Celebrant: May the Lord God uncover his face to you and bring you peace.
ALL: AMEN
Celebrant   Let's give each other a sign of peace.

A sign of peace is shared among the congregation.

CAMAS: LIVING THE LITURGY

Rachel McCann

Originally quarry-workers' cottages, then a salmon-fishing station, the Camas Centre on the Isle of Mull is run by a staff group with specialist skills, helped by several volunteers. Young people from the city and elsewhere, and other groups too, come to Camas for an adventure holiday with outdoor opportunities for canoeing, walking, swimming and camping, a visit to Iona, and the experience of exploring issues, building relationships, and facing new challenges through living and working in community.

Rachel McCann is a former Camas Coordinator.

Liturgy in the living

Walking down a boggy track for two miles in the pouring, west-of-Scotland rain with a group of young people – half filled with excitement, half filled with anxiety – singing, complaining, asking questions, laughing and shouting …

This may not be the first image that springs to mind when thinking of the justice and peace commitment and liturgy so strongly associated with the Iona Community. Yet, for me, having walked the track to Camas many times, this experience is grounded in justice and peace and is the very embodiment of liturgy.

Camas is a place where relevant, radical spirituality and worship are rooted in the everyday experiences of the young people who visit each week, where a deep commitment to care for the earth is lived out in practical ways, where those who are marginalised can be heard and made to feel welcome, and where community is built and shared. The liturgy is in this living – in the encounters and exchanges between people and place. The outer adventure of Camas often facilitates a profound inner journey. At a time when young people face so many pressures – homelessness and poverty; debt and drugs; questions about identity, belonging and worth – safe places to relax and rest, to explore and grow, are invaluable. Camas is one of these places.

Making a space

There are many creative ways to enable young people to explore spirituality. At Camas the emphasis is on being alongside people, on creating a dialogue and learning and sharing with young people in a safe and open space. Many of the young people who visit Camas come from situations of personal and political disadvantage and poverty. Many are worldly wise beyond their years. Tough shells often hide vulnerable and painful stories. Many come from places where they have had no experience, or a negative experience, of church and Christianity. One young man who came to Camas had spent many years sleeping rough in the porch of his local church but had never been inside.

So, in a place where physical safety is paramount, spiritual and emotional safety also become central. Camas is a place where the spiritual – that which is rooted in the core of all – can be explored and expressed freely; where respect, understanding, difference and diversity are honoured and encouraged. For many young people just being listened to in this environment is a new and moving experience.

A time to reflect ...

'Reflections' take place at Camas each morning and evening. Reflections are short, focused times when young people can explore spirituality. Taking their themes from the pattern and experiences of the day, reflections can enable learning, growth, freedom of expression, and a change of heart. Using ideas from liberation theology and experiential learning, reflections offer a creative way of 'growing in love, awareness and respect of God, self, others and the earth' (from Camas mission statement). This is the aim of all that takes place at Camas. For example, a reflection on trust uses the experiences of the day's abseiling; a reflection on friendship uses the feelings generated by pitching a tent together. Using symbolism of materials around them, young people are encouraged to create a physical space at the start of the week in which to meet for reflections; a safe space that is their own for the week.

For young people, who may have faith, who may know God, who may have a sense of the Spirit, but who may not express this in traditional religious terms, these reflections offer an honest and meaningful way to engage. There are none of the usual visual symbols of church services – no sermons, books or collection plates – but there is the naming of hurts and of hopes, there is laughter and love, there is the sharing of dreams and doubts. For me, this is prayer at its most beautiful and simple. For me, this is sacred space: where love is, God is.

Reflections mirror the way in which Jesus used the environment around him to teach his listeners of the nature of God and of the path of peace; the way in which he shared dialogue with those whom he encountered, meeting them where they were and refusing to place meaningless rituals or empty words as a heavy burden on their shoulders. Young people learn what it means to be true to oneself, to build relationships, to share responsibility, to know the love of the 'otherness' of God. As one young person said in a reflection: 'Camas is our spiritual home, where we can be who we are without fear and without prejudice.'

Worship as washing-up

'Reflections' are just one part of the daily rhythm of the liturgy of life at Camas, which is rooted in the rhythms of nature – the cycles of the sea and moon and changing seasons. The programme of activities works with this rhythm in helping young people to explore and grow. Yet it is often in the more informal times, in between structured activity, that young people find the space to relax, lower their masks and meet with themselves and nature.

Defining what people experience at Camas is not easy because it is not about words. Often, as the staff team that I was a part of waved goodbye to a group leaving Camas, we would say that the 'Camas magic' had worked again. The 'Camas magic' is of course the song of the Spirit and the music of the Mystery weaving its way through conversations, tree-planting, bread-baking, kayaking and washing-up! It is here, in the ordinary, everyday, down-to-earth things that we come to know God in our midst, the presence of Love. As one of the early Camas staff members said of his time working there in the 1950s, the Camas experience is about 'being together with one another in freedom and respect and God being present in that'.[1]

In a place dependent on rainfall for water and natural sources for heat and light, young people learn to care for the earth and honour creation in real ways, and to care for and honour themselves and one another. The first time I met one young man at Camas he was waving a knife at me and shouting. Despite my fear, what struck me most were the scars all over his hands and arms. With a lot of hard work from the staff, with the gentle touch of the earth, and with the 'Camas magic', he eventually began to relax and enjoy the week safely (also cooking us all an amazing curry on the final night). Another young person was so lacking in self-confidence that he refused to try any of the activities on offer. His fractured self-esteem meant he felt he would fail. Towards the end of the week he asked if he could share some of his poems with me. In one poem, he had written that the week at Camas had shown him he was 'a valuable person who could live out all that was inside me and care for the world around me'.

These are snapshots of the stories of the young people who visit Camas; they are glimpses of healing and freedom. If young people take even a fraction of these messages away with them, then their visit is worthwhile. Camas cannot provide answers for the many complex issues young people face today, but it can offer a safe place in which to explore them and a place which complements the ongoing work of the many dedicated youth workers who bring young people to Camas. In the terminology of youth work, Camas is about personal development, group building, and issue-based work. In the language of the Spirit, it is about healing, hope, affirmation and acceptance, freedom and friendship; it is about justice and peace in loving relationship.

Written, structured liturgies don't usually come out of Camas, but I hope what I have described here paints a portrait of the life-filled liturgy of love that is lived out there.

Notes

[1] 'Being together with one another in freedom and respect and God being present in that' – by Stewart McGregor, in *And They Never Ran Away, An Interview with a Camas Pioneer*, © Rachel McCann (ed.), 2002.

ADDITIONAL RESOURCES

RESPONSES, AFFIRMATIONS, LITANIES AND DIALOGUES

GATHER US, O GOD

Leader: Gather us, O God
ALL: AND WE WILL KNOW YOUR LIFE THAT MAKES US ONE

Leader: Gather us, O God
ALL: AND WE WILL CELEBRATE OUR VARIETY AND UNIQUENESS

Leader: Gather us, O God
ALL: AND WE WILL GIVE YOU THE PAIN OF OUR BROKENNESS

Leader: Gather us, O God
ALL: AND WE WILL SHARE THE GIFTS OF YOUR SPIRIT.

Leader: Trinity of love bind us as one

ALL: THAT OUR BROKENNESS BE HEALED BY YOU;
THAT OUR FEARS BE HELD BY YOU;
THAT OUR GIFTS BE USED BY YOU;
THAT OUR LIVES BE OFFERED TO YOU;
SO MAY THE WORLD BELIEVE.
AMEN

Ali Newell

GATHER IN OUR HEARTS, LORD

Gather in our hearts, Lord
BRING PEACE THROUGH OUR WORDS

Gather in our hearts, Lord
BRING PEACE THROUGH OUR LISTENING

Gather in our hearts, Lord
BRING PEACE THROUGH OUR TOUCH

Gather in our hearts, Lord
BRING PEACE THROUGH OUR SILENCE

Gather in our hearts, Lord
BRING PEACE THROUGH OUR LIVES

Ewan Aitken

YOU ARE A WONDER AND A JOY TO US

Lord God, creator and sustainer of life, we stand in awe before the touch of life you have given to our world, and your goodness to us shown in delights we enjoy daily.

How did you teach birds such melodious song as pleasures the heart-strings and thrills all our senses?

YOU ARE A WONDER AND A JOY TO US

How did you teach sunbeams to dance among grime and dust transforming their nature into a curtain of shining stars?

YOU ARE A WONDER AND A JOY TO US

How did you teach water to dash among rocks, dancing and delighting – exultantly dispersing itself in fronds of white foam, or resting in pools deep, tranquil, fish-laden?

YOU ARE A WONDER AND A JOY TO US

How did you teach trees to garb themselves in delicate lacework of blossom – and then cast their petals to the wind like flurries of snowflakes?

YOU ARE A WONDER AND A JOY TO US

How did you teach the wind to howl through caverns, and sooth fevered brows with its cool caress?

YOU ARE A WONDER AND A JOY TO US

How did you teach the air to sustain life so silently, accommodating itself to the different bodies of creatures?

YOU ARE A WONDER AND A JOY TO US

You, Lord God, the creator, are also the great craftsman continually shaping the fabric of our lives so that we may speak your glory.

WE EXULT IN YOU. YOU ARE A WONDER AND A JOY TO US.
WE BLESS YOUR HOLY NAME. AMEN

Ian M Fraser

SING PRAISE AND THANKS TO GOD

Leader: All waves that break on the seashore, gulls that screech on the wind,
            all seals and dolphins, whales and minnows;
            bless the Maker.
ALL: SING PRAISE AND THANKS TO GOD.
Leader: All streams and rivers, lakes reflecting the sky,
            all fishes and wriggling things, tadpoles and beetles;
            bless the Maker.
ALL: SING PRAISE AND THANKS TO GOD.
Leader: All mountains and rolling hills, larks singing on the wing,
            all badgers and foxes, hedgehogs and rabbits;
            bless the Maker.
ALL: SING PRAISE AND THANKS TO GOD.
Leader: All trees and green growing things, flowers scenting the air,
            all creeping and crawling things, bee, butterfly and moth;
            bless the Maker.
ALL: SING PRAISE AND THANKS TO GOD.
Leader: People of God, short, tall or growing still, skin black, brown or beige,
            full of creative talent, free to make choices;
            bless the Maker.
ALL: SING PRAISE AND THANKS TO GOD.
Leader: For all that is made, free to be as they were made to be;
            praise the Maker.
ALL: PRAISE THE MAKER'S SON.
            PRAISE THE HOLY SPIRIT.
            GOD, THE THREE-IN-ONE.

Chris Polhill

PROCESSIONAL: IN MEMORY OF HER

Scripture reading: Mark 14:3—9, ending with the words 'What she has done will be told in memory of her.'

Leader: Let us now praise great women
            And our mothers who lived before us
ALL: WHAT SHE HAS DONE WILL BE TOLD IN MEMORY OF HER

Voice 1:   She took heart and was healed by her faith
            Come, all women of heart and faith
ALL: WHAT SHE HAS DONE WILL BE TOLD IN MEMORY OF HER

Voice 2:	She had courage and great faith, and saved her daughter
	Come, all you mothers and daughters
ALL:	WHAT SHE HAS DONE WILL BE TOLD IN MEMORY OF HER

Voice 3:	She did a beautiful thing for Jesus
	Come, all women who make an offering of love
ALL:	WHAT SHE HAS DONE WILL BE TOLD IN MEMORY OF HER

Voice 4:	She, out of poverty, gave everything she had
	Come, all you women who have little but give much
ALL:	WHAT SHE HAS DONE WILL BE TOLD IN MEMORY OF HER

Voice 5:	There were many women there, watching by the cross
	Come, all you women who wait faithfully on the Lord
ALL:	WHAT SHE HAS DONE WILL BE TOLD IN MEMORY OF HER

Voice 6:	The women ran from the tomb, in fear and great joy, to tell others
	Come, all you sisters with a gospel to proclaim
ALL:	WHAT SHE HAS DONE WILL BE TOLD IN MEMORY OF HER

Leader:	Let us praise great women
	And our mothers before us
	The generations of women
	Through whom God's glory has been seen
	Come, faithful people, women and men
ALL:	LET US WORSHIP THE LORD

Kathy Galloway

WE ARE SO PRIVILEGED

Leader:	Lord God, we waken to warm homes and food and family; and so many waken to homelessness and hunger and loneliness.
ALL:	WE ARE SO PRIVILEGED

Leader:	We waken to spring flowers and green fields and distant hills; and so many waken to crowded bedsits and wastelands of rubbish and squalor and polluted air.
ALL:	WE ARE SO PRIVILEGED

Leader:	We waken to the singing of birds; and so many waken to the sound of cannon bombardments and the cries of the wounded and dying.
ALL:	WE ARE SO PRIVILEGED

Leader:	We waken to a village of friendly people; and so many people waken to a lonely, friendless life in the city, in housing estates, in outlying rural areas.
ALL:	WE ARE SO PRIVILEGED
Leader:	We waken to security of our person and our home; and so many waken to violence and threats of violence, to menaces from extortionists and racketeers.
ALL:	WE ARE SO PRIVILEGED
Leader:	That we are so unthankful for all the blessings we enjoy
ALL:	FORGIVE US, GOOD GOD
Leader:	That we keep wanting more instead of appreciating more gratefully what we have
ALL:	FORGIVE US, GOOD GOD
Leader:	That we so rarely take the small steps open to us to establish justice on earth
ALL:	FORGIVE US, GOOD GOD
Leader:	That we do not uphold in prayer those who are striving for a better world, and do not persist in prayer
ALL:	FORGIVE US, GOOD GOD

Lord Christ, enter into our lives and change us. Get rid of the carelessness and laziness in us. Let your forgiveness deal with our past sins and your grace make a different way of life possible.

We sum up our prayers in the prayer that Jesus taught us:

Lord's Prayer …

Ian M Fraser

BREAK THE CHAINS OF DEBT

Leader: Lord, must we starve our children to pay our debts?
ALL: BREAK THE CHAINS OF DEBT!
Leader: How long must this go on?
ALL: BREAK THE CHAINS OF DEBT!
Leader: It's one law for the rich and another for the poor.
ALL: BREAK THE CHAINS OF DEBT!
Leader: Debt destroys our families and our way of life.
ALL: BREAK THE CHAINS OF DEBT!
Leader: We defend our roots as our country's true base of growth.

ALL: BREAK THE CHAINS OF DEBT!
Leader: Debt tears down our clinics and schools as in war.
ALL: BREAK THE CHAINS OF DEBT!
Leader: Now external debt becomes eternal debt!
ALL: BREAK THE CHAINS OF DEBT!

From a service about the injustice of poor-country debt to rich countries and banks,
Iona Abbey, 1998

KNOCK, KNOCK ... WHO'S THERE?

(Responses for a children's service, Iona Abbey. These responses could be adapted to another place.)

Leader:	Knock, knock
Group:	*(three or four people – adults, children)* Who's there?
Leader:	Iona
Group:	Iona who?
Leader:	Iona doorbell, why don't you use it?!

Leader:	Knock, knock
Group:	Who's there?
Leader:	Teresa
Group:	Teresa who?
Leader:	Teresa Green.

Leader:	Knock, knock
Group:	Who's there?
Leader:	Teresa Green.
Group:	Teresa Green who?!
Leader:	Teresa Green, but I can't see them because I work in a factory 14 hours a day, seven days a week.

Leader:	Knock, knock
Group:	Who's there?
Leader:	Hans
Group:	Hans who?
Leader:	Hands are for holding and loving not pushing and shoving.

Leader:	Knock, knock
Group:	Who's there?
Leader:	José who collects in a dump for a living. Heather who sleeps on the street.

(Pause)

Leader:	Knock, knock
Group:	Who's there?
Leader:	Jesus
Group:	Jesus who?
Leader:	Jesus!

Who was born in a stable,
Who escaped the death squads of Herod.
Jesus, who says:

'Knock, and the door shall be opened.
Ask, and it shall be given.'

And: 'He who receives you receives me,
and he who receives me receives the one who sent me.'

ALL: COME IN, JESUS.

Helen Lambie, Vincent Manning, Neil Paynter

A PRAYER AFTER THE MORECAMBE BAY TRAGEDY

On 6th February, 2004 eighteen Chinese cockle pickers lost their lives at Morecambe Bay in England. The following prayer is from a service of remembrance that was held on 22nd February 2004 in the Cathedral Church of St Peter in Lancaster. Participating in the service were representatives from the local and national Chinese community; the Buddhist, Christian, Jewish and Muslim communities; the emergency services; the local fishing community; the Transport and General Workers' Union; the media; local Members of Parliament, local councillors, and other local dignitaries; and about 1300 members of the public. The aim of the service was to provide not only a memorial for the victims of Morecambe Bay, but also a rallying call for justice – an opportunity for faith communities to come together and to speak out against the exploitation of vulnerable migrant workers by gangmasters, and to recognise the underlying injustices and prejudice in our society and in our immigration policy and law, which allow this network of exploitation to flourish.

Reader: Eternal Father, open our eyes to see those around us who are suffering.
ALL: LET US OPEN OUR HEARTS TO LOVE THEM, AS GOD LOVES US.
Reader: Eternal Father, open our ears to hear the cry of those who are oppressed and exploited in our society.
ALL: LET US OPEN OUR MOUTHS TO SPEAK WORDS OF PEACE AND JUSTICE.
Reader: Eternal Father, inspire us with your Wisdom.
ALL: LET US, WHO ARE COMMITTED TO JUSTICE, EMBRACE THE DIFFICULTIES

OF THOSE WHO SUFFER, AND RESPOND WISELY TO THIS CHALLENGE WITH GENEROSITY OF HEART.

Reader: Eternal Father, may we who long for justice:

ALL: CHALLENGE OUR SOCIETY TO SHOW MORE RESPONSIBILITY FOR ONE ANOTHER.

Reader: Eternal Father, may we who speak of justice:

ALL: LET OUR VOICES BE RAISED ON BEHALF OF THOSE WITH NO VOICE.

Reader: Eternal Father, may we who believe in justice:

ALL: USE OUR LIVES AND GIFTS TO ESTABLISH A MORE JUST SOCIETY FOR ALL.

Reader: Eternal Father, may all of us gathered here today do all we can to safe-guard the dignity and welfare of your people.

ALL: GIVE US THE STRENGTH, HOPE AND THE COURAGE NECESSARY TO DEFEND THOSE WHO ARE VULNERABLE IN OUR COMMUNITIES.

Bishop Patrick O'Donoghue

FOR YOU ARE A GOD OF JUSTICE

Here's a mystery, Lord: how to manage our lives.

We know we have been given them to fulfil different parts of your purpose, and that, at the end of our days, we will have to give account of the way we have led them. We know that human beings have been put in charge of the earth and are meant to look after one another. So we look for mercy, not judgement.

At the supermarket, may we play our part in making sure that those who supply our needs are not exploited.

FOR YOU ARE A GOD OF JUSTICE

At our work, may we be concerned about the unemployed, or those unfairly treated in their employment, or those who, to survive, have to do work which they feel is wast-ing their lives and talents.

FOR YOU ARE A GOD OF COMPASSION

In our homes, make us alert to the needs of the homeless, supportive of bodies that seek to provide for them, appreciative of the work of builders, joiners, labourers, architects …

FOR YOU ARE A GOD WHO CARES

In our health, remind us of those who have to cope with weakened bodies and minds, and those who care for them.

FOR YOU ARE A GOD WHO STAYS WITH THEM

In the peace of this place, enable us to do what we can for communities torn by war and bitterness, supporting parties negotiating for a just peace and the establishing of true relationships, giving money to aid their work.

Lord, teach us what you want of us, and, by your Holy Spirit, enable us to do what seems beyond our power. Amen

Ian M Fraser

PRAYER FOR HEALING AND PEACE

This prayer was first written for a regional church gathering on the Central Coast of New South Wales, Australia, where the pelican, a traditional symbol of Christ, is ubiquitous.

Leader: Holy, healing God
ALL: THROUGH OUR LIVES AND BY OUR PRAYERS, YOUR KINGDOM COME.

(Pause)

Leader: Holy, healing God
              we give thanks that, through your servant Paul,
              you spoke words of healing and renewal.
              We pray for your troubled world,
              and for all whose lives are disfigured by war, poverty or oppression,
              remembering especially, at this time, the peoples of the Middle East,
              and all whose power and decisions impact upon the poor.
              May the way of the crucified Christ be honoured in our world,
              and hope be found in the Prince of Peace.

(Pause)

Leader   Holy, healing God
ALL: THROUGH OUR LIVES AND BY OUR PRAYERS, YOUR KINGDOM COME.

(Pause)

Leader: Holy, healing God
              we give thanks for this region of …
              in which we live:
              for its natural beauty and human endeavour,
              its commerce, councils and communities.
              And especially we pray for those who are excluded,
              or who feel cut off from fullness of life,
              remembering the hurts and hardships of the unemployed,
              of victims of violence,
              and of so many young people in our midst.

We lay before you those in particular need this day,
and those who are sick in body, mind or spirit
whom we name in the silence of our hearts.

(Pause)

Leader: Holy, healing God
ALL: THROUGH OUR LIVES AND BY OUR PRAYERS, YOUR KINGDOM COME.

(Pause)

Leader: Holy, healing God
we give thanks that through your Holy Spirit
you make us one body in your Son,
and equip us with various gifts for shared love and service.
We pray for your Church here and throughout the world,
that it may grow in health and spiritual vitality.
And especially we pray for one another,
that, recognising the gifts of the Holy Spirit amongst us,
we may grow as fellow pilgrims of your grace.
Build us up in love,
draw us out in mission to others
and enable us to be a sign of your holy, healing love.

(Pause)

Leader: Holy, healing God
ALL: THROUGH OUR LIVES AND BY OUR PRAYERS, YOUR KINGDOM COME.

(Pause)

Leader: Christ, our Holy Pelican,
where you dwell is living water.
You come to us.
Enable us, in the power of your Holy Spirit,
to walk with you in sorrow and in joy,
to move upon the waters of your new creation,
and to fly into your heavenly freedom,
empowered by your love
and in unity with one another.
This and all our prayers
we ask in the name of Jesus Christ.
ALL: AMEN

Jon Inkpin

ALREADY HERE

Leader: Violence,
            War
            Hunger
            Slavery
            Homelessness –
            O Lord, why don't you deliver us?
            O Lord, why do you hide your face?

ALL: O LORD, WHERE IN THE WORLD ARE YOU?
            WHY DON'T YOU COME DOWN AND SAVE US?
            CAN'T YOU SEE YOUR PEOPLE SUFFERING?
            CAN'T YOUR HEAR THEIR CRIES OF PAIN AND LONELINESS?

            (Pause)

Leader: Or, Lord, could it be that you are already here?

ALL: CHRIST, YOU *ARE* ALREADY HERE.
            WE ARE YOUR BODY –
            WE ARE YOUR EARS AND EYES AND HANDS AND FEET.

            CHRIST, UNITE US.
            HELP US TO WORK FOR JUSTICE AND PEACE
            IN YOUR DIVIDED, SUFFERING WORLD.
            AMEN

Neil Paynter

PEACE BE AMONG US

Where children squabble
PEACE BE AMONGST US

Where races fight
PEACE BE AMONGST US

Where neighbours argue
PEACE BE AMONGST US

Where nations disagree
PEACE BE AMONGST US

Where lovers quarrel
PEACE BE AMONGST US

Where people struggle
PEACE BE AMONGST US

Where Christ's disciples gather
PEACE BE OUR WAY
AMEN

Ewan Aitken

LET YOUR PROPHET BE HEARD
(Based on Isaiah 65:17–25)

Creator God of all,
your prophet Isaiah described a world full of joy.

In places of sorrow,
places of sadness,
places of suffering,
LET YOUR PROPHET BE HEARD

Your prophet Isaiah described a world without weeping.

Where the tears of the lonely,
the tears of the lost,
the tears of those longing for peace
fall on dry ground,
LET YOUR PROPHET BE HEARD

Your prophet Isaiah described a world
where all people had enough to eat and a home to live in.

In the lives of the rich,
in the souls of the wealthy,
in the actions of those who have enough to share,
LET YOUR PROPHET BE HEARD

Your prophet Isaiah described a world
where those who lived to one hundred years old
would still be considered young.

Where injustice kills the young –
physically,
emotionally,
mentally –
LET YOUR PROPHET BE HEARD

Your prophet Isaiah described a world without conflict,
where wolves and lambs ate together.

In places where decisions of war are taken,
in the minds where decisions of war are accepted,
in the hearts where decisions of war are implemented,
LET YOUR PROPHET BE HEARD

Your prophet Isaiah described a world
where prayers were answered before they were said.

In this, your world,
in which your prophet and your son
walked and were heard,
let us be heard,
let your disciples be heard.
By our words and actions,
let your world know
that we have heard your call
and that we shall speak up for the justice that is your kingdom.

GOD, LET YOUR PROPHETS BE HEARD
AMEN

Ewan Aitken

WHO ON EARTH IS BLESSED?

Blessed are the poor in spirit
for theirs is the kingdom of God.

GOD BLESS MY SOUL,
BECAUSE I AM SPIRITUALLY BROKE.

Blessed are those who weep
for they shall be comforted.

GOD BLESS MY SOUL,
I WEEP WHEN I SEE HOW WRONG WE HUMANS HAVE GONE.

Blessed are the meek
for they shall inherit the earth.

GOD BLESS MY SOUL,
AND TO HELL WITH HAVING MY OWN WAY IN LIFE.

Blessed are those who hunger and thirst for righteousness.

GOD BLESS MY SOUL,
I'M SO SICK OF THE WRONGNESS IN ME AND IN THE WORLD.

Blessed are the merciful
for they shall obtain mercy.

GOD BLESS MY SOUL,
FOR I, TOO, AM GETTING THINGS WRONG.

Blessed are the pure in heart
for they shall see God

GOD BLESS MY SOUL AND
BE THOU MY VISION, O LORD OF MY HEART.

Blessed are the peace-makers
for they shall be called the children of God.

GOD BLESS MY SOUL AND TEACH ME TRUE PEACE-MAKING.

Blessed are those who are persecuted for righteousness' sake
for theirs is the kingdom of heaven.

GOD BLESS MY SOUL AND DELIVER ME FROM SELF-RIGHTEOUSNESS.
AMEN

Ian Cowie

I AM

Leader:	I am the Bread of life.
ALL:	FEED US, LORD,
	THAT WE MAY PLAY A PART IN FEEDING THE HUNGRY.

Leader:	I am the Light of the world.
ALL:	SHINE THROUGH US
	TO HELP BRING SOME LIGHT INTO THE DARK PLACES OF THE WORLD.

Leader:	I am the Good Shepherd.
ALL:	KEEP A GRIP ON US, LORD,
	THAT WE MAY FOLLOW YOUR WILL.

| Leader: | I am the Resurrection and the Life. |
| ALL: | RAISE US UP TO LIVE FOR OTHERS AND FOR YOU. |

Leader: I am the Way, the Truth and the Life.
ALL: STRENGTHEN US TO STEP OUT ON YOUR WAY,
           TO TAKE THE RISK OF RELYING ON YOUR TRUTH,
           AND TO LIVE THE JESUS-LIFE.

Leader: I am the True Vine; you are my branches.
ALL: TOGETHER WE WILL BEAR FRUIT,
           AND THE CUP WE SHARE WILL BE INTOXICATING WITH JOY.

Leader: I am the Alpha and the Omega,
           the beginning and the ending.
ALL: RIGHT, LORD, YOU ARE THE BE-ALL AND THE END-ALL OF OUR LIVES.
           SO HERE IT GOES FOR SOME REAL LIVING!

           IN THE NAME OF THE FATHER
           AND OF THE SON
           AND OF THE HOLY SPIRIT.
           AMEN

Ian Cowie

JESUS SAID

Leader: Jesus said:
ALL: I HAVE COME TO BRING GOOD NEWS TO THE POOR

Leader: Jesus said:
ALL: I HAVE COME TO PROCLAIM LIBERTY TO THE CAPTIVES

Leader: Jesus said:
ALL: I HAVE COME TO GIVE RECOVERY OF SIGHT TO THE BLIND

Leader: And so they took this Jesus –
           the one who wanted to overthrow the order of the world –
           and brought him to a cliff to throw *him* over
ALL: BUT JESUS WALKED THROUGH THE CROWD AND WENT ON HIS WAY

Leader: And so the powers arrested and beat and bound him,
           and spit in his face and stripped him bare,
           and nailed him to a cross and left him for dead …
ALL: AND AFTER THREE DAYS
           HE ROSE FROM THE GRAVE …

Leader: Jesus Christ, we are your body on earth,
            help us to do your work:
ALL: TO HELP BRING JUSTICE TO THE POOR AND DISPOSSESSED;
            TO FREE THE SLAVES OF CAPITALISM AND 'THIRD WORLD' DEBT;
            TO OPEN THE EYES OF THE COMFORTABLE AND APATHETIC –
            TO TURN THE WORLD UPSIDE DOWN.

Leader: And when things get tough,
            in our home towns
            or far away in the great cities of the world,
            help us to stand firm,
            and not be moved by intimidation and threats of violence.
ALL: KEEP US SAFE, LORD CHRIST.

Leader: And if following you should someday lead us to a place
            where we are persecuted or arrested,
            or where our lives are in danger because of our affiliation with you,
            give us the strength not to deny you,
            and the peace to know that,
            whatever happens,
            we have lived our lives for you.
ALL: LORD JESUS, SEND US OUT IN CONFIDENCE, HOPE AND JOY TO DO
            GOD'S WORK. AMEN

Neil Paynter

OPENING AND CLOSING RESPONSES FOR A SERVICE ABOUT HOMELESSNESS

Two people in the crossing of the church: one person sitting begging for change (Voice 2), the other walking past her/him (Voice1).

Voice 1:   Hey, bum! Get a job.
Voice 2:   So, what do you do?
Voice 1:   *(proudly)* I own my own business.
Voice 2:   Well, how's about *you* givin' *us* a job, then? [1]

Leader: God, who calls us by our name;
            God, in whose image we are made.
ALL: COME IN FROM THE COLD, MAKE YOUR HOME IN OUR HEARTS.
Leader: God, who does not pass us by;
            God, who hears the cries of the poor.

ALL:	COME IN FROM THE COLD, MAKE YOUR HOME IN OUR HEARTS.
Leader:	God, who isn't impressed by our savings, properties and pension plans.
ALL:	COME IN FROM THE COLD, MAKE YOUR HOME IN OUR HEARTS.
Leader :	God, who has given us unique talents and skills and gifts to share;
ALL:	COME IN FROM THE COLD, MAKE YOUR HOME IN OUR HEARTS.

Leader: Jesus of no fixed address,
            come into this house, your home.
            Take refuge and shelter with us here –
            your feet must be tired,
            your heart must be heavy.
            Sit down with us, Lord.
            Tell us your stories,
            open our eyes to you.
ALL: MAKE YOUR HOME IN OUR HEARTS.

Closing responses

Leader: God, who welcomes us home with open arms –
            no matter where we've been or what we've done.
ALL: COME IN FROM THE COLD,
            MAKE YOUR HOME IN OUR HEARTS. AMEN

Neil Paynter

HOMELESSNESS IS YOU, HOMELESSNESS IS ME: A LITANY
(In this litany, use many different voices)

Leader: Homelessness is you, homelessness is me
Voice: Homelessness is Dan who was a miner
Voice: Homelessness is Eric who was a computer programmer
Voice: Homelessness is Emily who was a student
Voice: Homelessness is Brian who worked packing meat for a while,
            and worked picking fruit for a season,
            and works in construction when they can use him
Leader: Homelessness is you, homelessness is me

Voice: Homelessness is Jack who fought in the Falklands war
Voice: Homelessness is Harry who fought at Normandy and in Korea
            and in the east end of Glasgow
Voice: Homelessness is Jane who fought and survived the mental health system
Voice: Homelessness is Maggie who says:

| | If there's one thing she's learned – it's that she's a survivor |
| Leader: | Homelessness is you, homelessness is me |

Voice:	Homelessness is David who sees guardian angels in the trees; seraphim perched on fences
Voice:	Homelessness is Sarah who sees no way out
Voice:	Homelessness is Eric who jumped from a bridge in London
Voice:	Homelessness is Chan whom they found frozen in a dumpster
Leader:	Homelessness is you, homelessness is me

Voice:	Homelessness is Ewan who has travelled to South America and China and Alaska, and has so many stories he could fill a book
	Two books!
Voice:	Homelessness is Victor
	who has a tattoo of a butterfly he reveals –
	like he's baring his soul
Voice:	Homelessness is Jenny who is dying of AIDS,
	and whose last wish is to travel to Skye,
	to sit on a beach near Portree
	and watch the sun setting
Leader:	Homelessness is you, homelessness is me

Voice:	Homelessness is Mohammed who sleeps in his car,
	and has to keep moving on when the cops come
Voice:	Homelessness is Ray who sleeps in the graveyard
Voice:	Homelessness is Vernon who lives in a tidy squat where he likes to read the *Evening Times* and cook sausages
Leader:	Homelessness is you, homelessness is me

Voice:	Homelessness is Sittina who escaped the war in Sudan
	and is scared of being deported by the Home Office
Voice:	Homelessness is Susan who escaped her husband in Manchester
	and is scared of being found and killed
Voice:	Homelessness is Jessica who escaped her stepfather
Voice:	Homelessness is Curtis who works at a charity shop and can fix anything – radios, TVs, bicycles, washing machines …
	Homelessness is Curtis who has lived for forty years with the labels stupid, defective, disabled, broken …
Voice:	Homelessness is Neil who loves to sit and talk about 60s' music –
	and knows his stuff

Voice: Homelessness is Nicola who loves the ballet

Voice: Homelessness is Sylvester who plays joyful, jangly ragtime piano in the
          shelter chapel

Voice: Homelessness is Paul who writes the most sensitive, beautiful poetry

Leader: Homelessness is you, homelessness is me

Voice: Homelessness is Craig who never speaks or smiles
          and has an abused collie dog he takes excellent care of

Voice: Homelessness is Ian who wanders the streets looking for a hit –
          and has a distant light in his eyes when he remembers:
          playing football with his mates, walking in the hills, fishing for salmon …

Leader: Homelessness is you, homelessness is me

Voice: Homelessness is Chaz and Barry and Lynne,
          who spent their childhoods in and out of foster care,
          their teenage years in and out of institutions,
          and all of their adult lives inside either jails or shelters

Voice: Homelessness is Albert who spent 10 years in Belmarsh,
          where he learned to hate
          and how to play
          the whole dirty, rotten game

Voice: Homelessness is Dave who wants to work with children

Voice: Homelessness is Lewis who can't pay his council tax

Voice: Homelessness is Norma who can't pay her electric

Voice: Homelessness is Elizabeth who is eight months pregnant

Voice: Homelessness is Miles who misses tucking his kids in

Voice: Homelessness is Robbie who says:
          when he wins the lottery he's gonna buy his own tropical island,
          and give what's left to the nuns –
          who accepted him for who he is,
          who treated him like a human being again

Leader: Homelessness is you, homelessness is me

Voice: Homelessness is Dick who says:
          'I was staying with friends but they get sick of you.'

Voice: Homelessness is Chris and Nina who take good care of each other
          and make love where
          (and when)
          they can

Voice: Homelessness is Matt who says you feel like 'the invisible man'

Voice: Homelessness is Vincent who says:
'It could happen to anyone, people don't realise –
lose your family, your job, your mind …
People have no idea –
how close to the edge they're walking.'
Leader: Homelessness is me
Homelessness is you

Neil Paynter

The phrase 'homelessness is you, homelessness is me' is taken from a story by Ed Loring of the Open Door Community.

A HOLY WEEK LITANY CHALLENGING FEAR AND PREJUDICE
(based on Mark 14:32–42)

After each line from Mark's gospel spoken by Voice 2 (with the exception of the final section) the lights in the room are dimmed a little more. This can be done using either electric light or candles.

Voice 1: What is it?
What is that feeling that creeps into us?
Why when we approach a Big Issue[2] vendor, do we lower our eyes and pretend we don't see?
Voice 2: They went to a place called Gethsemane; and he said to his disciples, 'Sit here while I pray.'

Voice 1: Why does anger rise at the thought of a gay couple holding hands? Why would we choose to condemn love of any sort?
Voice 2: And he said to them, 'I am deeply grieved, even to death; remain here, and keep awake.'

Voice 1: Why does a group of teenagers on the corner warrant the checking for wallets?
Why do we assume that young people are up to no good?
Voice 2: And going a little farther, he threw himself on the ground and prayed that, if it were possible, the hour might pass from him.

Voice 1: Why do men get paid more than women for the same jobs?
Why are women still looked upon as inferior in so many cultures?
Voice 2: He said, 'Abba, Father, for you all things are possible …'

Voice 1:	How did we get to this stage of fear?
	Why do we laugh at the pain of others?
Voice 2	'... remove this cup from me; yet not what I want, but what you want.'

Voice 1:	Why is depression confused with laziness?
	Why do we make people who are schizophrenic outcasts?
	Why are adults with learning difficulties treated like children?
Voice 2:	'Simon, are you asleep? Could you not keep awake one hour? Keep awake and pray that you may not come into the time of trial ...'

Voice 1:	Why are we so afraid of homeless people?
	Why are we disgusted by newspapers and shopping carts and toeless shoes and cardboard boxes?
Voice 2:	'... the spirit is indeed willing, but the flesh is weak.'

Voice 1:	Why do we grumble self-righteously at the lifestyles of those caught in poverty's trap, yet whine as well about those who are rich?
	Why are we so comfortable surrounded by diverse objects, but so uncomfortable with diverse people?
Voice 2:	'Are you still sleeping and taking your rest? Enough! ...'

All the lights in the room are relit.

| Voice 2 | '... The hour has come; the Son of Man is betrayed into the hands of sinners. Get up, let us be going. See, my betrayer is at hand.' |

Katrina Crosby

LITANY OF HUMAN LABOUR

The different sections of this litany could be spaced throughout a service, for example on the theme of work, or used as a single block.

1. Family life and education

God, our Maker, you knitted our bones together in our mother's womb;
WE PRAISE YOU FOR THE GIFT OF LIFE.
God, our Maker, you surround us with the abundance of creation that provides
    for all our needs;
WE PRAISE YOU FOR THE GIFT OF LIFE.
God, our Maker, you encourage and sustain the life you have set within our hearts
    and souls;
WE PRAISE YOU FOR THE GIFT OF LIFE.

Living God, set your blessing on all who encourage and care for the life of children.

On all parents and grandparents: in their caring; and in their letting go when the time
is right;

LIVING GOD, SET YOUR BLESSING UPON THEM.

On all nurseries and play-groups, and on the leaders and parents who organise them;

LIVING GOD, SET YOUR BLESSING UPON THEM.

On all schools: on the teachers, governors and pupils; on the leaders and members
of youth clubs and youth groups;

LIVING GOD, SET YOUR BLESSING UPON THEM.

On all colleges and universities, on all courses to develop human skills;

on those who teach and those who learn;

LIVING GOD, SET YOUR BLESSING UPON THEM.

On our homes, that, in our joys and in our sorrows, we may know your blessing
and welcome you among us.

LIVING GOD, SET YOUR BLESSING UPON US.

WE PRAISE YOU FOR ALL THE NURTURING WE RECEIVE.

MAY YOUR LIFE, YOUR WAY, YOUR WILL SHAPE AND INFORM OUR LIVES. AMEN

2. Farming, industry and commerce, community life

Christ the carpenter, we thank you for walking beside us in our daily labours.

THANKS AND PRAISE TO YOU, O CHRIST.

Christ the worker, we thank you for showing us the way to work together.

THANKS AND PRAISE TO YOU, O CHRIST.

Christ the teacher, we thank you for teaching us priorities about wealth and its use
for the kin-dom.

THANKS AND PRAISE TO YOU, O CHRIST.

We give thanks for the work of farmers and all involved in food production.

Hallow the work of their hands and protect them from harm, from blight on the fields,
and from all the diseases that can afflict food.

JESUS, OUR LIVING BREAD, BLESS AND PROTECT THEM.

We give thanks for industry and manufacturing, for their labour and their creating.

Hallow their labour and protect them from harm, from injury, from greed
and mismanagement.

JESUS, THE MASTER CARPENTER, BLESS AND PROTECT THEM.

We give thanks for business and commerce, for shops and all who deal with finance.

Hallow their work and protect them from harm, from greed and shady deals,
from systems that deny your values.

JESUS, THE REDEEMER, BLESS AND PROTECT THEM.

We give thanks for all in management and organisation, those on boards
and in government.

Hallow their processes and protect them from harm; keep them within your concern
  for all people.
JESUS, OUR LORD, BLESS AND PROTECT THEM.
We give thanks for all who guard the boundaries and laws of our community life;
may your justice be served in all their work.
JESUS, OUR SAVIOUR, BLESS THEM AND PROTECT THEM.
LIVING GOD, WE PRAY FOR ALL THE WORKINGS OF OUR COMMUNAL LIFE.
MAY YOUR LIFE, YOUR WAY, YOUR WILL SHAPE AND INFORM OUR COMMUNITIES.
AMEN

3. Working for healing

Holy Spirit, we praise you for the love you awaken among us.
WE PRAISE YOU FOR THE GIFT OF LOVE.
Holy Spirit, we praise you for the compassion you encourage within us.
WE PRAISE YOU FOR THE GIFT OF LOVE.
Holy Spirit, we praise you for the healing you breathe upon us.
WE PRAISE YOU FOR THE GIFT OF LOVE.
Bless those who serve and care for others in our life together.
Prosper those employed in the medical profession; all who work in hospitals, hospices
  or general practice.
Enable your healing and shield them with your love;
GRACIOUS SPIRIT, SURROUND THEM WITH YOUR BLESSINGS.
Prosper those who listen and counsel, day and night: psychiatrists, Samaritans
  and all with gifts of listening.
Enable your healing and shield them with your love;
GRACIOUS SPIRIT, SURROUND THEM WITH YOUR BLESSINGS.
Prosper those who care for the elderly and the vulnerable, the homeless
  and those addicted to drugs.
Enable your healing and shield them with your love;
GRACIOUS SPIRIT, SURROUND THEM WITH YOUR BLESSINGS.
Prosper those who serve the broken, and who give compassion and support
  to people who have turned to crime.
Enable your healing and shield them with your love;
GRACIOUS SPIRIT, SURROUND THEM WITH YOUR BLESSINGS.
Prosper those who encourage faith in the living God; bless the work and witness
  of the churches and the care they offer.
Increase their faith and shield them with your love;
GRACIOUS SPIRIT, SURROUND THEM WITH YOUR BLESSINGS.
Prosper those who serve our communal needs through voluntary work.
Pour your blessings upon them and shield them with your love;
GRACIOUS SPIRIT, SURROUND THEM WITH YOUR BLESSINGS.

LIVING GOD, WE OFFER GRATEFUL THANKS FOR ALL THE SERVICE WE RECEIVE
    FROM OTHERS.
MAY YOUR LIFE, YOUR WAY, YOUR WILL BE ALWAYS SERVED. AMEN

4. Working for leisure

Within the dance of the Trinity we offer thanks for all who bless our leisure
    and our resting with their creativity and labour.
Those who work in leisure centres and fun parks.
Protect and bless them Living God;
WITHIN THE DANCE OF THE HOLY TRINITY WE BLESS THEM.
Those who work in travel, on railways, ships, planes and roads.
Protect and bless them Living God;
WITHIN THE DANCE OF THE HOLY TRINITY WE BLESS THEM.
Those who work in tourism or for holiday companies.
Protect and bless them Living God;
WITHIN THE DANCE OF THE HOLY TRINITY WE BLESS THEM.
Those who work in the arts to inspire and entertain us.
Protect and bless them Living God;
WITHIN THE DANCE OF THE HOLY TRINITY WE BLESS THEM.
Those who have retired from paid labour –
that they may enjoy to the full the freedom given them;
WITHIN THE DANCE OF THE HOLY TRINITY WE BLESS THEM.
Those who suffer from stress and over-work, and those who cannot stop
    because they see themselves as indispensable;
WITHIN THE EMBRACE OF THE HOLY TRINITY MAY THEY KNOW THE RECREATION
    AND HEALING THAT THEY NEED.

GOD THE CREATOR,
WHO RESTED ON THE SEVENTH DAY,
WE BLESS AND PRAISE YOU.
JESUS THE CHRIST,
WHO LAUGHED AND JOKED WITH THE DISCIPLES,
WE BLESS AND PRAISE YOU.
LIFE-GIVING SPIRIT,
WHO LEADS US INTO WHOLENESS,
WE BLESS AND PRAISE YOU.
HOLY TRINITY,
FOR ALL THE FUN AND REST WE ENJOY,
WE BLESS AND PRAISE YOU.
MAY YOUR LIFE, YOUR WAY, YOUR WILL SHAPE AND INFORM OUR PLAYTIME. AMEN

Chris Polhill

MAGNIFICAT AFFIRMATION
(Luke 1:46–55)

A: My heart praises you, O God,
B: My spirit rejoices in you, my saviour

A: You have remembered me in my lowliness,
B: And now I will be called blessed.

A: You have done great things for me
B: And shown mercy to all those who trust you.

A: You have stretched out your right arm
B: And scattered the proud with all their plans

A: You have brought down the mighty from their thrones
B: And lifted up the lowly.

A: You have filled the hungry with good things
B: And sent the rich away with empty hands.

A: You have kept your promise to our mothers and fathers,
B: And come to the help of your people,
to Abraham and Sarah,
and to all generations for ever. AMEN

The Iona Community, adapted

AFFIRMATION
(Luke 4:18–19)

The Spirit of the Lord is upon me
HE HAS CHOSEN ME TO BRING GOOD NEWS TO THE POOR.
HE HAS SENT ME TO PROCLAIM LIBERTY TO THE CAPTIVES
AND RECOVERY OF SIGHT TO THE BLIND;
TO FREE THE OPPRESSED
AND ANNOUNCE THAT THE TIME HAS COME
WHEN THE LORD WILL SAVE HIS PEOPLE
This is the word of the Lord
THANKS BE TO GOD

GOSPEL RESPONSES OF PEACE

Leader: You have heard it said, an eye for an eye and a tooth for a tooth.
ALL: BUT I SAY TO YOU – DO NOT SET YOURSELF AGAINST THE ONE WHO
            WRONGS YOU.

Leader: If someone strikes you on the right cheek,
ALL: TURN TO THEM THE LEFT CHEEK ALSO.

Leader: If someone takes your coat away,
ALL: GIVE THEM YOUR SHIRT AS WELL.

Leader: If anyone makes you go one mile,
ALL: GO WITH THEM TWO MILES.

Leader: As you wish people to treat you,
ALL: TREAT THEM JUST THE SAME WAY.

Leader: You have heard it said, love your neighbour and hate your enemy.
ALL: BUT I TELL YOU THIS: LOVE YOUR ENEMY AND PRAY FOR YOUR
            PERSECUTORS.

Leader: Only in this way can you be children of the Father,
ALL: WHO MAKES THE SUN SHINE ON THE GOOD AND EVIL ALIKE.

The Iona Community

THE SPIRIT OF LOVE UNITES US

LET US RENEW OUR RESOLUTION
TO BE REAL BROTHERS AND SISTERS,
REGARDLESS OF ANY KIND OF BAR
THAT SEPARATES US FROM ONE ANOTHER.
IN THIS HOLY RESOLVE MAY WE BE STRENGTHENED,
KNOWING WE ARE GOD'S FAMILY,
THAT ONE SPIRIT, THE SPIRIT OF LOVE, UNITES US.

Norbert Capek,
a Unitarian minister killed by the Nazis at Dachau concentration camp

MILLENNIUM INTERFAITH AFFIRMATION

*This affirmation could be adapted to include readings from other traditions –
the Sikh tradition, Taoism, Confucianism ...*

Women:	We gather impelled by visions of holiness and horror. Children of many traditions, we inherit both wisdom and tragic misunderstandings.
Men:	Give us aspiration for what is universal and true. Draw us to light, to love, to beauty. *(Hindu)*
Women:	I forgive all living beings. Let all living beings forgive me. Let all in this world be my friends. *(Jain)*
Men:	God, may I strive to make the enemy a friend; may I strive to make the wicked righteous; may I strive to help the ignorant understand. *(Zoroastrian)*
Women:	May all beings be happy! As a mother protects her children, may we cultivate an open heart towards all beings. *(Metra Sutra: Buddhism)*
Men:	Hatred is never appeased by hatred; it is appeased by love. This is an eternal law. *(Dhammapada: Buddhism)*
Women:	Worship inspired by fear is worship, but does not rise to the highest heaven. That is reserved for worship inspired by love. *(Zohar: Judaism)*
Men:	You have heard it said 'Love your neighbour, hate your enemy.' I say: 'Love your enemies and pray for those who torment you.' *(Jesus: Christianity)*
Women:	The humble, meek, merciful, and devout souls are everywhere of one religion; and when death has taken off the masks, they will know one another. (*William Penn: Quaker)*
Men:	O God, it is thy word that humankind is a single nation. All human beings are born free and equal in dignity and rights. They are endowed with love and conscience. They should act toward one another as children of one family. *(Koran: Muslim)*

Adapted by Richard Boeke from an affirmation used during an interfaith celebration
at Friends House in London, England, April 1999.

ON HIS WAY
(Luke 4:16–30)

A: It began all right

B: Nothing out of the ordinary then?

A: Oh no – it's always nice to see one of our own young people helping with the service.

B: He did a reading?

A: That's right. A lovely clear voice. I could hear every word in the back pew.

B: Were there many there?

A: All the usual folk. His family of course.

B: His mother must have been proud.

A: Well yes, but then …

B: Was it something he said?

A: He was reading from Isaiah. We'd heard it before. I mean, it's traditional. But he made it sound different.

B: 'The Spirit of the Lord'?

A: 'The Spirit of the Lord'.

B: Some people go on a bit about the spirit. And waving their arms. I am sure they're sincere, but I can't be doing it at my age.

A: What worried me more was 'He has chosen me to bring good news to the poor.'

B: Chosen you?

A: No, that's what the prophet said, and that's what he read, but as though he meant it … and what does it mean anyway by 'the poor'.

B: Well, we're none of us well off. We all have to pay these terrible taxes. And keep up appearances.

A: Quite – but 'poor' are them out there. The ones who don't pay taxes.

B: Don't care about appearances.

A: Scroungers.

B: Too many children!

A: Well, what's good news to them? Us having to cough up a bit more!

B: Of course there are widows and orphans and strangers at the gate. Tragic, really.

A: Charity – that's different. It's heart-warming to give to a good cause.

B: It's more blessed to give than to receive.

A: And our people are ever so good at giving.

B: Though it's one appeal after another.

A: But what's 'good news' to the poor, for goodness sake? And what's it got to do with us? We are doing our best. Surely we are not expected to change.

B: Did he go on?

A: Go on? It got worse. I couldn't believe my ears: 'He has sent me to proclaim liberty to the captives.'

B: That's what it says in Isaiah.

A: But I always thought it was about the Messiah, some time in the future, a good way off. When he read it I suddenly thought, 'What if it happened now?'

B: There's a lot of folk that are better off behind bars. There's no smoke without fire.

A: Quite. And I can't see the authorities taking kindly to this liberation talk.

B: I just don't see the need.

A: 'And recovery of sight to the blind.'

B: Eh?

A: What does it mean?

B: You never asked that before!

A: 'To set free the oppressed.' Who's oppressed? Them out there? But that's part of the system. You've got to have some on top to give orders, and some underneath to carry them out.

B: That's the way the world keeps going.

A: But who are we? Are we the oppressors or the oppressed?

B: No one's calling me an oppressor – I'll soon settle them … But why are you worrying? This is an old prophecy. It's about then and there, not here and now.

A: Unless 'The time has come when the Lord will save his people.'

B: Come on now!

A: But that's what he said, when he finished reading and sat down. He said 'This passage of scripture has come true today, as you heard it being read.'

B: I don't get it.

A: Nor did we. First we were impressed. After all we'd known him since he was so high. But he was right when he said we'd find it hard to understand him. All we wanted to do was to hear comforting words about God at work far away.

A: I know. Nothing political. Nothing that makes you feel got at or guilty – though you might take up a special offering for some project.

A: But he was bringing it all home. And then having the cheek to tell us that we are only on the edge of what God is doing.

B: You must have been mad.

A: We'd had enough. We showed him just what we thought of his 'good news'. We have a way of dealing with folk who dare to say we are in God's way.

B: And Jesus …

A: He went on his way!
       He went on his way …

Jan Sutch Pickard

FAIRTRADE DIALOGUE

Two people stroll into the centre of the worship space, one of them pushing a supermarket trolley. They converse as they are walking around, giving the impression of browsing the shelves in a supermarket.

Shopper: Umm. What do I need? I fancy something a bit different today – I'm bored with carrots and frozen peas. *(Pauses)* What's this? Mainge Toot.

Friend: I think it's called mangetout.

Shopper: Yeah, that's what I said. Product of Zambia. Wow, I'm surprised they can grow greens somewhere like that. I thought there was always drought there. That's why all those poor kids are starving.

Friend: I don't think that's the real reason for hunger in poor countries. I think it's down to poverty. And a lot of that's caused by unfair trade. We don't get to hear the real story. You see –

Shopper: *(interrupting)* I'll have these bananas. Good old Del Monte. *(Puts on a fake Central American accent)* 'The Man from Del Monte, he say yes!'

Friend: Actually, he's more likely to say, 'The world market price has fallen again so I'll pay you even less than I did this year.' Hey, look, they've got Fairtrade bananas now. Why don't you get them instead?

Shopper: *(moving on without taking much notice)* I need more coffee again – right caffeine addicts we are. So many brands to choose from though. What's on special this week? Nescafe? Maxwell House? Oh look, Kenco's offer is even better this time. 20% extra free. I'll take that.

Friend: You should get Cafédirect[3] instead. Then you know the farmers will get a fair price and be able to feed their families.

Shopper: *(snorts)* They have too many kids you know. That's the real problem.

Friend: No, I told you, the real problem is the unfair world trade system and the power of multinational companies.

Shopper: Oh, for God's sake, stop lecturing me, will you? You know what? Ever since you became a Christian you've become a real drag, you know that? I mean, we can't even go shopping any more without you making a big deal about it. Do we have to be thinking about everything we buy and where it comes from and who makes it? You know I'm not into politics. And was Jesus political? Was he sitting around worrying about unfair trade? *(Laughs)* Um, I don't think so. Yeah, the world's unfair, so what? I can't change it, can I?

Friend: Yes, you can! If you and me, and everyone we know, and everyone they know, always bought Fairtrade goods we *would* change the world. All the big companies would realise that people don't want unjust trade so they'd start to trade fairly, paying producers a decent price for their products. And one day all trade would become fair trade. That's how much of a difference we can make through what we choose to buy!

(Pause)

Shopper: *(Sighs)* Look, I do care about other people in the world, I really do. It's just … it's so hard to know where to start, you know?

Friend: Yeah, I know. It *is* hard … Well, why not start here? *(handing her a jar of Fairtrade coffee.)*

Helen Boothroyd

PRAYERS

COME, HOLY SPIRIT

Come, Holy Spirit,
give us a new breath
of freedom,
a new heart of fire,
a new strength of purpose,
to see the story of God,
in the people of God.

Come, Holy Spirit,
show us the patterns of your presence
in the places of our lives
where we work and serve,
as much as where we worship and pray.

Come, Holy Spirit,
make us a sign of God
in the darkness and poverty
in our world,
where hope is frail
and daily life
a struggle to survive.
Amen

Yvonne Morland

THIS NEW DAY

Here we are before you, Lord. We are always before you. You hold in mind each one of us as if there were no one else in the world. But we are often unaware of your presence. Here, together, coming to meet with you, we become conscious of you as the reality, the true basis of life.

You bring us into this day. Oh, the light does it coming through the curtains, footsteps in the corridor, maybe the alarm clock. But they are all your servants to awaken us to the gift of the day. How gracious is your giving.

The world brought us into the day. Cotton from Egypt, wool from Australia, coffee from Colombia – our needs were furnished by a multitude of unknown people. And in a world of hunger there was breakfast for us, food in abundance. We could not live without our neighbours. We are privileged, over-privileged, in such a world as this.

We brought ourselves into the day. Life is your gift – air to fill our lungs, bodies which can transform it into energy: but the gift was made ours. We have chosen life. Not just eternal life. Red-blooded, food-loving, friendship-seeking life – such as Jesus enjoyed at the feasts of publicans and sinners. We affirm life, we choose life, we are here for one more day of life and we say 'yes' to it.

So help us to use it well: not bothering about making a good impression on others but bringing to this day our authentic selves; and, at the end of this day, may we give it back to you as something preciously received, preciously used, preciously offered – a period of time such as has never been before in human history and never will be again, alive with your presence and purpose.

In the name of Jesus Christ, we ask it. Amen

Ian M Fraser

REVEAL YOURSELF TO US THIS DAY
(A prayer of confession)

We are here, God the Lord, because we want to get straight with you. In the end we know we will have to face you and account for the way we have lived our lives. For our lives are entrusted for a purpose. We are not to use them in any way we want, but to help make the world a place you will be proud to acknowledge as your own. That seems a distant dream. Yet you trust us to be partners in your purpose.

We come to worship because we want to get straight with you about that purpose. It is when we open ourselves to you and give you your due that we can see truly what we have been born to be, what part you want us to play.

Reveal yourself to us this day. For we are often absorbed in ourselves – what we are doing and what we are planning, so that we do not give you the place in our lives that you should have.

Reveal yourself to us this day. For we are often preoccupied with getting and spending and making life more comfortable for ourselves, however badly the rest of the world suffers.

Reveal yourself to us today. For we can forget the love which calls us and claims us, so that we are not marked in our lives with resurrection joy, which others might see in us to be a sign of your presence.

Reveal yourself to us this day in your forgiving grace. Put us straight with you and straight with ourselves and straight with our neighbours. In your compassion, make us better people. By your forgiveness give us a new start. Amen

Ian M Fraser

ACROSS THE BARRIERS

Living God,
grant us the grace to see your image
not just in those we know and like
but in those across the barriers of our making.
Forgive the prejudices that divide and exclude,
and help us to reflect your outrageous love
that reaches out to embrace enemies.
So may we truly follow Christ.
Amen

Chris Polhill

THE FINAL REALITY

What's your game, Lord God? Why do you tease us with visions and then waken us to reality? The vision becomes a mirage. We grasp it and then it disappears: racism is rampant, war and famine stalk the earth, schoolchildren gun each other down … How can we live in hope of a Kingdom of justice, love and peace when life-in-the-raw is all around?

And your Son let people down. They gave him his chance and their support. They wanted freedom from the Roman yoke – and that was meant to be what the Messiah would bring. They wanted justice, which the prophets promised – and the Messiah was to bring it. They wanted peace, the peace of sitting under their vine and fig tree and no one making them afraid. It was not to be. Jesus represented a promise but he did not deliver.

How like we are to the folk Jesus knew: wanting things to work out in the way which suits us; seeing the world's evil and sin, but not the work of the Holy Spirit.

We need to be turned round in our tracks like Paul on the Damascus road; so that we may see the Holy Spirit at work and join in that work of grace in the world, and the kind of freedom, justice and peace which the coming of Jesus Christ delivered.

Forgive us, we pray. Give us new eyes to see things your way. For beyond all the disheartening realities of life is this substantive and hopeful fact: You are the final reality. Forbid that we open our eyes to life's harsh realities without opening them to you, the reality that determines our future.

Ian M Fraser

FACES

All these faces, Lord God, passing us in the street. Over generations, millions upon millions and no two the same. Resemblances, yes. Strong resemblances, yes. Look-a-likes, yes. But no repeats.

What a craftsman you are, Lord God, to work in such a small space as is afforded by a human face and yet make each one of us unique. There has never been, there never will be, a reproduction of our human face. It is a sign from you.

Each one of us is special to you, each given a distinctive part to play in life, each one particularly loved.

Special to you, Lord God, are the drawn faces of the hungry, the terrified faces of those who suffer violence, the blank faces of those counted failures, all precious.

God, forgive us if we forget that we are special to you. And forgive us if we treat anyone else we meet as being other than special to you.

Ian M Fraser

HOPE FOR A TORMENTED WORLD

Lord God, we give thanks that you are active in your world through the Holy Spirit; that you keep touching people to life where despair seems to rule; that the oppressed gain new dignity when they realise they are made in your image, and stand up straight, confronting oppressors, claiming their inheritance in your name and by your power.

We give thanks that the Bible is a new dynamic resource in so many hands, freeing up people's gifts for ministry, leading them in new ways of life.

Through the Spirit and the Word provide hope, we pray, for a tormented world.

We pray for the people of Ireland, Iraq, Russia, America ...

Ian M Fraser

WE'RE CAUGHT IN SYSTEMS

We're caught in systems, Lord, doing what systems demand, whether you demand it or not. We confess our unwillingness to struggle to find your way, and to take risks of rejection by systems, because they also sustain us in comfort and with security.

We're caught in tides of emotion, Lord, moving this way and that as the wind blows, making judgements that are not carefully enough examined, wished on us by radio and TV and our favourite newspaper. We confess our unwillingness to find your truth, to take the risk of confronting popular opinion.

We're caught in the allures of consumerism, Lord, offers we supposedly cannot afford to reject, without which our lives would supposedly be impoverished – as if life consisted of getting more and more. We confess our unwillingness to struggle to find what makes true life, to take the risk of affirming priorities that people in general will despise.

So, unconsciously at times, thoughtlessly at others, we fall into ways which deny you as the Way, Truth, and Life.

Forgive us Lord, and restore us to the true ways of living.

We pray for those caught in systems:

We pray for those caught in systems of history which produce mindsets in conflict with one another (Northern Ireland …)

We pray for those enslaved to intransigent hatreds and prejudices (Rwanda, Burundi, Democratic Republic of the Congo …)

We pray for people oppressed by systems of aggression (Palestine/Israel, Zimbabwe …)

We pray for those caught in systems of weather change …

We pray, Lord, but what do we do?

We begin with communion with you.
In communion, Jesus enters into our beings,
and then we are sent out into the world
to a whole different system of living.
Amen

Ian M Fraser

ABUNDANT LIFE
(a prayer of intercession)

Look, Lord on your world – then look on us. How can we match up to the world's needs? We cannot even identity them adequately. Come to our aid!

We pray for those caught up in war, those whose homes have been destroyed; those grieving the deaths of family members and friends.

We pray for those deprived of food, especially when it is the result of others' greed; we pray for those who cannot find clean water to drink.

We pray for those suffering from preventable diseases, especially AIDS; for those left orphaned.

We pray for those around our doors who are ill, lonely, neglected, denied such friendship as we enjoy.

Take the time and gifts you have entrusted to us, and teach us how to use them to give others the abundant life which Jesus Christ came to bestow on all – so that your people may rejoice in the new life you give, for you are the life-giver and we are your servants. Amen

Ian M Fraser

THE STONE THE BUILDERS REJECTED

Let us pray for those whose lives are wilderness ...
Those who are hungry and thirsty ...
Those who are all alone ...
Those who are prevented from being the people God made them to be ...
For the stone which the builders rejected is made the cornerstone

Let us pray for those whose own will not receive them ...
Those who are not listened to ...
Those who are under constant threat ...
For the stone which the builders rejected is made the cornerstone

Let us pray for those whose calling is denied ...
Those who cannot speak their name ...
Those whose gifts are not recognised and affirmed ...
For the stone which the builders rejected is made the cornerstone

Let us pray for those who are judged and condemned ...
Those who are blinded by their own self-righteousness ...

Let us pray for ourselves …
For the stone which the builders rejected is made the cornerstone

O Christ, you lived as an ordinary man,
not in style but simply,
yet you still caused an uproar, and questions everywhere;
you drew the expectations of hungry crowds,
and brought buried conflicts to the light.
May we, who are sometimes swayed by the crowd's approval,
and who often avoid conflict
for fear of its cost to us,
stand firm in the gospel of justice and peace
and follow faithfully in your way of compassion and solidarity
with those who are poor and excluded,
wherever it may lead us.
Amen

Kathy Galloway

PRAYER AFTER A TERRORIST INCIDENT

Merciful God,
giver of life and bearer of all pain,
we lay before you the violence of our world,
the horrors and hatreds of our time,
the hurts we inflict upon one another
and the anger and aggression of our own hearts.
Bind up the wounds of your warring children,
grant us wisdom in seeking the way forward
and breathe upon us your word of peace.

God of tender consolation,
we especially lay before you today the horrors of this week in …
the tragedy of so many lives destroyed or torn apart,
the pain and anguish of relatives and friends.
We give thanks for the courage and self-sacrifice
of so many in seeking survivors, and in bringing relief.
May their example comfort and strengthen the hearts
of those most deeply afflicted,
and may your grace support and surround them
in the depths of their grief.

God of peace and righteousness,
we lay before you the violence of the wider world,
remembering especially the peoples of ...
e.g. the Middle East, Burma, the Sudan
and all places where poverty, oppression and discrimination hold sway,
where hope is fragile and hard to find
and where the seeds of terrorism are thus so easily sown.

In the face of such horrors,
we ask forgiveness for our own part in maintaining violence and injustice,
remembering especially
those whose suffering is sustained on our behalf,
and those whose continued oppression provides the ground and riches we live upon.
Turn the hearts of the powerful nations of our world
to finding ways towards lasting peace and justice,
and grant us all a greater will to lay aside the weapons of violence and fear.

God of wisdom and understanding,
we lay before you the anger of so many across the world
in the face of acts of terrible horror.
We pray that, without adding to the spiral of violence,
those responsible may be brought to justice
and their works of terror speedily ended.
May the firm determination to respond to the evils of terrorism
be guided by wisdom and mercy,
and all anger leavened by deeper understanding.

Jon Inkpin

INVISIBLE TO US

God the Lord, you sustain us invisibly by the air we breathe, the energy granted for daily tasks and conversation, the capacity to relate to you and to one another. This is the Lord's doing and it is wonderful in our eyes. The day itself is a gift of grace, not guaranteed, for we might not have wakened to it. We give thanks.

We give thanks for those who are servants of your sustaining grace, not only those we see but those who are invisible – bakers, butchers, candlestick makers, who supply our needs.

We switch on the light and the cooker, scarcely giving a thought to those who bring electricity to our homes – except in times of storm when the lines are down and we crouch in the cold. Now we take time to thank you for them.

We remember with gratitude those who drive vans, buses, trains, trucks, allowing networks of contact to be maintained and goods and people to be moved to where they can meet and work and be of use to you. We give thanks for those who maintain our highways, those who resurface roads …

We bless you for those who make and sell clothes; for voluntary workers in charity shops; and for all kinds of service in shops that supply our daily needs and wants.

We pray for those who, invisible to us, seek to heal divisions in and between nations – in Northern Ireland, in Palestine/Israel, all those working to make peace sustainable and just.

God, who sustains us, we give thanks for all those working behind the scenes.

Ian M Fraser

LIKE THE MOTHER EAGLE
(A Eucharistic prayer)

In the face of your mysterious presence, Creator God, we have so little understanding of the wonder of your awesome love for us. You care for us with the fierce protectiveness of the mother bear defending her cubs. Yet, like the mother eagle, you would push us from our cosy nest and make us fly for ourselves. And when we struggle in the treacherous gusts you glide beneath us ready to catch us and lift us and help us try again.

COME, HOLY SPIRIT, AND BLESS THIS TABLE AND THOSE AROUND IT.
TEACH US TO FLY ON THE WIND OF YOUR SPIRIT,
TEACH US TO DANCE WITH GOD THE DANCER,
TEACH US TO WONDER AT YOUR UNENDING LOVE FOR US.
AND WHEN WE DO NOT UNDERSTAND YOUR SECRETS,
WHEN WE SEEK TO LIMIT AND DEFINE AND CONTAIN YOU,
WHEN WE HIDE IN FEAR OF OTHERS AND OURSELVES,
GATHER US UNDER YOUR WINGS, NURSE US AT YOUR BREAST,
THEN PUSH US OUT AGAIN TO LIVE FOR YOU.

We gather round this table as Jesus gathered with his friends in an upper room. They gathered to remember the Passover and we gather to remember the Last Supper. For them, as for us, the ritual is one that has taken place many times, in many ways and in many places – always unique and always the same.

We remember Jesus' words and actions when he took bread, the ordinary staple diet, and blessed and broke it, and said:

'Take this all of you and eat it. This is my body, which is given for you; do this and make me real in your lives.'

Then he took the cup, filled with wine, made of the abundant good things of the earth for us to drink in celebration; he gave thanks and said:

'Take this all of you and drink it. For this is my blood, the blood of the new and ever-lasting promise of God; do this and make me real in your lives.'

So we, too, celebrate in wonder, the mystery of God's transcendent love brought to us in the ordinary things of life.

IN THE CRUCIFIED CHRIST, GOD MAKES FOOLISH OUR WISDOM,
WITH THE RISEN CHRIST, GOD INVITES US TO JOIN THE DANCE OF LIFE,
AND WE WILL ENCOUNTER CHRIST AGAIN AND AGAIN AS THE SPIRIT LEAD US
     AND ENFOLDS US.

Sharing of the bread and wine.

Linda Hill

ONE LIFE
(A communion prayer)

We know we have only one life, Lord God. It is meant to spell out your glory. At the end of our days our thoughts and actions will be offered to you in a kind of bundle and we will see what you make of it. It may be a surprise. A single mother who brings up her kids against all the odds, or a man spending his days clearing waste may outshine an important professor with all his academic degrees.

We don't want to use the gift of life carelessly, selfishly, and so let you down.

Open our eyes to the needs of your beloved world, which Jesus Christ lived and died for.

Enable us, through the Holy Spirit, to discern with his eyes the ways in which people, all made in your image, exploit and oppress one another.

We pray now for people and situations in ... *(e.g. Israel/Palestine, Sudan, Bangladesh, the Democratic Republic of the Congo ...).*

Lord God, teach us to stand with people in their desolation, and to share the resources entrusted to us, which are provided for the needs of all.

Around our homes, make us sensitive to those who, like Jesus, have no place to lay their heads; who, like Jesus, have sorrow and pain to bear; who, like Jesus, are despised and rejected.

We would need to be different people to live this way. Weakness in our natures holds us back.

So we give thanks to you Lord Christ that we can gather here in worship to get straight what life is for.

We give thanks that you can penetrate our natures, entering into them to endow them with your grace and power; that, as we receive the blessed bread, which will be for us your bodily life, and the blessed wine, which will be for us your sacrificed life, we need no longer live for ourselves but for you who died for us; that we might be collaborators with you in transforming life, so that it becomes the life abundant for all which you promised.

We rejoice in the fact that that promise is not just words, but that there is a spread table before us.

Lord God, here, take us, shape us, remake us
that the world may be glad that we were born,
that angels may dance,
that we may hear at the end of our day your greeting,
'Good for you. Come, share my joy.'
Amen

Ian M Fraser

ROLL UP YOUR SLEEVES AND GET GOING

God said: 'I made you in my image and called you to be my friend and fellow worker. Hold your head high. You are beloved by God.'

We responded with: 'But we have let you down. You made us trustees of the earth: it is full of war, torture, rape, violence, fear.'

You said: 'The power of the Holy Spirit is still at work. Ask sincerely for my forgiveness and you will find fresh hope and courage to share with me in the world's transformation. Roll up your sleeves and get going. I'll be alongside.'

So, Lord, we come to seek your forgiveness and to ask for new power to do and dare in your name. Heal us and help us. Since our own natures are not up to the challenge, nourish us with the life of Jesus Christ in the sacrament, that his indwelling might make all things possible for us.

It is in his name and depending on his prevailing grace that we ask this.

(Lord's Prayer)

Ian M Fraser

PRAYER FOR GOING OUT

Holy Spirit of God, mysteriously, wonderfully you commune with our spirits. You take the things of Christ and bring them home to us; and our spirits are refreshed and strengthened as Christ takes hold of us through your indwelling, to make us his own. We praise and bless your holy name, you who renew our innermost being.

You send us in mission to the ends of the earth. We are not up for it. Our heart fails us at the magnitude of the task. But you give us heart, remind and assure us that we have one another to turn to, we have you: all things are possible to those who believe. We take heart and soldier on, blessed by your presence within us.

You are like a refreshing stream. We bathe in you, we frolic in you, we drink of you and renew our strength. You are an unfailing source of hope and promise for our often tatty lives, for the often tatty life of the world.

You do not overbear us. Like a sensitive lover you wait for our response. Like a lover you rejoice in it. Like a lover you give it full value so that we are warmed and enriched and encouraged to go further on the road of obedience. Not a step of that road do we take alone; you travel with us, our guide, our comforter, our friend.

We bless you, Holy Spirit of God, who renews the whole earth and makes us sharers in the renewal of all things.

Ian M Fraser

WILD CARDS FOR THE KINGDOM

Lord Christ, God's wild card, help us to follow in your way:
You overturned concepts of divinity, coming so weak and small;
you overturned notions of prestige, working in a carpenter's shop;
you overturned assumptions of appropriate company, 'a gluttonous man and a wine-bibber', you associated with the punters.
Foxes and birds had shelter –
    you identified with the homeless.
Women and children were devalued –
    you gave them place and status.
The religious kept rules for self-serving justification –
    you saw through their game and condemned it.
When the safety of Galilee beckoned, you set your face to go to Jerusalem.
When you were tried, it was your accusers who were put on trial.
The flogging and crucifixion put you at one with
all who are tortured and murdered.
You submitted to death; then gave death its comeuppance.

Lord Christ, who gave integrity of life its meaning,
make us wild cards for the Kingdom, we pray.
Amen

Ian M Fraser

DOWN TO EARTH (Analysis Paralysis)

Read: Matthew 25:31–46 or Luke 4:16–19

(Silence)

Lord, it seems pretty obvious what we should be doing.
It's plain what you require.

Jesus, made it plain.
Jesus, brought it all down to earth.

Lord, although your work is never easy or straightforward,
may we never become confused and uncertain
about why your son,
our saviour,
came
and lived
and died on the Cross

Lord, may we never become side-tracked with theology.
Lord, lay your Spirit upon us.
Amen

Neil Paynter

EYES BIG WITH WONDER

God, the promise of life in unfurling poppy petals,
spreading butterfly wings,
    bursting buds,
    and tiny, trusting hands,

Give us
sensibility
    that we may learn to think fragility;
    understanding
    that we may know our part

in the intricate pattern of being;
companionship
that we may live gently and simply
alongside all living things;
Give us
eyes big with wonder
that we may truly see
    the small things of our earth;
    ears sharp to hear
    what lies on the other side
    of silence;
    hearts of flesh
    that we may feel suffering
    and beauty;
for what we truly see, hear and feel
we will not pollute, exploit or destroy
but will care for tenderly.
We will cherish
this fragile and finite planet
which is our only home
and know the holiness of becoming
fully and integrally human.

Joy Mead

YOUR RECONCILING ARMS

Used at the national release of the Decade to Overcome Violence, Australia,
March 2003.

Holy God, of holy dreaming,
through your breath of life you bring creation into being.
You shape the myriad forms and features of this land,
and form its rainbow of many colours, cultures and peoples.
Through your redeeming love you give us peace in Jesus Christ, your only Son,
    our Lord.
You reconcile us together in one body by the Cross,
giving us grace for our journey of healing.
Through your Holy Spirit you enable us to grow and to flourish in your service.
You bring forth fruits of love and grains of joy.
In this Decade to Overcome Violence,
help us, we pray, to prune back all which brings destruction,

and to turn to your renewing springs:
that we may seek you in all we meet,
and cultivate a culture of peace.
Holy God, of holy dreaming,
breathe through us,
and in your mercy
hear our prayer.

Holy God, of holy journeying,
you travel with us through darkness and despair.
Hear our prayer for your children, here and elsewhere,
caught up in the violence of our world.
You call us to move out beyond our boundaries,
to walk with others in their journeys, sharing your Spirit of reconciliation.
Breathe your Holy Spirit upon us, we pray, and open our hearts to your presence,
that we may be released from our warring passions,
and journey onward in the freedom of your love.
Encircle us with your peace,
enfold us in your reconciling arms,
and enlarge the circles of our love.
Amen

Jon Inkpin

GOD OF HOLY JUSTICE

First used at the Sydney Palm Sunday protest during the Iraq war, 2003.

God of Holy Justice,
you inflame our hearts with righteous anger,
and breathe upon us the gentleness of your peace.
In this trying hour,
give us care for one another,
commitment to others,
and courage to challenge the powers of evil:
that we may comfort the afflicted,
and afflict the comfortable,
transforming our world's warring madness.
In the name of Jesus Christ,
who, riding on a donkey,
turned the world upside down.
Amen

Jon Inkpin

THE DOVE OF PEACE

Used at the national release of the Decade to Overcome Violence, Australia, March 2003.

God of reconciling love,
whose covenant with us is an everlasting covenant,
and whose peace passes all our understanding,
release, we pray, the dove of peace in our hearts and lives;
pour out your love upon your warring children;
touch with your healing Spirit the violent places of our world;
enable us to link our hands in your service,
and lead us in the ways of true and lasting reconciliation, now and for ever.
Amen

Jon Inkpin

GRACE OUR LIVING TOGETHER

God, the Holy Trinity,
within your dance is both unity and community.
So grace our living together
that, from village to city,
there may be your harmony,
and compassionate understanding
of all differences.
So may our lives worship you,
Father, Son and Holy Spirit.
Amen

Chris Polhill

YOUR GRACE AND GRITTINESS

Lord Christ,
in your earthly life you failed to come up to people's expectations.
Faced with testing situations you were outrageously inventive.
In human relationships you were outrageously imaginative,
compassionate and straight-speaking.
Your love for the poor showed you to be outrageously committed to justice.

You lacked balance, were short of diplomatic skills.
Yet you are the Way, the Truth, the Life.
In light of your life it is human expectations that need to be revised.
So make us unbalanced, we pray:

Not saying 'on the one hand, on the other hand' to excuse inaction.
Not pandering to social prejudices of racism and sexism.
Willing to jettison advancement, promotion, prestige in favour of truthful living.
Prepared to spend our lives sacrificially to share in the coming of God's Kingdom
and the doing of God's will on earth, for we want to follow in your footsteps.

O Christ, our saviour and friend,
clothe us with yourself that your grace and grittiness
may enter into us and make the kind of living possible
which is ready to face persecution, false charges, vilification –
whatever might come, as we seek to do your will;
because it is in your name and to God's glory that we act.
Amen

Ian M Fraser

REFLECTIONS AND MEDITATIONS

THE WOW OF CREATION

Each of us is made of stardust –
atoms built millions of years ago in hot stars,
thrown randomly into space,
collected by all-pervading gravity
and taken in as food, drink, air,
and recycled again and again by nature;
spread out for reuse,
during our lifetimes and after.

Start with a hydrogen atom
and an oxygen atom or two,
and carbon atoms for fire and fuel;
add nitrogen atoms and the stage is set
for the finger of God to bring the chemistry to life –
DNA molecules which can reproduce,
but only when living in community with others.

When you think of the simplicity of the basic building blocks of the universe,
such as the hydrogen atom –
and the fact that its potential for change is limited
to the rise and fall of its energy levels,
and reflect that with this are made:
the hummingbird and the whale
the mind of an Einstein
the music of Handel
the words of Shakespeare
the Iona landscape
the laughter of children
the courage of people in suffering,
then no miracle
no sign
can ever arouse more wonder
than the facts of the natural universe
and the mystery of the human soul.
Dust to dust
Atoms to atoms

We all share the atoms again and again.
When you eat and drink you become one with those atoms –
you receive what you already are,
you become more of what you already are.

Some of the atoms in your body may once have been part of a dinosaur.

When you breathe in, you breathe life-giving oxygen atoms –
do you breathe in some of the atoms that Jesus breathed?

David Hawkey

DO NOT RETREAT

Do not retreat into your private world,
that place of safety, sheltered from the storm
where you may tend your garden, seek your soul,
and rest with loved ones where the fire burns warm.

To tend a garden is a precious thing,
but dearer still the one where all may roam;
the weeds of poison, poverty and war
demand your care, who call the earth your home.

To seek your soul, it is a precious thing,
but you will never find it on your own;
only among the clamour, threat and pain
of other people's need will love be known.

To rest with loved ones is a precious thing,
but peace of mind exacts a higher cost;
your children will not rest and play in quiet
while they still hear the crying of the lost.

Do not retreat into your private world,
there are more ways than firesides to keep warm;
there is no shelter from the rage of life,
so meet its eye, and dance within the storm.

Kathy Galloway

(Tune: Sursum Corda, COSH)

SEPTEMBER 11TH, 2002

A year ago today
a strange new world was born
at the heart of global wealth.
A world of misunderstanding,
of alienation,
where 'the other' was no longer
our sister and brother,
but one whose face is feared.
And one year on
those who control our lives
plan revenge; global revenge
on our connected planet.
And as the bombs are loaded
we hear again
the tears
of the One who holds us all.

Peter Millar

LEWIS THE BOOK

I have a friend whom I have known for ten years. When I first knew Lewis he was home-less and sleeping in the various hidden corners of one of our cities. One night he was set alight in his sleeping bag. He had very nasty burns and was in hospital for some time. When he was well again he wrote this poem. I think it shows the spirit and courage of some of the so-called socially excluded homeless people in our neighbourhoods.

Viv Davies

Nay Asking

Ther's nay need to haud yir pockets lads,
Am no gonny ask yi fir chinge
Cos a know yir in a hurry
Tae git an catch yir trains.

But some day yi'l huv tha' pleasure
Tae pit some money in ma hat,
An a wul huv tha pleasure
O thanking yi fir that.

It may jist be coppers, silver or even gold
But ma lads am sorry
Yir fortune can't be told
Fir yir copper, silver or gold.

Aye ma lads av got ma Freedom
O which a dearly hold.
Aye ma lads yi canny buy it
Wi yir copper, silver or gold.

Lewis the Book

Lewis did value his freedom and retains it, and now has a tenancy, a part-time job, which he enjoys, and a little dog. I still see him and I like to feel he will always be my friend.

Pray for those who have no homes;
that they may find people willing to help them
and offer them the hand of friendship.

ALL PEOPLE, ALL HUMAN

I'm telling the people with power
that I have power too.
If you stifle my voice,
and deny me a voice,
I will show my power to you.
I will not come with a weapon,
I will not come in fear.
I will come with others
as brothers and sisters
and a voice you will have to hear.

I'm telling people with knowledge
that I have knowledge too.
If you ignore my words,
and deny what you've heard,
my knowledge will be lost to you.
I will not come in anger,
I will not come in pain,
I will come as me,
with dignity,
and your denial will be to your shame.

I'm telling the people with control,
that I have control too.
If you put me in chains,
then hatred reigns,
and fear gains control of you.
I will not come as a prisoner,
I will not come broken to you,
I will come with pride,
and stand by your side,
because I am human too.

ATD Fourth World member

WORDS FROM A SHOP DOORWAY

I envy you that overcoat, you know.
Thick, black and buttoned to the neck –
just right to stop the wind that cuts me like a knife.
And I envy you those fancy gloves as well.
Leather, with a soft fur lining I imagine.
A Christmas present, I expect, from a loving, caring wife.

And I have to say I envy you those shoes.
I bet they don't let water in
and soak your socks so that your feet are always damp and cold.
And I envy you as well the fact that,
although we're much the same age,
you look young and well-kept … while I look ragged, tired, old.

The woman on your arm's a looker too.
Flowing hair, and, although her coat is firmly fastened,
I can well imagine that, in a velvet dress with those high heels, she looks a lovely sight.
You're off downtown, the two of you, to where the pretty people go.
You've got your lady, I've got my dog.
I envy you.

But I do not envy you the problem that you have
with your eyesight, because as yet it's not quite dark,
and I'm here clearly to be seen.
Is there some reason why you can't see me? Perhaps you need new lenses.
And I don't envy you the fact that your hearing's not too good.
I'm calling out, from just a yard away, and it's clear you can't hear

or you'd look in my direction.
Have you a problem with all your senses?

But wait, perhaps it's neither sight nor hearing that's at fault.
Perhaps it's the muscles in your neck
that won't let you turn your head towards me.
Or your back, perhaps it's clicked
and you can't turn at all.
Bad luck. I don't envy you that.
There must be something, after all, that's physically wrong.
What other reason could there be?
For when all's said and done, we're both human beings,
although your world is warm and rounded, and mine is cold and flat.

'Pass on, you fat and greasy citizens, pass on.'
No, they're not my words, Shakespeare wrote them long ago.
How do I know that? Ha! you make the mistake, my friend,
of equating my present plight with foolishness or lack of education.
When you look at me – if you'd look at me – you'd see,
behind these eyes, a brain like yours, but one which, at the moment,
no one needs or wants.
You thought you understood my situation.
'Idler', 'waster', good-for-nothing', 'parasite'.
Look in the thesaurus and increase the range of words that you can use.
But, while you're there,
take time
and find the word 'compassion' –
that, at least, would be a start.
Find 'love', find 'care', and then find 'understanding'.
Search through for others, there are plenty to be found.
But what would truly change this ugly city's face would be
if you could find these things not just in books,
but in your heart.

Stephen Cornish

THE POWER OF PROTEST

In my teens I joined others my age
in Trafalgar Square
to protest for an end to the Vietnam war.
There were only a few of us.
We wore bells around our necks and flowers in our hair.
The sun beat down and the pavements were hot
and incense of peace wafted through the air.

I was ridiculed when I returned home.

My friend was a young mum
when she joined with others in the Women's Peace Camp
at Greenham Common.
They were all women
who wept for their children as they cried for nuclear disarmament.
It was dark and cold by the wire
but they lit candles and kept them burning.
I wish I'd been there –

Even though she was ridiculed when she returned home.

Now it's almost the millennium, the year 2000.
I joined with others linking hands in a six-mile chain
in Birmingham
to protest for an end to third world debt.
There were no age or gender limits this time.
We all wore red, and broken chains and carried red balloons.
The sun beat down and the pavements were hot.
Music and car horns, whistles and church bells filled the air.

And I was ridiculed when I returned home.
But over 50,000 people sang a song for justice!

Time moved on and I joined with others
in Glasgow
on a peace march to stop the war in Iraq.
Mixed races, mixed classes, mixed creeds – together;
beating drums and singing 'All You Need Is Love'.
Rainbow colours in bright sunshine.
Politicians flee before the army of peace protesters.
And this time, there was solidarity when I returned home.

Christine Green

DO WE SEE ... WILL WE LISTEN?

Sung to the tune of 'Where have all the flowers gone?', with strong guitar accompaniment as a protest song, or reflectively as a lament. In the latter case, the last verse should be sung more firmly.

Do we see the young folk here, living in poverty?
Do we see the young folk here, struggling with life?
Do we see the young folk here, lost and discontented?
When will we listen well?
When will we listen well?

Do we see the young folk here, excluded from community?
Do we see the young folk here, lost to our homes?
Do we see the young folk here, disabled by society?
When will we listen well?
When will we listen well?

Do we see the young folk here, the bright ones who have left us?
Do we see the young folk here, for whom the dark has come?
Do we see the young folk here, falling into mystery?
When will we listen well?
When will we listen well?

Do we see the young folk here, going to 'serve their country'?
Do we see the young folk here, tense and afraid?
Do we see the young folk here, sacrificing for our fear?
When will we listen well?
When will we listen well?

God can see the young folk here, reflections of God's image.
God can see the young folk here, lost and alone.
God can see the young folk here and cries out for our listening.
When will we ever learn?
When will we ever learn?

Yvonne Morland

SHE CALLED ME ON THE PHONE

She called me on the phone
The same phone
The same phone that she was beaten with
The same phone that caused her bruises
What could I say?
(Silence)
She told me
She told me that he hit her
He said it was the last time
She believed him
What could I say?
(Silence)
He told me
He told me he didn't want to
He just couldn't stop himself
What could I say?
(Silence)
She came to me
She came to me crying
She was walking where she always had
Now she never can again
What could I say?
(Silence)
She told me
She told me it was her fault
She shouldn't have been there
She shouldn't have said that
She shouldn't have worn that
She should have known
And now everything is different
Everything
What could I think?
(Silence)
I saw them
I saw them on the news
Their husbands were murdered
They were beaten
They were raped
What can I do?

(Silence)
I tell you
Every woman I know
Every woman I know has suffered
Every woman I know has suffered physical or sexual abuse
What do you say?

Katrina Crosby

OLD MAN

My old man
worked for the same firm
for thirty-seven years
hated every minute of it I suspect
out on his ear
(his arse actually)
at fifty-five
surplus
to requirements

Was there dignity there?

The dignity of labour
certainly
at the beginning
the dignity of belonging
loyalty too
comradeship

But indignity
ultimately.

And where are they now
those dinosaurs of industrial decline
and what of their dignity?
Consigned perhaps to the scrap heap
of technological change
at eighteen years old
aspirations stillborn, energies squandered.

Or what of the 'lucky' few?
Stressed

beyond bearing
year on year
performance targets
competition
running
to stand still
looking increasingly
like prey
hunted
by generations to come
hot on their heels.

It needn't be like that.
It should be possible
to order things
as if people mattered
as if dignity mattered.

We have to try.

Pete Anderson

MAKE NO MISTAKE: PEACE, JUSTICE, LOVE
FOR THE GOSPEL TELLS US SO

In 1928, A.J. Muste, one of the organisers of the Fellowship of Reconciliation, wrote, 'In a world built on violence, one must be a revolutionary before one can be a pacifist.'

And so we pray.

Make no mistake,
in a world dominated by the
powers of fear, war, and money,
where leaders speak openly
and proudly of the American Empire,
the gospel messages of Peace and Justice and Love
are the building blocks
of revolution, non-violent revolution.
Revolution may sound like too strong a word
to gospel people
who base their lives on action and reflection
for Peace and Justice and Love.

But make no mistake,
those who struggle for the gospel
of Peace and Justice and Love in action and reflection
are engaged in a non-violent revolution.

What about gospel justice?
In a time when we lead the world
with over two million people in jail
when millions have no work
when millions more who do work
do not earn enough to support their families
when we lead the world in executions
when public housing is destroyed
and education is slashed
when refugees die alone in deserts,
and die in our cities by the trailer full
when our lesbian and gay sisters and brothers
are condemned for wanting to commit to each other
when our international sisters and brothers get
harassed and get night visits from the FBI
when our sisters and brothers of colour
are told to just forget about centuries of oppression
when millions of our sisters and brothers
live on less than $2 a day
when corporations purchase and shape
the laws of the world
when 'the invisible hand of the market'
is our certified god
Make no mistake
gospel Justice is revolutionary.

What about gospel Peace?
In a country that spends $12,000 a second
on the military
In a time when unelected leaders
use and re-use the horrible 9-11 deaths
of innocent mothers and fathers
to scare tens of millions
by fanning the searing flames of insecurity
and then order tens of thousands
of our sisters and brothers

(who are in the army to be able to go to college
and to get enough money to live on)
to march and shoot and bomb and invade
and occupy countries
where we have already starved by sanctions
hundreds of thousands of children
in the name of a perpetual war on terrorism
a war that was mapped out
before terrorists ever struck
(and then – instead of bringing home
our sisters and brothers –
leave them out in the deserts and in cities
with no water or electricity
guarding oilfields with their lives)
Make no mistake
gospel Peace is revolutionary.

What about gospel Love?
In a time
when we are told that our sister the immigrant
is a threat to our jobs
When we are told that our brother the stranger
has a bomb for us
When we are told that this religion says
the world is better off without others of that religion
When we are told that executing other people
is for the common good
And when they dare to tell us
that dropping bombs and murdering thousands
is liberation
Make no mistake
gospel Love is revolutionary
For the gospel tells us so.

The gospel tells us
that Jesus was born poor –
so we are to love the poor – and not just love the poor
but bring justice so there are fewer poor.
The gospel tells us
that Jesus was a refugee –
so we are to love the refugee – and not just love the refugee

but bring justice so there are few refugees.
The gospel tells us
that Jesus said the prisoners are to be set free –
and so we are to bring justice and set the prisoners free.
The gospels tells us
that Jesus said we are to love our enemies –
so we are to love them not kill them.
The gospel tells us
that Jesus said blessed be the peacemakers –
so we are to make peace.
The gospel tells us
that Jesus said nothing is greater than love –
so we are to love, and love, and love.

Our world, our country, our churches,
our families, our selves
deeply need the action and reflection of
Peace and Justice and Love
In this, Gandhi was a revolutionary
Martin Luther King was a revolutionary
Dorothy Day, Oscar Romero,
Kathy Kelly are all revolutionaries
Make no mistake
Nothing is more revolutionary
in the world we live in today
than struggling in action and reflection
for the true gospel of Peace and Justice and Love
And so we together again
try to take up the struggle with our lives
try to live lives committed
to Peace and Justice and Love
Make no mistake
Peace Justice Love
For the gospel tells us so.

Bill Quigley

THE LIGHT OF THE WORLD IS SHINING

We placed candles on a map –
the world spread out on a damp, dusty floor,
held down by sea-gifted stones and shells,
circled by the old and young,
the searchers and seekers,
the dreamers and healers

We placed candles on a map
because we knew that wars were raging
and hate and shame and fear were rising
because we knew our brothers were dying
and in their arms their children were crying
because we knew our sisters were starving
whilst greed and wealth and violence were harming
because we knew our land was taken
and trees were cut and gifts were stolen
because we knew of pain and sorrow
and our neighbours' fears of facing tomorrow

Because we knew,
we placed candles on a map
chartered the contours of care
marked lines where love lived
pinpointed places where
people and projects made peace

We placed candles on a map
one in each spot:
for the bridge builders in Belfast
and the soul-healers in Sarajevo
for the young women of Washington Heights
and the earth-carers of Kerala
for the life-lovers of Liverpool
and the ministers in Maputo
for the sister in San Francisco
and the believers in Beijing
for the joy-givers in Johannesburg
and the campaigners in Chiapas …
for love, for truth,
for justice, for peace
we placed candles on a map

We placed candles on a map
and in our humble act of honouring hope
we saw the Light of the world was shining.

Rachel McCann

THE NOT-SO-NEW SONG

He said,
    'Thou shalt love the Lord thy God with all thy heart …
    and thy neighbour as thyself.'
He did not say,
    'God bless America – only.'
He said,
    'A certain man fell among thieves … was stripped of his
    raiment … and left half-dead … two passed on the other
    side. A certain Samaritan took care of him.
    Who do you think was the real neighbour?
He did not say,
    'Shock and awe – destroy, kill, dehumanise.
    Collateral damage is necessary.'
He said,
    'You have heard it said, "Hate thine enemy" … But I say,
    what reward have you if you love them who love you?'
He did not say,
    'Together we stand – no one else matters.'
He said,
    'To whom much is given, much is required.'
He did not say,
    'Might makes right.
    America should use the world's resources for its own luxuries.'
He said,
    'Blessed are the peacemakers.'
He did not say,
    'Pray for peace.'
He said,
    'And why beholdest thou the mote in thy brother's eye …
    Thou hypocrite, first cast out the beam from thine own eye …'
He did not say,
    'They are evil. We are right.'

He said,
>   'Ye shall know them by their fruits.'
>   'In as much as you have done it unto one of the least of these,
>   you have done it unto me.
>   Inasmuch as you did it not to one of the least of these,
>   you did it not to me.'

And he never said
>   That it would be easy.
>   That it would not take courage.
>   That it would be popular.
>   That you might not be crucified.

And he never said
>   That he would do it for us.

Faith Dowdy Armstrong

O AMERICA, I LOVE YOU
(after Allen Ginsberg)

O America, I love you –
not as you are now
but the dream of you.
No, not the dream –
what you could be.

What you truly could be.

O America, I love you:
I love Henry David Thoreau, I love Walt Whitman,
I love Jackson Browne, I love Thomas Paine.
I love your prophets.
O America, when will you listen to your prophets?
O America, you are breaking my heart.
O America, what have you become?
O America, have you gone mad?

O America, maybe you were always crazy and I didn't fully realise it,
    didn't want to believe it –
wars in Vietnam, Cambodia, Nicaragua …

coups in Chile, Indonesia, Haiti ...
deals with dictators in Panama, Guatemala,
Iraq ...

O America, I read you gave 3 billion to Osama Bin Laden and his fellow terrorists.
O America, I read you gave millions to Saddam Hussein.

O America, when will you repent of your great wealth built on slavery?
When will you repent of the genocide of the Native American people?
O America, when will you stop sending the poor to die for you?

O America, I am full of light and dark too,
I understand, in a way –
I've enslaved others,
I've slaughtered friends.
I understand.
We understand.

O America, will you humble yourself
or will you be humbled?

O America, the world is waiting for you to be true to your word.

O America, if you only did what you said.

O America, there is still something about you so beautiful and great:

O America, I want to dance with you all night at Mardi Gras.
O America, I want to drive with you down Highway 61 with the windows open
and the warm, fragrant night wind flowing
through our long, starry hair.
O America, I want to eat and laugh with you in a corner booth in a diner
      in New York City.
O America, I want to sleep with you under the evergreens in Washington State.
O America, I want to kiss you in the morning in a cottage in New England.

O America, remember when they used to call you the New Jerusalem?
Now they call you the great Satan.

O America, you had such promise.

O America, I love you.

I love you.
For God's sake
you spend $12,000 a second on the military.
Are you so bloody insecure?
O America, choose Life not rapture.
(Make it a slogan if it helps, make it a T-shirt.)

O America, when will you really save the world?
You could, you bastard, you bitch,
you could!
You could save the world.
You could feed every starving child.
It's your manifest destiny.
You could feed the world.
O America, you want to be God's chosen;
well, go ahead, be God's chosen.
Well, go ahead – do it!
Feed the hungry,
free the slaves,
shelter the poor huddled masses,
the hunted refugees,
the tortured.
O America, are you blind?
It is within your power.
Don't you realise?
O America, you have the power, the resources, the money,
the intelligence, the spirit
to save the world.

O America, your leader told the world:
'You are either with us or against us.'

O America, what's next?
Iran?
Syria?
North Korea?
Apocalypse?

O America, I can no longer abide you.
O America, I never dreamed your neurosis would win out in the end.
O America, I want to tell you something.

But before I do, I want to say this:

Everything you want I want –
democracy
peace
freedom
an end to terrorism.

'You are either with us or against us.'

OK, America,
if that's the way it has to be,
then
I am against you.
There, I've said it.
It breaks my heart.
Does that make me a terrorist?

O America, there are so many others like me.
Your daughters and sons are fleeing by the plane load.
I meet them in pubs,
I meet them on the road.
They are embarrassed to be your children.
They deny you.
O America, they look up at me and ask:
'But where in the world is there left to go?'
O America, they look so sad.

O America, we will come together.
O America, we will never give in to sadness, hopelessness and fear.
O America, we will stand in the way of your capitalist tanks.
O America, we will live in communities and affirm and love one another.
O America, we will take to the hills and live as ascetic peace-monks, if need be.
O America, we will use guerrilla media tactics.
O America, we will fight your giant and beastly corporations
with the power and beauty of the human Spirit,
and the holy weapon of non-violence.

O America, we are immune to security and comfort.
O America, you will never enslave us with cocaine, junk entertainment, sick sex ...
O America, we will work and never tire.
O America, we will stay rooted in prayer and meditation.

O America, we will a keep a sense of humour in this dark age.

O America, everything you say you want we want.
Everything you say you are working for we will work for:

We will work to topple dictators and bring democracy.
We will work to bring an end to terrorism.
We will work to free the oppressed and enslaved of this world.
We will work for justice and peace and a new world order
modelled on the Kingdom of Love.

O America, we will turn your world
upside down.

Neil Paynter

LESSONS: A MEDITATION

To have been
at the
centre
of things
and to find yourself
at the periphery,
that is a lesson
in humility.
To have had
power
and to have
relinquished
that power
readily,
that is a lesson
in grace.
To have been

wronged
and to have learned
to love the wrongdoer,
that is a lesson
in godliness.

Pete Anderson

WHEN THERE IS PEACE

'I know whenever peace comes, flowers will be planted instead of mines.'
12-year-old Afghan student

When there is peace
they will plant flowers
instead of mines.
And they will explode
in silence, and blow us
quite off our feet.
Their colours will blind
our eyes, their scent
will sing in our nostrils,
cling to our clothes
and linger in the air.
Fragments will fall
as petals
and none shall be afraid
to walk, though beauty
too shall require
our gentleness
when there is peace.

Alan Horner

STORIES AND READINGS

LIVING STONES

'I am a stone!' shouted Marta, this dumpy young woman from El Salvador, rolling up her sleeves, shaking with frustration and pointing her finger in accusation. 'You [Europeans] must be intentional about working together with us [the poor of the third world]. You must get clear about what you are doing. Do you not know that the European Community is in an all out war against the poor? You are out to kill us! But as Christians we are one body, and if one part hurts the whole body hurts … Is that not what the Bible tells us?'

In the stunned, embarrassed silence she went on: 'I need to shake the world to a new reality and if you are not expecting to shake the world, why are you here?

'While we are hungry, you go on diets. My mother is just a simple peasant woman. She does not understand the gringos. They use things to fatten up their cattle, then they eat the meat and get fat. Then they all go crazy for diets.

'One day stones are going to speak … Well, here is a stone talking to you … I am begging you really to listen to us, to read the signs. Unless you really listen to us you can talk yourselves to sleep.

'I am alive thanks to God and it is one of the tricks of God that I can still call you brothers and sisters. I am bringing you not the helplessness but the hopefulness of the struggling people. We don't need help, we need brothers and sisters in the struggle to change the world.'

Erik Cramb

TESTING BY HUMAN OPPRESSION
(A story from Guatemala when it was one of the Killing Fields)

As I entered Guatemala City, news came through of the assassination of a priest, Fr Faustina Villanueva Villanueva. Deaths of priests made the headlines. Hundreds and thousands of Christian catechists, delegates of the Word, leaders of small ecclesial communities were being eliminated too but these deaths went largely unreported. Still it is important that the need to remove priests existed. It showed that they were with the people. For the official church to be with the people is always a threat to repressive regimes.

Those killed need not have been particularly radical. This priest was not. But he was greatly loved by the Indians in his area, and he greatly loved them. The people in that area were terrorised. Troops would enter a village, herd the men out, rape the women, browbeat the children and take anything of value they could find in the poor houses. Nuns had had their Centre raked with bullets.

The priest had been at a meal when the two men called. When he enquired as to their business, one shot him through the side of the head. He fell forward and the other opened the back of his head with a close-range shot.

The floor where he had fallen forward was covered in blood. His people gathered earth sufficient to absorb the blood. The blood and earth were put in a box. They held a vigil beside it all night. The next day it was buried in front of the altar.

At the funeral four bishops and forty-seven priests were on parade. It was public affirmation to such killers that there were plenty more who stood by the faith who were ready to die if need be.

I asked, 'What is the effect on people of these murders, which are only the tip of an iceberg?' I was told: 'We are both more scared and more firm. With the example of our martyrs before us and the resurrection of Jesus Christ at the heart of our existence, we know that evil will be defeated – with or without our life.'

Ian M Fraser

KUMARI'S EVICTION
(A story from South India)

Kumari usually comes to see us after her work is over, about 7 pm. The other day she came very early in the morning and in great distress. Her landlord was about to evict her because he wanted to pull down her small mud and thatched hut and build a larger one in order to get a higher rent. Her hut is very basic. No running water, no electric light, no toilet and a roof that lets in the monsoon rain, but for the last four years it has been her home and that is what matters. Kumari and her three children moved into this house after the death of Kumari's husband, Mohan, from TB. It costs Rs.200 (about five pounds) a month to rent.

For the last few years, Kumari has had a sewing job repairing clothes, which brings her about Rs.200 a month. It is a full-time job, starting at 8 am, and it takes her 30 minutes to walk to work from her home to the tailoring shop. She usually gets up at about 4:30 a.m. to pump the water from the street well and to make the day's food. Her children attend the local government school (70-80 students in a class) and at night study under the baker's light in the shop next to their hut. In the school holidays, the two other children do a sweeping job and earn about Rs.3–5 a day. Most days, the family manages one meal of rice and dahl, but if the children are ill and medicine needs to be purchased, Kumari goes without her food. They never have a holiday and they seldom buy new clothes and they certainly don't have any luxuries.

Now, because of the landlord, Kumari is forced to find another place to stay. A next to impossible task in an overcrowded city, unless you have money. Where to find the 'advance money' or 'key money' – the down payment given to a landlord before occupancy? The minimum advance is Rs.500 and that will be for a tiny mud hut. One room. No windows and an earth floor. A toilet shared with many families and a water pump on the road.

After many disappointments and days of weary walking about the city after work, Kumari found a place. At least it is a shelter if very little else. Life with its myriad obstacles goes on. A new day begins.

Kumari's plight is the plight of millions. In some ways, she is better off than others. She also reveals to us the way in which perpetual struggle and human hope are bound together. On the evening of finding her new hut, Kumari's face was lit up with pure joy! In circumstances like hers, many of us would despair, but Kumari is far from despair, and her home – small and bare as it is – is a place of warmth, love and laughter. She has found life – despite the poverty of her surroundings.

This is not to advocate that we should all dwell in thatched huts in an Indian slum. There is nothing romantic about living in such conditions, yet we have to admit that as we begin to learn how the Kumaris of our world do manage to live with hope in their hearts, many questions arise.

Peter Millar

GAMBLING WITH LIFE
(A story from Chile)

Jacques Chonchol, Minister of Agrarian Reform in Salvador Allende's government in Chile, answered my question by dodging it. I represented the World Council of Churches. The heart of the interview was the takeover of agricultural land.

I had visited three areas of agrarian reform about 200 kilometres south of Santiago. Conversations with peasants, who now worked the land as their own, revealed an impressive change in their mentality as well as their material situation. Their forebears had for centuries been treated as hewers of wood and drawers of water. From nowhere it seemed they had developed gifts of leadership, capacities for communal initiative. I have heard of deserts that had not had rain for fifty years. When the rains came the deserts blossomed. It was like that in Chile.

At times the state took over the farms and divided them among the workers. At times the workers organised and took over the farms themselves, while the state came in later and confirmed their ownership. Jacques Chonchol clearly preferred the latter. Peasants who organised a takeover would have developed skills for acting as a community and for managing the land they seized. He must have felt that, in his official position, he had to give equal emphasis to both methods of redistribution. But his unstated preference was clear.

The vast latifundias that were appropriated contained great stretches of land which had not been cultivated or put to any alternative use, but yet they had been denied to peasants. I learned of landlords who had broken up their agricultural machinery when the land was seized, leaving peasants only basic tools to work with. In spite of this, at the end of the first year, they had increased productivity.

It was a revolution with too much promise in it. So it was bloodily squashed.

Prayer

Lord God,
what a spirit you have put into human beings!
Did your eyes go round with delight, did you clap your hands and tap your feet when Miriam led the rout after crossing the Red Sea; when Mary sang of promised deliverance for oppressed people; when your beloved community in this century risked life and limb to establish on the earth truer governments, fairer systems?

Do you rejoice with one another in the Trinity when you see positive results from the gamble taken breathing your own life into us: your own daring reflected in the daring of your human family, your own sense of justice reflected in their fights for justice, your own community expressed in their common coordinated action to overturn false and establish fair structures?

Does your heart leap when you see the poor, once derided and set aside, claiming the place in the sun which you have prepared for them; looking to you for light and hazarding their lives to live by that light?

And does your heart break when you see the bloody response of the powerful to such action which, they realise, threatens their policies of domination?

Then Father, Son and Holy Spirit, we can delight in you, and believe in you and trust our cause to you for it is from you that we have learned to love and to gamble at love's insistence. Amen

Ian M Fraser

WATER AND LIGHT
(A story from Brazil)

In Brussels, Margaret and I met a Solima nun who worked in Pueblo Joven, Brazil. She told us, 'There are very poor people there. There is no water, no light. It is terrible. We had to return there because the bishop did not want to renew the contract with us.

'One of the things he said was: "You are no longer involved in things that are holy." I told this to one of the women of Pueblo Joven. She was very angry. She said, "For the bishop what is holy is all that is happening inside his church. For me what is holy is the future of my people."

'This Saturday before Easter I came back to my convent. It's a big convent. They had the celebration of Easter with water, light, etc. There is a priest in the convent who is a very artistic man. In the chapel there was a beautiful scene, beautiful vestments, water, a very beautiful lighted candle and beautiful music. I came from Pueblo Joven where there was no water or light. I left the chapel and afterwards I said, "This is the degeneration of the liturgy."'

Ian M Fraser

CRUSHED IN CAMLACHIE
(A story from Glasgow)
John 1:14

As everyone knows, Glasgow, Europe's city of culture, is *miles better* – than Edinburgh, that is. But it wasn't always seen to be so and indeed, as late as the middle 1970s, huge chunks of Glasgow were centres of decay and dereliction rather than of culture. Amongst the worst areas of decay was the east end.

A Labour government, struggling, and with an election in prospect, launched a new initiative declared to be the creation of a new town in the inner city, and with the inspiration that goes into political cosmetics, announced the G.E.A.R. Project, the Glasgow Eastern Area Renewal. Lumping together all the funding set aside for projects that were already in the pipeline, and adding very little new money, a multi-million pound package was announced. A cornerstone of this new package was that the people were to be consulted. To the astonishment, and I expect the consternation, of the politicians and planners, the people took this commitment to consultation seriously. It has to be said now that G.E.A.R. has been a great success, but it did have dubious and fragile beginnings.

One of the early consultations took place in the Camlachie Institute in the Gallowgate. The hall was packed. On the platform was a young town planner, with the good suit, the collar and tie, and the flip board by his side. The poor guy was finding it hard to concentrate; he was forever casting anxious glances out of the window to where his new car was parked. He was feart to death that the kids outside would scratch it or jump on it or something.

Anyway, the guy was introduced. He stood up, and his chest started to puff out as, with very obvious pride, he began to describe the new Health Centre that we were to get. It was to be in Abercrombie Street, near the meat market. Under the one roof would be all the doctors, dentists, district nurses, chiropodists, health visitors and so on. There was no doubting his pride.

When he finished, he asked if anyone had any questions.

This wee woman got up and said, 'Hey son.' (There's nothing that pricks your balloon quite as effectively as being addressed as 'son'.) 'Hey son, do you drive a motor?' The guy got up, very wary, as if he knew he was about to be gubbed *(trounced)*, but not knowing quite how, and said tentatively, 'Yes, madam, I do.'

'Have you ever had a corn on your foot?' More bewildered than ever he replied, 'No, I haven't.'

'Naw, I didnae think so,' she said. 'If you didnae huv a motor, and if you had a corn on yer foot you'd know your plan was bloody stupit. You just try walking from Stamford Street tae Abercrombie Street with a corn on yer foot an' y'll know whit am talking about.'

Exit one humble, but wiser, young town planner.

Erik Cramb

THE MODEL AND THE SPARROW
(A story from Scotland)
Luke 12:4, 6

A shock wave reverberated around Scotland at Christmastime in 1986 when the giant American multinational Caterpillar Corporation announced that it was closing its profit-making factory at Uddingston, near Glasgow.

It was not of course that we were unfamiliar with closures in Scotland; closures in themselves may sadden, but they no longer shock us. What shocked us all about Caterpillar was that only a few months before no less a figure than the Secretary of State for Scotland had been holding them up as model employers and investors and was trumpeting a massive investment of some £60+million in the plant. In just a few months, a complete turnaround from massive investment to total closure. How could such a thing happen in so short a time and so few know about it? Even the Secretary of State was acutely embarrassed by the unexpectedness of it all. The explanation given by the management to the workers was that 'they were victims of remedy' and they asked the workers to participate in a 'humane and orderly run-down' of the plant.

As all Scotland now knows, the workers dismissed as incomprehensible nonsense the notion that they were 'victims of remedy'. 'What the hell does that mean anyway?' they asked. They dismissed the plea to participate in 'an orderly and humane run-down' – and what the hell does that mean? Instead they decided to occupy the plant and fight for their jobs.

In early February 1987, the Scottish Trades Union Congress called a meeting about the situation. In a packed and smoke-filled room, every seat was taken. The walls of the room were lined with those standing and among the crowd overflowing out into the corridor there gathered the men and women who bore the battle scars of the struggle to preserve jobs: men and women from the coalfields, the shipyards, the steel works; from British Telecom, from the printing trades, from the hospitals, from the classrooms. Present also were Members of Parliament and the clergy. The battle for Caterpillar was on.

A white-collar union representative painted a graphic picture of the gulf between Caterpillar management and the aspirations of the workers.

'In a Glasgow hotel,' he said, 'we have management in good suits and being paid, talking about an orderly and humane closure, and outside on the streets, unpaid, the workers talking about defending their jobs. That's the way it always seems to be: on the one hand management with their smooth, urbane, civilised talk, whilst the workers are portrayed as a noisy, unruly rabble. But, who has right on their side? Let the media ask themselves that.'

Arising from that meeting, a lobby of Parliament was arranged for the 5th March and I was part of the churches' representation on that lobby.

As I boarded the train in Glasgow's Central Station on the night of March 4th, I wondered if it was an omen that only an hour earlier Jim MacLean's 'corner shop team', Dundee United, had just defeated the 'supermarket giants' from Barcelona in the European Cup game at Tannadice. Can the mighty battalions be overturned? Tackling a multinational giant like Caterpillar was certainly taking on the big battalions. It was a tribute to the resilience and determination of the Caterpillar workers and their supporters from all over Scottish industry that they set off for London in such buoyant mood.

The Palace of Westminster is impressive, even intimidating, a cathedral of politics around which it takes little imagination to listen for the echoes of Empire. It's a bold punter who isn't put in his place by the atmosphere, but together we were all bold punters. Into the splendour of the Grand Committee Room we filed. The bunnets might have been doffed, but the mouths remained unzipped, and it would be true that for anyone with an ear for biblical echoes, such was the justified anger of the cause that I'm sure that even if the workers had remained silent, the very stones would have cried out.

Was the lobby a gesture journey? someone asked. Well I find it hard to know, but if it was a gesture journey, it was a fine gesture, one I was proud to be part of. The Glasgow working man's affinity for the bevy is legendary. To travel for six hours in a train to London, to have time free in the afternoon, and then another six in the train home, would seem to be an invitation to a big bevy, a blow out of memorable proportions, but that didn't happen. Of course it wasn't a dry trip, but it was disciplined, dignified, full of courtesy and humour. It would have been good for the 'righteous' in our land, who are so ready to dismiss the workers as 'bears'[4], to have been with us, journeying to London.

During that afternoon free time I mentioned a moment ago, I went for a walk in St James's Park with Norman Orr, the industrial mission organiser. It was a gorgeous day and we wandered down beside the Serpentine to watch old men and little girls feeding the great variety of wild fowl that congregate in the park.

To tell the truth, it was some big girls who caught my eye, and even although they looked as though they had just stepped off the front page of *Vogue* magazine, it was not for that obvious reason that they caught my eye. It was their excitement. For, you see, one of these girls (there were three of them, very much sophisticated ladies of the world) had, on the palm of her outstretched hand, a sparrow – yes, a sparrow – eating away at whatever crumbs or seeds she had. I looked on transfixed at the sight of these young sophisticated ladies, who would no doubt take a night at Stringfellows nightclub in their cool stride, wide-eyed in a childlike wonder, transported in delight by a simple sparrow.

What is it the Bible says about God's foolishness being wiser than human wisdom? Could not even what seems a gesture journey have power we cannot immediately recognise? Why not, why not indeed? Are workers not worth much more than sparrows?

Erik Cramb

THE CROSS OF NAILS
(A story from Coventry Cathedral)

On the night of November 14th 1940 the medieval cathedral of Coventry was hit by incendiary bombs. Much of the rest of the city was also bombed and hundreds of people were killed.

In the morning, the cathedral staff stood in the still smouldering remains of their once beautiful, beloved place of worship. The walls and spire still stood, but the roof and the insides of the church were reduced to rubble by the enemy.

The enemy ...

Yet their reaction and resolve were not of anger and desire for revenge, but of reconciliation:

Two charred roof beams had fallen in the shape of a cross. These were bound together and stuck upright in a bucket of sand.

Provost Howard wrote *Father Forgive* on the soot-covered wall behind the burnt-out altar.

'It should be *Father Forgive Them*,' he was told.

'No,' he replied. 'We *all* need forgiveness in war.'

Three big, ancient handmade roof nails had fallen amongst the rubble. Someone bound them into a cross, using wire from the shattered windows. This cross of nails has become a symbol of costly reconciliation across the world in centres committed to reconciliation; it forms the centre of the altar cross in the new cathedral, which was built alongside the ruins of the old.

The ruins of the old, with the charred cross and the words 'Father Forgive', remain as a quiet place of contemplation, inspiring thousands of visitors to seek and work for reconciliation. A litany of reconciliation is said at Coventry Cathedral every Friday.

Frances Hawkey

SEA GLASS
(A story from Iona)

This reflection was written in the months leading up to the war on Iraq in spring 2003.

I stroll along the beach. A twinkle catches my eye. It is a piece of sea glass. Broken shards of old bottles, jars, windows ... broken ... white, blue, green, brown, clear, yellow. Bits that are so tiny you almost miss them ... large chunks with a few letters of some unknown word. Some have been there for years and years, smashed against the rocks and abraded by the sand, until they are smooth ... each piece unique and beautiful.

I would not call myself a political person. I try to ignore the news because it brings out all those 'nasty' emotions: anger, sadness, pity, hate ... the side of myself I prefer left unopened. I don't always understand all of the terminology ... the lingo of war. Instead, I like to be strolling along the beach, looking at all the interesting things that the tide leaves behind.

As I search out these bits of treasure, my mind wanders. I start to face my frustrations as I turn a bit of glass through my fingers ... there are pieces of wire running within it. I see the faces ... the faces of civilians. Ordinary people. Living in terror, without enough resources to sustain them, and not knowing what will happen next.

I bend down to pick up another piece. This one is green. I imagine the soldiers ... following orders, wearing confining gas masks, digging holes for trenches ... or graves, loading weapons to fire into the distance ... beyond their vision. I slip the glass into my pocket.

I wander along for a while scanning the sand. I think of those in power ...Tony Blair ... George Bush ... Saddam Hussein ...

An amber piece catches my eye. I only know what the news tells me. What else do these reporters see, that I will never know? I wonder if they've lost their faith ... or if they ever had any. Do they even know what the truth is? Oh, a bright blue one ... these are hard to find ... like truth.

Another bit of brown ... there are so many brown ones that they fill my pockets. All the faces of protesters filling the streets. What are they saying? Who is listening?

I find a cloudy bit. Where do I fit into all of this? What do I want to say?

My pockets and mind are full and heavy. But even if the world leaders don't hear, I know that God is listening.

Katrina Crosby

TWO WORLDS MEET
(A story from England)

'Olton Stadium' is a lawn-sized island of grass with a telephone box where Olton Avenue meets Faulconbridge Avenue right next to our house. Every fine evening the youngsters gather there to play football, to let off steam, to relate to each other – the boys and girls aged about 10 to 14.

One week the African Children's Choir came to visit our town and church, and some of the children stayed in our house. The African Children's Choir were from villages in Kenya and Uganda; the children were small for their age, but skilled and fearless footballers – and keen Arsenal supporters.

Every evening that week the doorbell rang halfway through supper. 'When are you coming to play?' And there was an international fixture at Olton Stadium! The numbers increased each day – to about 15 or more. The all-white local children were fascinated to meet real Africans and were much impressed by their enthusiasm, joy and skills. The girls were full of questions about their country and the forthcoming concert. 'I did Kenya at school last term, but I've never met anyone *from* Kenya.' Joseph (9), Nicolas (10) and Paul (8) enjoyed the games and good-humouredly tried to answer all the questions. Ivan and Barnett, the two adults from Uganda, learned the names of all the footballers and the air rang with: 'Here, pass here, Barry.' 'Sam, shoot!' 'Well saved, John.'

Every morning and evening in our home, the African children led us in prayers – their normal routine – and then at the church, where they rehearsed, standing in a ring of 24 children and adults. On the evening of the concert, we were led by the youngest, John, aged 6, in joyful choruses, and then, suddenly, in a quiet devotional song; with his eyes closed, swaying slightly, John led us into a prayer time where each person murmured personal prayers aloud. During this time, I prayed:

O, what a dream to have all the children from both worlds praying around Olton Stadium together, singing and laughing after a friendly match.

O Lord, show us the way.

David Hawkey

THE SECOND COMING
(A story from Hong Kong)

With Raymond Fung, of the Hong Kong Industrial Mission, and others, 600 factory workers in that colony, who had become Christians in the last four years, worked on the interpretation within their own situation of the main doctrines of the Christian faith. Incarnation, crucifixion, resurrection, justification – these could be made recognisable realities, full of meaning in the Hong Kong industrial context. It was exciting to find old doctrines come alive within that very special context.

But one doctrine baffled them – the Second Coming. They found it hard to pray 'Even so, come Lord Jesus.' In their experience, that had been a get-out for facing life and coping with it exactly as it is. Jesus would come and put everything right – so you need not be bothered about sufferings now, either of others or of yourself. How could those who hungered and thirsted for justice be content to sit passively under conditions as they existed and just wait for the return of Jesus Christ? In their Bible study periods, the factory workers came back again and again to the theme. But that doctrine seemed alien. It did not come alive, as the others did.

Then came a terrible industrial accident. Six workers, including a Christian, were killed. There was a mass funeral with 1000 people attending. Both the pastor and the chairman of the Communist trade union were given the opportunity to speak.

The pastor spoke for an hour. His speech was divisive. He spoke of heaven and hell, the narrow and wide gates. Those who were of his kind and view would be saved, others would be lost.

The chairman of the Communist trade union spoke for only three or four minutes, but with great effectiveness. He pledged his union to fight for better legislation and better safety regulations; and ended with the communist exhortation to the relatives to go on living courageously.

The Christian workers were furious. Here was a time to express solidarity in the human family and Christians had been divided off from unbelievers. An opportunity had been passed up of witnessing to Christ's justice and judgement and healing.

Some of the new Christians met afterwards to give vent to their anger at the distortion of the gospel in the mouth of the pastor. One, in high indignation, blurted out, 'I wish Jesus had been here to speak for himself.'

At once, for many, the key turned in the lock of the doctrine of the Second Coming. The Christian group began to see how poorly they represented Christ on earth – not only the pastor, but all of them.

Ian M Fraser

A LETTER TO MORDECHAI

'I believed I was going to serve the human people, the Israelis and Arabs, because nuclear weapons kill everyone.'

Mordechai Vanunu

Mordechai Vanunu is usually described as Israel's nuclear whistleblower. He was born in 1954 into a Jewish family in Morocco and ten years later moved to Israel. He worked as a technician at Israel's Dimona nuclear facility and in the late 1980s revealed to a British newspaper some illegal photographs he had taken at that facility. These photographs proved that Israel had nuclear bombs.

Around that time Mordechai became a Christian. After being captured by Israeli agents in Rome, he was imprisoned for 17 years, 11 of which were spent in solitary confinement. He was released in the spring of 2004, and shortly after his release a friend and I had the opportunity to spend some time with him in St George's Cathedral in Jerusalem, where he was basically under house arrest. In time, Mordechai hopes to settle in Europe or the United States for he remains a distrusted person in Israel. His life continues to be in danger.

Dear Mordechai,

It was good to be able to have those long talks with you when I was in Jerusalem. I cannot believe that you are so well, both in mind and in spirit, after all that you have been through during the long, hard years of your imprisonment. It was particularly good to share the Eucharist with you and also to be able to share a bottle of white wine!

I know that your personal future is still very uncertain, but I wanted to tell you how much I learned from you about the Christian faith in times of persecution. What you have endured in prison, perhaps especially during the eleven years of your solitary confinement, is beyond my understanding. Although you were so welcoming and gracious when we met, I was fully aware that you carry the pain of your imprisonment. Most human beings would not have survived what you have gone through, and, even now, having served your time in prison, you continue to be the recipient of much hatred, abuse and regular death threats.

With millions of others around the world, we long to see our planet free from nuclear weapons. Thousands of us regard you as a hero, although what you did was seen as illegal by your government. Nuclear weapons in themselves are illegal if we are to accept the ruling of an international court. I myself am working, along with many others, for the day when my own country will be free of such weapons of mass destruction. As you say, 'Nuclear weapons kill everyone.'

Perhaps what struck me most in our conversations was the way in which you have come through these unspeakable experiences with your faith, laughter, intelligence, awareness, prayer and body still intact. You are a witness to the endurance of the human spirit. I asked you when we were together what had kept you going and you said that your faith in Christ has been a significant factor. I hope that when you are able to travel, you will share your knowledge of God with many people, for such a witness as yours is needed in our violent time. You are an inspiration.

With warm wishes, thinking of you,
Peter

Peter Millar

A LETTER TO COLUMBA

This reading was used in Iona Abbey in a service about refugees and immigration.

Date: June 12, 563
To: Mr Columba (or Columcille)
From: The Iona Immigration Department

Dear Mr Columba,
I am concerned about certain irregularities on the form which you and your fellow 'pilgrims' filled in for us recently:

Reason for stay:
> Mr Columba, I am afraid that fleeing from vengeful opponents is not a valid reason for entry to our island. We are reliably informed that you are, in some measure, responsible for 10,000 deaths in your country of origin. Your request for asylum here, therefore, seems bogus. And we see no reason to fear for your safety should you return to your homeland.

Reason for stay:
> Mr Columba, spreading the good news about a prophet who lived five hundred years ago is neither valid grounds for stay nor useful to us. We inhabitants of Iona have followed the gods of our ancestors for centuries and have no wish to be indoctrinated by the teachings of an obscure Palestinian sect. I should warn you that attempts to interfere with our established religion may meet with resistance and hostility from the islanders.

Financial support:
> Mr Columba, your reply that 'God will provide' is curious, confusing and flippant in the extreme. Inhabitants must be able to support themselves without the aid of handouts, housing benefits or income support. A group of 13 men such as yourselves must be able to demonstrate that you have the means and ability to earn your livelihoods. I should mention at this juncture that you will meet with opposition if you make advances to any of the local women.

Transport:
> Your coracle is not in possession of a Hebridean certificate of seaworthiness, and is
> therefore illegal. Therefore, we advise you to bury the said craft at your point of
> entry; failure to do so will result in severe penalties.

Mr Columba, you have two days to reply to this letter, or one week to return to your
country of origin. While we are happy to offer hospitality to tourists, we cannot be
seen to be a soft touch; we must protect our beautiful island from a flood of bogus
asylum seekers. We hope that you will enjoy the remainder of your stay with us, and
hope that you will be able to join us for worship any evening at the stone circle by the
Hill of the Fairies.

Sincerely,
The Iona Immigration Department

Helen Lambie

'HERE AM I'

... Never was a book so compacted of 'material' considerations as the history of the
Jewish people. Its true study reveals that it is rather the 'spiritualisers' who have
wrenched it from its purpose; as a nineteenth-century unconscious expedient to make
it harmless. That, surely, is one reason why it is so little read.

To study the Bible, as God's revelation of his plan, is to discover a social purpose in
almost every book. It was not only in the Person of Christ that the spiritual entered the
material world. God's chosen people were prepared through the centuries for the
understanding of that event by a social concern unparalleled in every previous or
contemporary religion. Where these last [religions] conceived of deities to be propiti-
ated by intricate sacrifices and strange ceremonies, the evolution of the Hebrew faith
made ever more clear that the right-ordering of the material relationships of man [sic]
to man was alone well-pleasing in the sight of God. The Jewish Law was compacted of
political and economic devices, to be accepted and obeyed, as a framework for the
only obedience that would satisfy the living God. 'Morality', for the Old Testament Jew,
was not a matter of sentiment; nor charity a response to the occasional moving of the
human heart. Religion, for them, was not, what we have made it, a sentimental matter.
Turn to the first five books of the Bible, and you discover it was not the human heart
that was to be moved: it was human landmarks that were not to be removed. The Year
of Jubilee was not a Jamboree: it was debt cancellation, an intricate economic obliga-
tion, whereby, every fifty years, there was a reorganisation of private property, alike to
prevent irresponsible ownership and a submerged tenth [of the population]. The value
of property was scaled to it, rising in value if a Jubilee had just occurred, decreasing if
a Jubilee was at hand – like the changing values of London property let on a ninety-

nine years' lease. 'Holiness' was thus, for them, not a supercharged emotional experience, but the result of obedience to legally enacted economic devices.

Or move to the message of the great Prophets. They lived when strict observance of the Law had been largely set aside; when all the economic strictures, designed to bring continuing health to the people, were more honoured in the breach than in observance. And what is the nature of their 'Recall to religion'? It is not a lashing of their neighbours to a higher pitch of emotional response; but a recall to the indissoluble relationships between holiness and social righteousness. Isaiah, in his fifty-eighth chapter, informs them why their days of National Prayer seem largely unrelated to any recognisable results. He tells them, in effect, that Lenten observances won't get them very far if they persist in divorcing them from business loans. He begs them to realise that so long as the 'Church column' in the newspaper is on a different page from the 'City column' all their holiness will fail to lead to wholeness in their national prospects. As a modern translation has it – God answers our modern questions as to the value of National Days of Prayer, saying, 'You ask me to direct you … you ask why I never pay heed to your penances. Why, on fast days you find time for your business … Fasting like yours today will never bear your prayers on high … to droop your head like a bulrush, is that what you call fasting? … Is not this my chosen fast – to loosen all that fetters people unfairly, to free poor debtors from their bonds and break what binds them? It is to share your food with those who are hungry, to clothe the naked when you see them, and never turn from any fellow-creature. Then shall light dawn on you, with healing for your wounds: the Eternal will answer when you call, and when you cry, he will say, "Here am I" … if you relieve those in misery, then light shall dawn for you in darkness, and the Eternal shall guide you and renew your strength till you are like a watered garden. Your sons shall build once more the ancient ruins; you shall be called the restorer of wrecked homes.'

Such is the burden of all the prophets, page after page. The Prophet Amos – after dealing with our essential peace-time problem of short production and ill distribution – gives serious (and topical to our day?) warning of what happens when people divorce the things of Communion from the things of Common Wealth. Were such a divorce to continue, he declares, the Lord would send a famine: 'Not a famine of bread, but of hearing the words of the Lord: and they shall wander from sea to sea, and from the north even to the south, they shall run to and fro to seek the word of the Lord and shall not find it.' It is 'this Bible' that must be opened again, if we are to find again the Word of God that our soldiers seek. In the very last book of the Old Testament the promise is made that God 'will open the windows of heaven to pour a blessing down on you, a harvest more than enough'. Such soldiers as have heard that familiar figure have heard it in only one place: at times of missionary revivals, as if the blessings God were offering were a harvest of souls: so departmentalised and spiritualised have we made the blessings of religion. But to read Malachi aright is to discover that what God is offering is what people today are seeking – a greater material abundance, which all know science has made possible, but which, by our present day emphasis, appears as only the interest of secular social reformers.

It is 'this Bible' that must be opened again, with its further projection of the same truths, into the New Testament; its figure of John the Baptist declaring a new age; and, when people came out to ask him what they must do about a new age, the first demands by John were economic. It is this Bible that reveals the Christ choosing, for his first sermon among his own people, Isaiah's central reference to the year of Jubilee, and declaring 'this day hath this scripture been fulfilled in your midst'; that reveals the Christ giving three quarters of his earthly ministry to the healing of bodies and to the feeding of multitudes; and that, finally, reveals the Christ identifying himself with bread shared at a common meal – that must be opened again. With the issue at Pentecost, the first response to which was an economic decision, as the key-point to open to our day the primary concern of the New Community if it is to be a Holy Community.

It is this material challenge that we must place before humankind – *not* as the only message of the Bible, but *as the relevant nexus by which there is made to live again* all the mystery that the Bible also declares about our own natures, about the need of our personal salvation, about the offer of an incorporation, in which we can be born afresh, and from a new starting point make our especial contribution to the urgent political and economic problems of our times.

George MacLeod, 1962

AND WHAT IS THE CONTINUING FIGHTING ALL ABOUT?

... Don't let's forget how it [the Vietnam war] started. In 1953 General Eisenhower (no idiot fringe man he) spoke to the Governors of the States in the USA who were restive about getting involved in Indo-China. He said to them 'If we lose Indo-China the tin and the tungsten would cease. So when we vote 400 million dollars to help the French we are voting for the cheapest way of preserving our security, our power to get the things that we need from the riches of Indo-Chinese territory.' In 1954 *US News and World Report* said 'One of the world's richest areas is open to the winner in Indo-China. That's behind the growing US concern. Tin, rubber, rice, key strategic raw materials are what the war is really about. The US sees it as a place to hold at any cost.'

(Strange isn't it how these motives can get elevated into 'the sad necessity to help the Vietnamese to freedom', which the mass media soon adopted and have consistently protested ever since!)

And don't let's forget how it has progressed:

	South Vietnam*	Laos**	Cambodia	Total
Killed	335,000	100,000	tens of thousands	450,000*
Wounded	740,000	250,000	tens of thousands	1,000,000*
Refugees	5,695,300	1,000,000	1,600,000	8,295,300
Totals	6,677,300	1,350,000	1,600,000	9,755,300*

The ongoing civilian toll (as of August 1971)

Killed, wounded, refugeed under Johnson (1964–1968)	5,655,300
Monthly civilian toll under Johnson (1964–1968)	95,000
Killed, wounded, refugeed under Nixon (1969–August 1971)	4,100,000
Civilian toll under Nixon (1969–August 1971)	130,000

*Kennedy Sub-Committee on Refugees
** Project Air War

To which must be added the massive bombings since January 1972.

Six million acres have been defoliated. Vietnam used to export 300,000 tons of rice for much needed foreign exchange. Vietnam now has to import 100,000 tons a year to survive. There is now the 15,000-ton super bomb. One kills everything in an area of 110 acres, men, women, children, beasts, crops. It causes injuries over 1,746 acres.

Then there are smaller smart bombs. Some aim themselves at a target illuminated by laser beam.

... Then there are gravel mines disguised as small bits of cloth. Some have been found stitched into dolls. If you stand on one, you do not die. Your foot is blown off. There are pleasant pictures of children's bodies after this exercise ...

To complete this funeral dirge about Vietnam here are the *US Defence Department figures*. In the thirty months up to December 1971, 200,000 tons of high explosives *a month* have been dropped on Indo-China, Cambodia, Laos, Vietnam. This is the equivalent of ten Hiroshima bombs *a month* for thirty months. There are now in the three countries a million refugees who have lost their homes for good ...

For why? For being Communists! Still the bombs rain down, while Mr Nixon drinks white wine in Peking and toasts eternal peace in Moscow, and orders the bombing to go on ...

What is the continuing fighting all about? Sub-marine oil! ... During the present eleven years (David Rockefeller has confirmed) the American oil interests are spending three BILLION dollars a year prospecting for oil off the coasts of Thailand and Cambodia. Russia must not get it or China ...

George MacLeod, 1971

I KNOW A CAT WHOSE NAME IS …

This is an example of the kind of story or testimonial that could be read during a service about mental health issues.

'One in four people will suffer from mental illness in their lifetime.'

Penumbra

John 1:4–5

There's a stigma to mental illness – still. People empathise but then back off. Like they suddenly smell something on you, like they're afraid of contagion.

People wonder why you don't just snap out of it. It's maddening, you can't snap out of it! You can't snap out of hell. On the outside you look in and don't believe, or want to believe, it could happen to you. Well, it can.

In 1996 I went through an 'episode' of clinical depression. I lost all confidence in myself, couldn't work for much of the time; I broke up with my partner – actually, she broke up with me; who can blame her? I'd become irritable, manipulative, needy as a child. At one point the depression got so bad that I started to self-harm, to cut the insides of my arms with kitchen knives. I'd tell people that the cat did it. I was just playing with the cat. I was playing with death.

How did I fall down so far? How did I go from someone who had worked as a nurse's aide and a counsellor, from someone who'd travelled through Yugoslavia solo, to someone who couldn't even take a city bus alone? … One thing was certain: I was sure that, down below, it was my fault. It wasn't of course, but I couldn't help feeling that I was a very weak person. Weak, defective, lazy, a loser. A failure: the shame of depression on top of the depression.

I did a lot of things to survive during that time: I talked to good friends, I fell back on family, I went through counselling, I took anti-depressants. One day, I woke up and started writing children's poems. I had always written, but I'd never once thought of writing children's poems. I was desperate. I was clawing for the light.

The depression lasted for about a year. I've been well since that time. These days I feel blessed: I have work I feel passionate about, a wonderful partner; sometimes I even do gigs as a stand-up comedian. If you had told me, back in the days when it was hard to get out of bed in the morning, that one day I'd be doing stand-up comedy, I never would have believed you.

Sometimes when I'm doing stand-up, I use the following poem in my act – one of the 'children's poems' I wrote when I was clinically depressed. I recite the poem and skip rope. Punters seem to enjoy it. That a poem I wrote when I was clinically depressed now makes people laugh is a miracle to me.

On the surface, this little poem may seem to have nothing at all to do with being a survivor of depression; for me, though, it is an embodiment of 'the light that shines in the darkness' …

Going through depression has rooted my faith, has brought me closer to Jesus Christ –
I have no problem in the world now in believing in resurrection.

I used to feel very guarded and ashamed of talking about mental illness. Now I
need to hold myself back. I want to shake people awake and tell them how close to the
edge we can all come, how normal it is – how human.

Skipping song

This poem is a performance piece. When I recite it in a club, I do things like throw peanuts,
drink milk, hand cans of tuna fish and salmon to the audience ...

I know a cat whose name is Mimi
she doesn't like tuna fish
I know a cat whose name is Mimi
what's her favourite dish?

(skip)

Pears Potatoes
Pizza pie
Falafels Capers
Ham on rye

Olives Pickles
Fried bananas
Rumballs Gumballs
Dried sultanas.

I know a cat whose name is Mingy
who likes his mozzarella stringy

I know a cat whose name is Leroy
who left the duck and ate
the decoy

I know a cat named Siamese Sam
who's lost his yen for corned beef and Spam
I know a cat named Siamese Sam
what sticks to his chops?

(skip)

Blue cheese
Toasted fleas
Chocolate-covered honey bees

Garter snakes
Frosted flakes
Pistachio-almond honeycakes.

I know a cat named Need-a-tail
who's trying to eat a lot of kale

I know a cat whose name is Oopik
who forgets how to hunt walrus and seal
I know a cool cat named Oopik Toopik
what's his favourite meal?

Cheese nachos All dressed tacos
Enchiladas Fried iguanas
Beef burritos Fried Tostitos
Corn tortillas Margueritas
Hot peppers! *(skip like mad)*.

I know a cat whose name is Kate
who plays with the sunlight on her plate

I know a cat whose name's Mad Manx
who struts from his bowl and never says thanx

I know a cat titled Rex The Third
who says that eating canned food's absurd
I know a cat titled Rex The Third
what does he rather fancy?

(skip)

Pheasant
Quail
Chinchilla under glass

Bouillabaisse
Mayonnaise
Refined sugar.

I know a Tom who's a tough Maine Coon
who picks at the garbage and cries at the moon

I know a cat named Davy Crocket
who keeps liquorice jerky in his pocket

I know a cat who's an opera singer
and always wears black coat and tail
I know a cat, half-alto, part-tenor
what does he like for dinner?

Rigatoni
Rice-a-roni

Fried baloney
Cold spumoni

Manicotti
Pavarotti

Late Puccini
Hot linguine

Cannelloni
Macaroni

Vermicelli
Cold spaghetti

Hot peppers!! *(skip like mad)*

I know a cat who likes a good pot luck
I know a cat who likes a good pot lick

I know a cat who smelt the smelts
(in the salty, fishy, kitcheny air)

I know a cat who's fond of airline peanuts

I know a cat whose name is Stevey
who crunches on Spice Mice watching late night TV

I know a cat called Hate-to-Cook
who'd rather shed on her deep, soft bed
I know a cat named Hate-to-Cook
what does she like instead?

(skip)

Take out
Drive through
Ready to eat

Dine in
Phone-up
Delivery free.

I know a cat who likes to lie
and dream of eating pie in the sky

I know a cat called Judy Star
who lives for caviar by soft guitar
I know a feline called Judy Star

I know a cat who's kinda finicky
I know a cat who's kinda picnicy

I know a cat who sucks out the marrow
I know a cat who picks like a sparrow

I know a jaded Abyssinian
who doesn't want to eat the same thing again

I know a cat who hisses at hot dogs
I know a cat who relishes relishes

I know the cat who owns Captain Cat Burgers
(but his name is Ed)

I know a cat who chatters for chocolate
I know a cat who's a milkaholic

I know a cat named Alabamy Sammy
whose vit'ls consit of grits and groats
I know a cat named Hamish McCaindish
who always eats stiff Quaker Oats

I know a cat who skips double Dutch
and never even stops for lunch
I know a cat who skips much double Dutch
and never even stops for lunch
and never even stops for lunch …

Neil Paynter

BLESSINGS

CLOSING PRAYER AND BLESSING

Living God, you have taught us that faith without works is dead, so temper our faith with love and hope that we follow Christ and give ourselves freely to people in their need: then the lives we live may honour you for ever. AMEN

May God bless us and keep us; may Christ smile upon us and give us his grace; may he unveil His face to us and bring us his peace. AMEN

The Iona Community

BLESSING

May prayer feed your actions
and may your actions feed the world.
AMEN

Neil Paynter

BLESSING

May you never feel alone in the struggle for justice and peace.
May you know the support of family, friends
and people who feel as passionately about the world as you do.

May you feel a part of the great cloud of witnesses who,
through the ages,
did God's work and prayed for the coming of the Kingdom.

May you never feel alone.
And if you do, may you carry in your heart
the words of Jesus, who told his friends:
'I am with you always.'

Neil Paynter

THE MUSTARD SEED

In times when you feel that your actions are small and inconsequential,
may you remember the mustard seed:
the tiniest of things that takes root and grows and
one day
becomes a great tree
sheltering all the birds of the air.
AMEN

Neil Paynter

SILENT WORDS

May our silence
speak the peace of God

May our silence
sing the peace of God

May our silence
bring about
the peace of God

Ewan Aitken

Dedicated to The Women in Black, an international peace network. The network began in Israel in 1988, with women protesting against Israel's occupation of the West Bank and has developed in many countries. Women, dressed in black as a symbol of sorrow, demonstrate in silent protest against war and violence and in solidarity with women throughout the world.

BLESSING

May the love of God surround you,
the passion of Jesus inspire you,
and the wisdom of the Spirit guide your thoughts and actions.
AMEN

Neil Paynter

BLESSING

May you never become cynical
May you never become jaded
May you never lose heart
May you never let the bastards get you down
May you never lose faith

May you see light and good in everyone
May you remain open to wonder and mystery
May you stand firm in the assault of the powers
(shielded with the armour of God
and a good sense of humour)
May you stay rooted in hope
AMEN

Neil Paynter

THE COURAGE TO SAY NO

May you have the courage to say no –
no to the madness of the arms race
no to shallow Christian experience
no to increasingly comfortable lives for ourselves
no to all those who have made security a god
no to policies that favour the rich at the cost of the dispossessed.
May you have the courage to say no to all these areas of death
and always,
through the way you live each day,
the courage to reaffirm life in all its hope and promise.
AMEN

Peter Millar

GOD'S MESSAGE

Although the powers own most of the TV networks, newspapers chains,
web servers, media conglomerates …
may their power and propaganda never overwhelm you,
may it never impress you,
may it never hypnotise you,
may it never lobotomise you.

May you keep tuned in to God's message.

May Jesus Christ,
who is the way, the truth and the life,
enter you
body, mind and spirit.
May Christ convert and change you for ever:

May you become a witness to the good news and transmit it freely.

May you go out into the world –
a living letter of God's Word.
AMEN

Neil Paynter

BLESSING

When you are deep in the earthy, messy thick of it,
may you remember to look up at the stars
and to wonder.

Neil Paynter

BLESSING

May you live a rich life full of passion, purpose, joy, mystery, wonder and love.

May you live a rich life full of these things,
because you only have one life.

One life on this beautiful, precious planet
full of beautiful, precious people.
AMEN

Neil Paynter

BLESSING

God of our lives,
bless our endeavours
to serve and to love,
when we ask, 'Where next?'
rather than, 'What cost?'

Jesus, our companion,
bless our holy anger
that we may sweep out hypocrisy
from our thinking and our deeds.

Spirit of liberation,
bless our restless journeys
as we ask the difficult questions
and resist the easy answers.
AMEN

Yvonne Morland

SOWING SEEDS

God who is the quivering voice of new life in all creation,
may we sow seeds of love and hope
and water them with tears of joy.

Joy Mead

Notes for Additional Resources

[1] Story told to me by a man who had been homeless.
[2] *The Big Issue* is a magazine sold by homeless people on the streets of the UK.
[3] A brand of Fairtrade coffee in the UK
[4] A dismissive term often used for manual workers, implying the need to keep them caged.

*'The light shines in the darkness
and the darkness will never put it out.'*

John 1:5

SOME SUGGESTED OCCASIONS FOR USE OF LITURGIES

Human Rights: Human Wrongs

Martin Luther King Day	20th January
Holocaust Memorial Day	27th January
Rwanda Genocide Memorial Day	7th April
Refugee Week	Middle week of June, commencing Monday
World Day Against Death Penalty	Date varies in October & November
Kristallnacht Anniversary	9th November
Prisons Week	Commences 3rd Sunday in November
World Migration Day	3rd December
World Human Rights Day	10th December
International Migrants Day	18th December
Holy Innocents Day	28th December

In an Unjust World

Fairtrade Fortnight	Commences first Monday in March
World Water Day	22nd March
International Labour Day	1st May
Christian Aid Week	Commences 2nd Sunday in May
World Debt Day	16th May
Harvest Festivals	Various in September and October
Child Poverty Action Day	1st October
World Food Day	16th October
One World Week	Penultimate week of October
World Aids Day	1st December
United Nations International Day for the Abolition of Slavery	2nd December

In Our Own Backyard

Homelessness Sunday	Last Sunday in January
Poverty Action Sunday	1st Sunday in February
Shaftesbury Sunday	Last Sunday in April
Harvest Festivals	Various in September and October
International Day for the Eradication of Poverty	17th October

In All Generations

Candlemas	2nd February
Feast Day of Polycarp	23rd February
International Day of Older Persons	30th September
Universal Children's Day	20th November
Youth Sunday	3rd or 4th Sunday in November

Blessed Are the Peacemakers

Peace Sunday	3rd Sunday in January
Ash Wednesday	Start of Lent
BAE Systems AGM	Late April / Early May
Arms Trade Day of Prayer	1st Sunday in June
Stop the Arms Trade Week	2nd week in June
Hiroshima Day / Feast of the Transfiguration	6th August
Nagasaki Day	9th August
Landmine Action Week	Commences 1st Monday in November
Armistice Day	11th November
Remembrance Sunday	2nd Sunday in November

With All Creation

Earth Day	22nd April
Rogation Sunday	Sunday before Ascension Day
World Environment Day	5th June
Environment Sunday	1st Sunday in June

Challenging Prejudice

Martin Luther King Day	20th January
International Women's Day	8th March
Gay Pride	Various, depending on location: London Pride is 1st Saturday In July
Racial Justice Sunday	2nd Sunday in September
Week of Action Against Racism in Football	3rd week of October
Kristallnacht Anniversary	9th November

Engaged Community

Corrymeela Sunday	Middle Sunday in March

SONGBOOKS

CAYP *Come All You People*, Wild Goose Publications, 1995
CFTC *Cloth For The Cradle*, Wild Goose Publications, 1987
CG *Common Ground*, St Andrew Press, 1998
COSH *Church of Scotland Hymnary*, 3rd edition, 1973
EOA *Enemy of Apathy*, Wild Goose Publications, 1988
FIC *Freedom is Coming*, Wild Goose Publications, 1990
IAMB *Iona Abbey Music Book*, Wild Goose Publications, 2001
LAA *Love and Anger*, Wild Goose Publications, 1997
LFB *Love From Below*, Wild Goose Publications, 1989
MAG *Many and Great*, Wild Goose Publications, 1990
OITB *One is the Body*, Wild Goose Publications, 2002
POPAP *Psalms of Patience, Protest and Praise*, Wild Goose Publications, 1993
SBTL *Sent by the Lord*, Wild Goose Publications, 1991
SOGP *Songs of God's People*, Oxford University Press, 1988
TIOAU *There is one among us,* Wild Goose Publications, 1998
TOEWK *The Only Earth We Know*, Stainer and Bell Ltd, London, 1999
WWB *A Wee Worship Book*, Wild Goose Publications, 1989

SOURCES AND ACKNOWLEDGEMENTS

Every effort has been made to trace copyright holders of all the items reproduced in this book. We would be glad to hear from anyone whom we have been unable to contact so that any omissions can be rectified in future editions.

LITURGIES

Refugee evensong

'God of all, where are your children?' responses – adapted by Helen Boothroyd from responses from Jane Bentley, 1998. Original source of responses unknown.

'God beyond borders' responses – © Kathy Galloway, from the liturgy 'Exile', *The Pattern Of Our Days*, Wild Goose Publications, 1996, ISBN 0947988769.

A vigil liturgy for the worldwide abolition of the death penalty

'The last hours of James Terry Roach' – from *When The State Kills... The death penalty v. human rights*, Amnesty International, 1989. Used with permission of Amnesty International.

Goodness is stronger than evil – „ 1995 by Desmond Tutu, from *African Prayer Book*, Doubleday. Used by permission of Lynn C. Franklin Associates Ltd., New York and Doubleday, a division of Random House, Inc.

Bible readings – from the New Revised Standard Version.

Mahmoud Mohamed Taha story – information from *When The State Kills... The death penalty v. human rights*, Amnesty International, 1989. Used with permission of Amnesty International.

Edward Johnson story – information from *When The State Kills... The death penalty v. human rights*, Amnesty International, 1989. Used with permission of Amnesty International.

Dante Piandong, Archie Buian and Jesus Morallos stories – information from Amnesty International website: www.amnesty.org Used with permission of Amnesty International.

Mukobo Putu story – information from Amnesty International website: www.amnesty.org Used with permission of Amnesty International.

John Spenkelink story – from *When The State Kills... The death penalty v. human rights*, Amnesty International, 1989. Used with permission of Amnesty International.

'In country after country' quote – information from *'When The State Kills... The death penalty v. human rights'*, Amnesty International 1989, and *'Killing With Prejudice: Race and death penalty in the USA*, Amnesty International 1999. Both used with permission of Amnesty International.

Mass public execution in Zhengzhou report – information from *'When The State Kills... The death penalty v. human rights'*, Amnesty International 1989. Used with permission of Amnesty International.

Thai construction worker story – from *When The State Kills... The death penalty v. human rights*, Amnesty International, 1989. Used with permission of Amnesty International.

Stoning to death report – from *When The State Kills... The death penalty v. human rights*, Amnesty International, 1989. Used with permission of Amnesty International.

The case for abolition – information from *Death Penalty Information Pack*, Amnesty International UK, 2001. Used with permission of Amnesty International.

'The forfeiture of life is too absolute ...' quote – from *Death Penalty News & Updates*: http://people.smu.edu/rhalperi/ Used with permission of Rick Halperin.

'I supported the death penalty ...' quote – from *Death Penalty Information Pack*, Amnesty International UK, 2001. Used with permission of Amnesty International.

'Thus is our God' (prayer for change and absolution) – adapted from words of Oscar Romero, 24th September 1978, 'God is kind', from *The Violence Of Love*, Fr James Brockman SJ, Orbis Books, 2004, by arrangement with Plough Publishing and The Society of Jesus. Used with permission of the Chicago Province of the Society of Jesus and Orbis Books.

'God giver of all life' (affirmation) – adapted from and inspired by some words of Helen Prejean in her book *Dead Man Walking*, © Helen Prejean, Fount, an imprint of Harper Collins, first published 1993, ISBN 000628003X. Used with permission of Helen Prejean. Adapted by Neil Paynter.

Twentieth Century crucifixion: A dramatic communion liturgy

Words of Dom Helder Camara – source unknown.

Lord make us instruments of your peace – prayer of St Francis of Assisi. From the *Iona Abbey Worship Book*, Wild Goose Publications, 2001, ISBN 1901557502.

'I am guilty of hypocrisy and untruthfulness in the face of force' – from *Ethics* by Dietrich Bonhoeffer, reprinted with the permission of Scribner, an imprint of Simon & Schuster Adult Publishing, and SCM-Canterbury Press Ltd. © 1955 by SCM Press Ltd. © 1955 by Macmillan Publishing Company.

'Every now and then' – quoted in *My Life with Martin Luther King Junior* by Coretta Scott King, Hodder and Stoughton, 1969. Reprinted by arrangement with the Estate of Martin Luther King Jr, c/o Writers House as agent for the proprietor, New York, NY. Copyright 1963 Martin Luther King, Jr., copyright renewed 1991 Coretta Scott King.

'I don't know what will happen now' – quoted in *My Life with Martin Luther King Junior* by Coretta Scott King, Hodder and Stoughton, 1969. Reprinted by arrangement with the Estate of Martin Luther King Jr, c/o Writers House as agent for the proprietor, New York, NY. Copyright 1963 Martin Luther King, Jr., copyright renewed 1991 Coretta Scott King.

'If I can help someone' – by Androzzo © Copyright 1944 by Lafleur Music Ltd. Reproduced by permission of Boosey & Hawkes Publishers Ltd.

'Brothers, you are from our same pueblo' – words of Oscar Romero, taken from *Cloud of Witnesses* by Susan Bergman, 1996. Copyright © Used by permission of The Zondervan Corporation.

'Be poor, go down to the far end of society' – words of Charles de Foucauld, a priest and hermit who was martyred in Algeria in 1916 while trying to build understanding with the local population. Source unknown.

From slavery to freedom

'Sing praise to God all you faithful people' responses – based on Psalm 30, *Iona Abbey Worship Book*, Wild Goose Publications, 2001, ISBN 1901557502.

AIDS/HIV: A liturgy of solidarity and justice

Opening responses (based on Psalm 121) – © Neil Paynter, 2003.

'Lord, we live in a world that is divided' prayer – © Neil Paynter, 2003.

A person of hope – from the chapter 'Sandy' in *Finding Hope Again* by Peter Millar, Canterbury Press, Norwich, 2003, ISBN 1853114383. Used with permission of Peter Millar and SCM/Canterbury Press.

Affirmation from South Africa – from the *Iona Abbey Worship Book*, Wild Goose Publications, 2001, ISBN 1901557502. Adapted extract from presentation by Alan A. Boesak to WCC VI Assembly on the theme of Jesus Christ, the Life of the World. In 'Gathered for Life: Official Report', WCC VI Assembly, Vancouver, Canada 1983. Ed. David Gill, copyright WCC Publications, WCC Geneva. Used by permission of the WCC.

'Watch now, dear Lord' prayer – St Augustine, from the *Iona Abbey Worship Book*, Wild Goose Publications, 2001, ISBN 1901557502.

Living water

'Creator Spirit, wellspring of our lives' – © Kathy Galloway, from *The Pattern Of Our Days*, Wild Goose Publications, 1996, ISBN 0947988769. Also in The *Iona Abbey Worship Book*, Wild Goose Publications, 2001, ISBN 1901557502.

Hawa Amandu case study – © Christian Aid, based on a case study in Christian Aid appeal letters and information sheets, 2003. Used with permission of Christian Aid.

The water of life – © Christian Aid, from *Water For Life* harvest appeal materials. Used with permission of Christian Aid.

'A blessing on you who are poor' responses – © Iona Community, adapted from closing responses, *Iona Abbey Worship Book*, Wild Goose Publications, 2001, ISBN 1901557502.

In the beginning

Litany of change – suggestions for change from the article 'The new peasants' revolt', The New Internationalist magazine, Issue 253, January/February 2003. Reprinted by kind permission of the New Internationalist: www.newint.org

Living letters

Prayer of confession – © Neil Paynter, 2004.

'For the Word of God in scripture' responses – © Wild Goose Resource Group, from *A Wee Worship Book: Fourth incarnation*, Wild Goose Publications, 1999, ISBN 1901557197. Used with permission of the Wild Goose Resource Group.

'May God write a message upon your heart' blessing – by Neil Paynter, © Iona Community, *Iona Abbey Worship Book*, Wild Goose Publications, 2001, ISBN 1901557502.

Choosing God or choosing mammon

'In 1999 Nelson Mandela asked the Davos World Economic Forum' – quoted by CAFOD in *The Rough Guide To Globalisation: A CAFOD briefing*. Used with permission of CAFOD.

'In arrogance the wicked persecute the poor' – adapted from a prayer of confession © Christian Aid, 2003. Used with permission of Christian Aid.

'My name is Paulo' story – based on case studies in the article 'Cutting the wire', The New Internationalist magazine, Issue 253, January/February 2003. Reprinted by kind permission of the New Internationalist: www.newint.org

'I am Miguel' story – based on a case study in CAFOD Action, autumn 2001. Used with permission of CAFOD.

'My name is Men' story – based on information in World Poverty (leaflet), World Development Movement, Used with permission of the World Development Movement.

'Christ has come to turn the world upside down' responses – adapted from responses by Neil Paynter, *Iona Abbey Worship Book*, Wild Goose Publications, 2001, ISBN 1901557502 © The Iona Community.

Give us this day our daily bread: A communion liturgy

Give us this day our daily bread liturgy by Oliver Fernandes of Church Action on Poverty – Used by permission Church Action On Poverty. From the booklet *Just Worship: Prayers, reflections and worship ideas for Unemployment Sunday*, 2003, published by Church Action on Poverty

Holy Ground: Praying for our cities

'In the peace and the bustle of island life' responses – © The Iona Community, from the *Iona Abbey Worship Book*, Wild Goose Publications, 2001, ISBN 1901557502.

'Our cities cry to You, O God' – © 1987 Hope Publishing Company, administered by Copycare, P.O. Box 77, Hailsham BN27 3EF UK. music@copycare.com Used by permission.

'Weeping for cities and working for justice' – © Ruth Burgess, from *Praying For The Dawn: A resource book for the ministry of healing*, edited by Ruth Burgess & Kathy Galloway, Wild Goose Publications, 2000, ISBN 190155726X.

'We believe that God is present' affirmation – by Jan Sutch Pickard and Brian Woodcock, © The Iona Community, from the *Iona Abbey Worship Book*, Wild Goose Publications, 2001, ISBN 1901557502.

'Visionary God, architect of heaven and earth' prayer – © Neil Paynter, *Lent & Easter Readings From Iona,* edited by Neil Paynter, Wild Goose Publications, 2001, ISBN 1901557626.

'Christ has come to turn the world upside down' responses – by Neil Paynter, *Iona Abbey Worship Book*, Wild Goose Publications, 2001, ISBN 1901557502. © The Iona Community.

'May the God who shakes heaven and earth' blessing © Janet Morley, from the *Iona Abbey*

Worship Book, Wild Goose Publications, 2001, ISBN 1901557502. Originally from *All Desires Known* (Movement for the Ordination of Woman, and Women in Theology, 1988; SPCK, 1992.) Used with the permission of Janet Morley.

A rural liturgy

'Your love is as high as the heavens, O God' responses – from the *Iona Abbey Worship Book*, Wild Goose Publications, 2001, ISBN 1901557502.

'O God, gladly we live and move and have our being in you' – adapted from a prayer by Phillip Newell, © The Iona Community, from the *Iona Abbey Worship Book*, Wild Goose Publications, 2001, ISBN 1901557502.

'O God, star kindler' responses – © Kate McIlhagga, adapted from a prayer in *The Green Heart Of The Snowdrop*, Kate McIlhagga, Wild Goose Publications, 2004, ISBN 1901557855.

'And now may the God of hope' blessing – adapted from a blessing in the *Iona Abbey Worship Book*, Wild Goose Publications, 2001, ISBN 1901557502.

Playful God

Alfie sang – © Save the Children, from *The Friday Miracle And Other Stories* by Kaye Webb (ed.), Puffin Books, 1969. Used by permission of Save The Children.

Lord I love to stamp and shout – words by Ian Fraser, © 1969 Stainer & Bell Ltd, London, England. Music by David Evans, © 1974 Stainer & Bell Ltd, London, England. Used by permission of Stainer and Bell, PO Box 110, Victoria House, 23 Gruneisen Road, London N3 1DZ.

Help us make a difference

'When the last dove of peace has flown' reflection – © John Young, 2002. Used with permission.

'A Native American grandfather was talking to his grandson' – Source unknown.

'God says: I will judge with fairness' responses – © Emma Wright, 2002. Used with permission.

'In many foreign countries' song – © Charles Ogilvie, 2002. Used with permission.

'I believe that unarmed truth and unconditional love will have the final word' – Reprinted by arrangement with the Estate of Martin Luther King Jr, c/o Writers House as agent for the proprietor, New York, NY. Copyright 1963 Martin Luther King, Jr., copyright renewed 1991 Coretta Scott King.

God of all Ages

Prayer of St Polycarp – Source of translation unknown.

Arming the war machine

'I lie huddled in a large shell hole' – abridged extract from *All Quiet on the Western Front* by Erich Maria Remarque, published by The Bodley Head. Used by permission of the Random House Group Limited.

All Quiet On The Western Front by Erich Maria Remarque. 'Im Westen Nichts Neues', copyright 1928 by Ullstein A,G.; Copyright renewed © 1956 by Erich Maria Remarque. All Quiet On The

Prayer vigil outside BAE Systems arms factory

Faslane Blockade

Nuclear weapons: An Ash Wednesday service of repentance

A simple liturgy challenging racism

The soul loves the body

Persecution in Zimbabwe – © The Big Issue, from a report in The Big Issue magazine, July 16-22, 1998. Used with permission of The Big Issue.

Jesus and Peter dialogue – © Neil Paynter, 1998.

'Society needs gay people because they are human' – by Michael Vasey, from *Strangers and Friends*, reproduced by permission of Hodder and Stoughton Limited.

Litany of celebration – some information and inspiration from *Religion Is A Queer Thing: A Guide to the Christian Faith for Lesbian, Gay, Bisexual and Transgendered People*, Elizabeth Stuart with Andy Braunston, Malcolm Edwards, John McMahon and Tim Morrison, The Pilgrim Press, Cleveland, Ohio, 1997.

(Other books which might be helpful in creating a litany of celebration are the following: *Another Mother Tongue*, Judy Grahn, Beacon Press, Boston, 1984; *Gay Men & Women Who Enriched The World*, Thomas Cowan, Wm. Mulvey, Inc., CT, 1988; *Gay American History*, Jonathan Katz, Avon Books, NY, 1976; *Hidden From History: Reclaiming the Gay and Lesbian Past*, Duberman, Vincinus, Chauney, eds., Penguin, NY, 1990; *The Gay Book of Lists*, Leigh Rutledge, Alyson Publications, Boston, 1987.)

'It happens all the time in heaven' poem – by Hafiz (fourteenth-century, Persian poet). From *The Subject Tonight Is Love*, by David Ladinsky. © David Ladinsky. Reprinted by permission of the author.

A silent desperation of the soul

Loneliness – A silent desperation of the soul – © Tony Chan, 2003. Used with permission.

The dark was clear – © Helen Campbell, 2003. Used with permission.

'May you come safely to shore' blessing – by Mary Taylor, © Mary Taylor, from *A Book of Blessings: and how to write your own*, Ruth Burgess, Wild Goose Publications, 2001, ISBN 1901557480. Used with permission.

Hearts and hands and voices

'Among the poor' responses – © Wild Goose Resource Group, from *Cloth For The Cradle: Worship resources and readings for Advent, Christmas & Epiphany*, Wild Goose Publications, 1997, ISBN 1901557014. Used with permission of the Wild Goose Resource Group.

'O Christ, may our minds never become closed by belief *(Open Mind)*' – by Joy Cowley, © Joy Cowley in *Psalms Down Under*, published by Pleroma Christian Supplies, 1996: management@pleroma.org.nz Used by permission of Pleroma Christian Supplies.

'On our heart and on our houses' responses – © Wild Goose Resource Group, from the *Iona Abbey Worship Book*, Wild Goose Publications, 2001, ISBN 1901557502. Used with permission of the Wild Goose Resource Group.

A new Psalm: Psalm 152 – © Deaf lay ministry students, October 1999; English translation © Gill Behenna.

A Deaf person's creed – © Hannah Lewis, 2000

We are all broken, we are all gifted

'If you enter into relationship with a lonely or suffering person' – by Jean Vanier, from *The Broken Body* by Jean Vanier, 1999. Reprinted with the permission of Darton, Longman +Todd.

Crucified Earth

'Jonathan Porritt, searching for the reasons …' quote – from the pamphlet *The Spirituality of Economics* by Kathy Galloway and Bernadino Mandlate, Christian Socialist Movement. CSM Lectures 2003.

'Invisible we see you, Christ beneath us' – extract from the prayer 'Man is Made to Rise', *The Whole Earth Shall Cry Glory* by George MacLeod, Wild Goose Publications, 1985, ISBN 0947988017 © Wild Goose Publications.

'O God, who called all life into being' responses – by Philip Newell, from the *Iona Abbey Worship Book*, Wild Goose Publications, 2001, ISBN 1901557502. © Iona Community.

'Wonderful God, creator, the whole earth declares your greatness' (Psalm 8) – from the *Iona Abbey Worship Book*, Wild Goose Publications, 2001, ISBN 1901557502.

'O Christ, there is no plant in the ground but is full of your virtue' – Celtic traditional prayer, from the *Iona Abbey Worship Book*, Wild Goose Publications, 2001, ISBN 1901557502.

'Deep peace of the running wave to you' blessing – from the *Iona Abbey Worship Book*, Wild Goose Publications, 2001, ISBN 1901557502.

Footprints in the cosmos

'O God, your fertile earth is slowly being stripped of its riches' confession – adapted from confession by Ali Newell in the *Iona Abbey Worship Book*, Wild Goose Publications, 2001, ISBN 1901557502 © The Iona Community.

'Creating God, you have given us a vision of a new heaven and a new earth' prayer – © David Pickering, CTBI Environmental Issues Network. Written for the 2002 Johannesburg Earth Summit on Sustainable Development. Used with permission of David Pickering and CTBI.

'The Earth does not belong to us' responses – adapted from responses in the *Iona Abbey Worship Book*, Wild Goose Publications, 2001, ISBN 1901557502.

'Bless to us, O God, the earth beneath our feet' blessing – from the *Iona Abbey Worship Book*, Wild Goose Publications, 2001, ISBN 1901557502.

What a waste!

'Creator God, in whose image we are made' responses – © Neil Paynter, 2004.

'This is the day that God has made' responses – from the *Iona Abbey Worship Book*, Wild Goose Publications, 2001, ISBN 1901557502. © The Iona Community.

An act of commitment to a common work of reconciliation

Liturgy © Corrymeela Community, from *Travelling the Road of Faith: Worship Resources from the Corrymeela Community*, edited by Jacynth Hamill, 2001. Used with permission of The Corrymeela Community.

Worship in a time of war

Excerpt from the Iona Community's Justice and Peace Commitment – from the Rule of the Iona Community.

A service of the washing of feet: The L'Arche Community

Liturgy © L'Arche Community. Used with permission of L'Arche and Jean Vanier.

Camas: Living the liturgy

'Originally quarry-workers' cottages, then a salmon-fishing station ...' introduction – taken from *What Is The Iona Community?,* Wild Goose Publications, 2000, ISBN 1901557324.

ADDITIONAL RESOURCES

Magnificat affirmation – adapted from the *Iona Abbey Worship Book,* Wild Goose Publications, 2001, 901557502.

The new law responses – from *The Iona Community Worship Book* ('The black book'), Wild Goose Publications, 1988 (out of print).

'The Spirit of Love unite us' affirmation – by Norbert Capek, from *Singing The Living Tradition,* Unitarian Universalist Association.

On his way – by Jan Sutch Pickard, from *Imaginary Conversations: Dialogues for use in Worship and Bible Study,* Methodist Church Overseas Division, 1989/90.

Do not retreat – © Kathy Galloway, from *Iona Abbey Music Book,* Wild Goose Publications, 2003, ISBN 1901557731. First published in *Love Burning Deep: Poems and Lyrics,* Kathy Galloway, SPCK, 1993, ISBN 0281046425 (out of print).

All people, all human – from *Out Of The Shadows: A Collection of Poems from the Fourth World,* edited by Liz Prest, ATC Fourth World, 2000, ISBN 095085145. *Out Of The Shadows* is an anthology of poetry from a creative writing project involving professional writers with over a hundred individuals who live in poverty in the UK. ATD Fourth World is a human rights organisation taking a holistic approach to poverty eradication. Copies of *Out Of The Shadows* available from ATD Fourth World atd@atd-uk.org

The power of protest – first published in *Coracle,* the magazine of the Iona Community, Ruth Harvey, editor. www.iona.org.uk

Old man – first published in *Coracle,* the magazine of the Iona Community. www.iona.org.uk

Make no mistake: Peace, Justice, Love: For the gospel tells us so – by Bill Quigley, from *Hospitality,* the newspaper of The Open Door Community, Atlanta, Georgia. www.opendoorcommunity.org

The not-so-new song – by Faith Dowdy Armstrong, from *Hospitality,* the newspaper of The Open Door Community, Atlanta, Georgia. www.opendoorcommunity.org

Lessons: A meditation – first published in *Coracle,* the magazine of the Iona Community. www.iona.org.uk

When there is peace – by Alan Horner, first published in the Epworth Review.

Living stones – excerpt from an article in *Coracle*, the magazine of the Iona Community. www.iona.org.uk

Testing by human oppression (A story from Guatemala) – by Ian M Fraser, from *Strange Fire: Life Stories and Prayers*, Wild Goose Publications, 1994, ISBN 094798867X.

Kumari's eviction (A story from South India) – by Peter Millar, from *Letters from Madras*, Dorothy and Peter Millar, 1988.

Gambling with life (A story from Chile) – by Ian M Fraser, from *Salted with Fire: Life-stories, Meditations, Prayers*, St Andrew Press, 1999, ISBN 0715207628. Used by permission of St Andrew Press.

Water and light (A story from Brazil) – by Ian M Fraser, from *Strange Fire: Life Stories and Prayers*, Wild Goose Publications, 1994, ISBN 094798867X.

Crushed in Camlachie (A story from Glasgow) – by Erik Cramb, from *Parables and Patter*, Wild Goose Publications, 1989 (out of print).

The model and the sparrow (A story from Glasgow) – by Erik Cramb, from *Parables and Patter*, Wild Goose Publications, 1989, ISBN 09479882335 (out of print).

The second coming (A story from Hong Kong) – by Ian M Fraser, from *Reinventing Theology As The People's Work*, Wild Goose Publications, first published 1980, republished 2005 ISBN 190501001X.

'Here am I' – by George MacLeod, from *We Shall Re-Build: The Work of The Iona Community on the Mainland and on Island*, 1962 (out of print), © The Iona Community.

'And what is this continuing fighting all about?' – by George MacLeod, from *The Future of the Traditional Churches: An Essay on Pentecostalism and Peace, September 1971*(out of print), © The Iona Community

Closing prayer and blessing – © Iona Community, from *'The Iona Community Worship Book'* ('The black book'), Wild Goose Publications, 1988 (out of print).

Women in Black description from *Making Peace in Practice and Poetry*, Joy Mead, Wild Goose Publications, 1901557847.

ABOUT THE CONTRIBUTORS

Ewan Aitken is a father, husband, minister, politician, writer and broadcaster.

Faith Dowdy Armstrong was born in Atlanta, Georgia. She and her husband and a collection of animals live in rural, southwest Virginia. Faith is a writer, artist, seeker, and, hopefully, a teller of truth, whatever that may be, and wherever it may be found.

ATD Fourth World is a human rights organisation taking a holistic approach to poverty eradication. www.atd-uk.org

Gill Behenna is ordained in the Church of England and works as chaplain with the Deaf community in the diocese of Bristol. She is also a freelance sign language interpreter, consultant and trainer.

Richard Boeke writes: 'I was born in Atlanta, USA, and was a U.S. Air Force Chaplain before becoming a 'Unitarian Peace-nik Minister'. I marched against war in California and London. I work for interfaith friendship as Secretary of the World Congress of Faiths www.worldfaiths.org. I enjoy my current ministry at the Unitarian Church of Horsham, UK.'

Ruth Burgess is a writer and editor who lives in the North East of England with a large and hungry black and white cat. She likes fireworks and growing flowers and food. Ruth is a member of the Iona Community.

Helen Campbell lives in Edinburgh and is a former teacher. She has a daughter and grand-daughter and enjoys writing and poetry.

Tony Chan is of Scottish/Chinese background, is married, has a daughter and has lived in Edinburgh for some years. He struggles with mental health problems and feelings of isolation.

Bev Chidgey is a free-spirited global wanderer from the land downunder. Her journeys have taken her to Iona many times as a volunteer and also as a participant in programmes offered by the Iona Community.

David Coleman is a parent to Taliesin and Melangell, married to Zam, and works with Barrhead United Reformed Church, near Glasgow. He longs to see a fully inclusive, united free catholic Church, and enjoys experimenting in making worship a more audio visually enriching experience, in order to uncover the subversive potential of orthodox Christianity. He is a member of the Iona Community.

Stephen Cornish is a Baptist lay-preacher, a professional railwayman and an occasional writer of poetry. He is married to Brenda and has two grown-up daughters.

Corrymeela Community – Corrymeela is people of all ages and Christian traditions, who, individually and together, are committed to the healing of social, religious and political divisions that exist in Northern Ireland and throughout the world. www.corrymeela.org

Ian Cowie came into the Iona Community on leaving the army and hospital back in 1945. He was the first Iona Abbey guide, then served as a minister in three parishes and finally as chaplain to the Christian Fellowship for Healing. He is married to Ailsa; they have 5 children.

Maxwell Craig, a minister of the Church of Scotland and a member of the Iona Community, has served parishes in Falkirk, Glasgow and Aberdeen. From its launch in September 1990 to

December 1998, he was General Secretary of ACTS (Action of Churches Together in Scotland); and, in 1999 and 2000, he served as minister of St Andrew's Scots Church in Jerusalem. He is now chairman of Scottish Churches Housing Action, the churches' ecumenical body to combat homelessness.

Erik Cramb was until recently head of Scottish Churches' Industrial Mission, the ecumenical arm of the churches that relates to working people and working life. He has been a member of the Iona Community since 1972.

Katrina Crosby is a former member of the Iona Community's resident group on Iona. (See the liturgy Living Water.)

John Davies is an Anglican priest in Liverpool and a member of the Iona Community. He writes at www.johndavies.org

Viv Davies – 'I am a small Welsh member of the Iona Community. Since retiring from midwifery, I have worked with and for homeless people and have found many friends.'

Mel and Georgia Duncan served as volunteer staff of the Iona Community during the summer of 1998. Georgia works as a social worker in schools in St Paul, Minnesota (USA). Mel is the founding director of the Nonviolent Peaceforce: www.nonviolentpeaceforce.org They have 8 children and 5 grandchildren.

Sandra Fox is currently a postgraduate student and practical-theologian-in-the-making. She is a former member of the Iona Community's resident group on Iona.

Ian Fraser – 'The main thing about my life is that Margaret married me, I have three children, nine grandchildren and two great-grandchildren. I became a member of the Iona Community in 1941.'

Jenni-Sophia Fuchs has been an associate member of the Iona Community since 1998. She holds degrees in Scottish Ethnology and Museum Studies and has lived and worked in England, Wales, the United States, and on the Isle of Iona, where she did various stints as children's worker for the Iona Community.

Kathy Galloway is the current leader of the Iona Community.

Louise Glen-Lee is a member of the Iona Community and current deputy warden for the Iona Community on Iona.

Yousouf Gooljary is a member of the Iona Community. He qualified as a solicitor in 1996 and currently teaches science in a comprehensive school in London.

Tom Gordon is a Church of Scotland minister who has worked as a hospice chaplain with Marie Curie Cancer Care since 1994. He is author of *A Need For Living* (Wild Goose Publications 2001) and *New Journeys Now Begin* to be published by Wild Goose in 2005. He has been a member of the Iona Community since 1973.

Christine Green is an associate member of the Iona Community living in the Lake district.

Sophia Griffiths spent three wonderful summers housekeeping in Iona Abbey. Now she works with disaffected young people in South London and volunteers at the London Lesbian and Gay Switchboard.

John Harrison is a member of the Iona Community and also supports, as a member and/or subscriber, many environmental campaign organisations. He and his wife try to practise what they preach: organic gardening, solar water heating, solar photovoltaic electrical generation and the 4 R's – reduce, reuse, repair, recycle.

Ruth Harvey is a mother of three, a member of the Iona Community, and editor of *Coracle*, the magazine of the Iona Community.

David Hawkey is an associate member of the Iona Community and is married to Frances. A science technology teacher by trade, he is always learning from children and sharing the deep magic of creation. He learnt a lot about candles and creative worship as Sacristan on Iona in 2000. He is now involved with the International Centre for Reconciliation of Coventry Cathedral.

Frances Hawkey is an associate member of the Iona Community who worked as the housekeeper at Iona Abbey for a year. She and her husband, David, now live in Coventry, where they are involved in local and world justice issues, and the work of International Reconciliation based at the Cathedral.

The Hexham Abbey Youth Group and Bridget Hewitt – A group of teenagers, and their adult enabler, who meet approximately once a month for discussions, attempting to be as free and open as possible, relating to faith and life.

Linda Hill is a counsellor who specialises in working with trauma, working part-time for the NHS and part-time in private practice. As a member of the Holy Metropolitan Community Church, Edinburgh, she leads worship regularly and enjoys writing and exploring creative ways to reflect on the gospel message.

Alan Horner was Chairman of the Methodist Synod in Scotland 1982–94. He retired from paid ministry in 1999 and moved to Milton Keynes to work for the Living Spirituality Network as Associate Staff.

Revd Dr Jonathan Inkpin is an Anglican priest, originally from the north-east of England, now living on the central coast of New South Wales. A member of the ecumenical Wellspring Community in Australia, he coordinates the Decade to Overcome Violence initiative for the National Council of Churches in Australia.

Helen Lambie is a baker and caterer, and a former member of the Iona Community's resident group on Iona.

L'Arche Community – L'Arche Communities, founded by Jean Vanier and Père Thomas Philippe, bring together people with a learning disability and those who choose to share their lives by living in the same home, and sharing the same work-place (from the L'Arche international website) www.larche.org

Hannah Lewis is an associate member of the Iona community and a Deaf priest working with the Deaf and hearing communities of Shropshire.

Christian MacLean is a member of the Iona Community living in Perthshire. She is involved in education, rural development and sustainability issues.

George MacLeod, the founder of the Iona Community, was a charismatic man of prayer and action whose life spanned the 20th century. Giving up a promising career as minister to the middle classes in Edinburgh, he took up a post in the poor and depressed area of Govan in Glasgow, where he moved inexorably towards socialism and pacifism and his theology became more mystical, cosmic and political. In 1938 he initiated the venture of restoring the ancient abbey on Iona, out of which the Iona Community developed.

Vincent Manning has a background in youth and social work, and had the privilege of working with the team at Camas in the 1999 season.

Rachel McCann is a member of the Iona Community.

Joy Mead, a member of the Iona Community, is a poet and a writer who also leads creative writing groups. She is involved in development education and justice and peace work.

Hugh Miall is Reader in Peace and Conflict Research at Lancaster University and Director of the Richardson Institute. He is a member of the Society of Friends.

Peter Millar is a member of the Iona Community.

Yvonne Morland is a poet and liturgist and a member of the Iona Community living in Edinburgh.

Ali Newell is a Church of Scotland minister and is a team member at the Ignatian Spirituality Centre, Glasgow. She is an associate member of the Iona Community.

Bishop Patrick O'Donoghue is the Roman Catholic Bishop of Lancaster.

Jean Oliver is a member of the Iona Community and of the Adomnán of Iona Ploughshares Affinity Group.

Elizabeth Paterson worked with the Church of Uganda for 16 years. During this time she was involved in AIDS and HIV education, including working for 3 years with an orphan support organisation. AIDS has affected many of her friends and colleagues. She has been a member of the Iona Community since 1986.

Jan Sutch Pickard is a poet and storyteller, and a learner-liturgist. A member of the dispersed Iona Community, she is a former warden of Iona Abbey. At the time of publication, she was Southlands writer in residence for one semester at Roehampton University. Following a period as an Ecumenical Accompanier in Palestine/Israel, she hopes to continue working freelance from her home in Mull.

Chris Polhill is a priest in the Lichfield diocese. With her husband, John, she runs the Reflections project linking Christian spirituality and environmental issues. She is a member of the Iona Community.

Prayer vigil outside BAE Systems arms factory – The group that vigils at BAE Systems grew from a campaign to stop the sale of Hawk aircraft to Indonesia during the occupation of East Timor. The group is comprised mainly of Catholics from parishes in Liverpool, Choley, Freckleton and Blackpool, though it is sometimes joined by people of other faiths and none.

Jane Rogers is a retired civil servant, and a mother and grandmother in her mid-sixties. She was also main carer for her widowed father until his recent death, aged 90. She is a member of the Iona Community.

Norman Shanks is minister of Govan Old Parish Church, Glasgow.

John Smith is a non-stipendiary Anglican priest who, before he was ordained, was County Librarian of Cumbria. He is a Franciscan tertiary and also chairman of the Brampton and District Justice and Peace Group, who enact the 20th century crucifixion liturgy every Lent.

Suet-Lin Teo has been involved with the Glasgow World AIDS Day Service since she moved to Glasgow from Birmingham in 1999. The Glasgow World AIDS Day Service Group is a made up of West of Scotland agencies, local agencies and enthusiastic volunteers.

Bill Quigley is a Professor of Law at Loyola University New Orleans School of Law. Bill is an active advocate for civil and human rights. Bill shared his prayer in this book when he was awarded the Pax Christi USA Pope Paul VI Teacher of Peace Award.

Veni Vounatsou is a German Greek who lives in Scotland and is currently splitting her time between working for a women's project and the National Museums of Scotland.

Zam Walker has been exploring new directions. In addition to being a parent to Taliesin (6) and Melangell (3) and partner to David, she is training for ministry within the United Reformed Church and discovering new ways to live life to the full. She particularly hopes that the Church will celebrate God's wonderful diversity in creation and become truly inclusive. She is a member of the Iona Community.

Wellspring was born in 1998 when Catherine McElhinney and Kathryn Turner began making resources, used in parishes and schools, available to the wider world, particularly through their website www.wellsprings.org.uk

Paul Whittaker is a Deaf musician who also enjoys the occasional challenge of being a relief musician on Iona. Paul says: 'It's interesting when you can't hear or see what's happening in the Abbey.' His proper job is running 'Music And The Deaf' www.matd.org.uk

Iain Whyte is a Church of Scotland minister and has been a member of the Iona Community since 1966. Married to Isabel and with three children, he has been Chaplain to two Scottish universities, worked in Ghana and with overseas students in Glasgow, been a parish minister in Paisley and Coatbridge, National Secretary for Christian Aid, and is now a Community Mental Health Chaplain. Iain has had a lifelong interest in Africa and is current Treasurer of the Britain Zimbabwe Society. A lover of travel, he served as unofficial chaplain to the Scotland football supporters on several campaigns from Brussels to Belarus.

Maire-Colette Wilkie is a former nun now married to another recidivist peacenik. Regular arrests at Faslane have provided the privilege of witnessing to Christ's message of peace and the opportunity to prepare liturgies. The Iona link with Adomnán and, of course, with the living Community members, has been for her both an inspiration and a blessing.

Brian Woodcock is a United Reformed church minister in St Albans. He is a member of the Iona Community and was warden of Iona Abbey from 1998 to 2001.

Woolman House Community – Alan Paxton, Craig Barrett and Kate Marks were members of the Woolman House Community from 1999 to 2004. They remain active supporting refugees.

Unfortunately it was not possible to obtain biographical details of every contributor.

INDEX OF AUTHORS

THE IONA COMMUNITY IS:

- An ecumenical movement of men and women from different walks of life and different traditions in the Christian church
- Committed to the gospel of Jesus Christ, and to following where that leads, even into the unknown
- Engaged together, and with people of goodwill across the world, in acting, reflecting and praying for justice, peace and the integrity of creation
- Convinced that the inclusive community we seek must be embodied in the community we practise

Together with our staff, we are responsible for:

- Our islands residential centres of Iona Abbey, the MacLeod Centre on Iona, and Camas Adventure Centre on the Ross of Mull

and in Glasgow:

- The administration of the Community
- Our work with young people
- Our publishing house, Wild Goose Publications
- Our association in the revitalising of worship with the Wild Goose Resource Group

The Iona Community was founded in Glasgow in 1938 by George MacLeod, minister, visionary and prophetic witness for peace, in the context of the poverty and despair of the Depression. Its original task of rebuilding the monastic ruins of Iona Abbey became a sign of hopeful rebuilding of community in Scotland and beyond. Today, we are about 250 members, mostly in Britain, and 1500 associate members, with 1400 friends worldwide. Together and apart, 'we follow the light we have, and pray for more light'.

For information on the Iona Community contact:
The Iona Community, Fourth Floor, Savoy House, 140 Sauchiehall Street,
Glasgow G2 3DH, UK. Phone: 0141 332 6343
e-mail: admin@iona.org.uk; web: www.iona.org.uk

For enquiries about visiting Iona, please contact:
Iona Abbey, Isle of Iona, Argyll PA76 6SN, UK. Phone: 01681 700404
e-mail: ionacomm@iona.org.uk

Wild Goose Publications, the publishing house of the Iona Community established in the Celtic Christian tradition of Saint Columba, produces books, CDs and digital downloads on:

- holistic spirituality
- social justice
- political and peace issues
- healing
- innovative approaches to worship
- song in worship, including the work of the Wild Goose Resource Group
- material for meditation and reflection

For more information:

Wild Goose Publications
Fourth Floor, Savoy House
140 Sauchiehall Street,
Glasgow G2 3DH, UK

Tel. +44 (0)141 332 6292
Fax +44 (0)141 332 1090
e-mail: admin@ionabooks.com

or visit our website at
www.ionabooks.com
for details of all our products and online sales